TRELAWNY
The Incurable Romancer

TRELAWNY
The Incurable Romancer

William St Clair

THE VANGUARD PRESS, INC. NEW YORK

Library of Congress Catalogue Card Number: 77-84020
ISBN: 0-8149-0792-X
Manufactured in the United States of America

Contents

Illustrations

Acknowledgements

In the preface to his great biography of Shelley the late Newman Ivey White declared that to record his thanks to everyone who had helped him would be impossible and might seem ostentatious. I too am very conscious that this book on Trelawny could not have been attempted without the generous assistance of large numbers of friends and acquaintances – who gave access to documents, answered my letters, gave permissions, arranged introductions, shared the results of their researches with me, suggested ideas and discussed Trelawny's character, who welcomed me into their homes and showed me round as I explored the places associated with Trelawny (a special thank you to the goatherds of Parnassus for directions on the mountain and to the Tithoreans who pulled my car out of a ditch and gave me dinner afterwards), who typed and retyped the drafts, who commented on the book as it was being written, and who all contributed in various ways to the fun and excitement of the search.

I should like to acknowledge my thanks to the staffs of the Athenaeum Library, London; Avon County Library; Beinecke Library, Yale; Bodleian Library, British Library and British Museum; British School at Athens; Brotherton Library, Leeds; Cambridge University Library; Columbia University Library; Cornwall Record Office; Folger Library, Washington; Gennadios Library, Athens; Houghton Library, Harvard; Humanities Research Center, Texas; Huntington Library, San Marino; Keats House, Hampstead; Keats House, Rome; King's College Library, Aberdeen; Lambeth Palace Library; London Library; Monmouthshire County Library; J. Pierpont Morgan Library, New York; National Library of Scotland; National Portrait Gallery, London; New York Public Library; Newstead Abbey; Public Record Office, London; Viareggio Municipal Museum; West Sussex Record Office; and Worthing Public Library.

The Carl H. Pforzheimer Library, New York, besides a great deal of other assistance and encouragement, generously gave me access to a mass of unpublished manuscripts relating to Trelawny without which the book would have been impossible, but, like others before me,

I sadly record that some relevant documents there remain closed owing to the restrictive policy of the Library.

I should like to thank especially Sir John Balfour, Dr Betty T. Bennett, Mrs Margaret Brown, Dr Vera Cacciatore, Miss Catharine Carver, Mrs Sybil Cookson, Mrs Imogen Dennis, Dr Rodney G. Dennis, Miss Margaret Duffy, Mr C. W. J. Eliot, Mrs Elston, Mr Guy Evans, Mrs Jean Fane, Dr P. R. Feldman, Mr E. Finopoulos, Mrs Doucet Fischer, Mr Tom Grey-Davies, Mr Mihai Handrea, Lady Anne Hill, Mr Peter Hopkirk, Mr P. L. Hull, Mr R. A. Hyde, Mrs C. M. Trelawny Irving, Miss Elizabeth Johnstone, Mr Andrew Kolesnikow, Mr A. C. Lascarides, Miss Elaine Ling, Mr Kenneth A. Lohf, Lady Mander (R. Glynn Grylls), Mr Leslie A. Marchand, Mr Max McCann, Mrs Doris Langley Moore, Mr John G. Murray, Mrs Patience Trelawny de Perez-Huerta, Mr Robert A. Picken, Mrs Louise Pleydell-Bouverie, Mrs Diana Pugh, Mr Donald H. Reiman, Dr H. L. Schanz, Mr Jon Stallworthy, Mrs Emily Sunstein, Miss Pamela Thomas, Mr Roger Tomkys, Dr Auguste Toussaint, Sir John Trelawny, Colonel Philip Trelawny, Mr Simon Trelawny, Dr Francis Walton, and Mr Francis Williams.

London
January 1977

Introduction

Some of his admirers still cling to the belief that Trelawny merely exaggerated his stories at the margin for the sake of effect, but this is too charitable a judgement. When he was young he embarked on a daring deception which he was to maintain and foster for the rest of his life, and all his genuine achievements were built on this insecure foundation.

But lies acquire a life of their own. They breed new lies, which in turn help to sustain their parents. Trelawny's stories were a response to the pressures of his real life, and his real life in turn was adapted to accommodate the stories until he came to believe them himself. So much so that in later life the quality for which he was most warmly admired was his blazing fearless sincerity, summed up by his first biographer with a quotation from *Hamlet*:

> This above all: to thine own self be true,
> And it must follow, as the night the day,
> Thou canst not then be false to any man.

The mask which he initially put on as a protection or disguise became his true face. Early in life he adopted a view of his own character which he then proceeded to live out in practice. As his view of himself changed, so did his behaviour. Shadow and reality chased one another until no one – not even Trelawny – could distinguish the two.

Obviously, in writing about such a man, special care is needed. The simplest statements have to be checked against independent sources if they can be found, and much must inevitably remain obscure and doubtful. Explanations, if there are explanations, are bound to be speculative and tentative, and based more often on circumstantial evidence than on hard facts. However, it would be unambitious merely to try to establish the events of Trelawny's life and to set alongside them a list of his punctured pretensions. That would be like plotting the route of Walter Mitty's drive through Waterbury on a map, reconstructing where he bought his overshoes and where Mrs Mitty went for her hairdressing appointment, and hoping thus to say something revealing about Walter Mitty. Somehow we must get behind the facts and try to disentangle the complex of ideas, hopes, ambitions, and fears which buzzed around in that handsome head.

I have therefore, from time to time, ventured suggestions which go beyond the evidence. Some, no doubt, are more persuasive than others. Many must be simply wrong. But in trying to project a picture of a man whose life and ideas were so strange and unsettling even to his own contemporaries, imagination must be given its chance. Trelawny himself, though he hated and attacked with unspeakable virulence anyone who came near to uncovering his secrets, would surely have advised boldness, and might even, I suspect, if he liked my ideas, have adopted them himself and made them true afterwards.

I

The Younger Son

My birth was unpropitious. I came into the world, branded and denounced as a vagrant, not littered by a drab in a ditch but still worse; for I was a younger son of a family so proud of their antiquity that even gout and mortgaged estates were traced many generations back on the genealogical tree as ancient heirlooms of aristocratic origin.

The opening words of Trelawny's account of his own life.[1]

He was born on 13 November 1792, it is not known where, although he himself usually said Cornwall. He was christened Edward John, although for a period in later life he called himself John Edward. To his family he was always John, but to his friends he was Edward.[2]

His father was a retired lieutenant-colonel, himself a younger son. He had sacrificed love to marry an unattractive heiress, but the money had turned out to be less than he expected and he soon ran through it. When Trelawny was born, the family were living a quiet country life in reduced circumstances waiting for their fortunes to improve, until in 1798, when Trelawny was not yet six, the death of Owen Salusbury Brereton, a cousin who owned extensive lands in Cheshire and elsewhere, brought the long-awaited reversal. Trelawny's father became a rich man, he changed his name to Brereton, established himself in a large house in London, and prepared to enter public life.

The long years of failure and disappointment had, however, taken their toll. Trelawny's father was vile-tempered, oafish, ignorant, and greedy. With his new wealth he became worse, and his wife and children lived in terror of his moods and rages. 'Selfish', 'tyrannical', 'stern and unforgiving' were phrases which Trelawny later used to describe him.[3] 'A man of most virulent temper and avaricious disposition' he was called by his brother-in-law,[4] and there is every reason to believe that these descriptions are accurate. Brereton was said to have carried a ready-reckoner of actuarial tables in his pocket and to have worked out the 'sterling' value of all his relations, their heirs, their next of kin, their ages and the state of their constitutions.[5] He was even suspected of having deliberately destroyed legal documents as part of his relentless desire for legacies.[6]

Trelawny's mother, the former heiress, is also an unattractive figure, tall, dark, awkward, and masculine, and she was generally disliked almost as much as her husband. She was always conscious of her great connections, her elder brother Sir Christopher Hawkins, who owned the magnificent house and estate of Trewithen in Cornwall, and her younger brother John Hawkins whose house at Bignor Park, Sussex, was scarcely less grand. Sir Christopher, like Trelawny's father, was a miser, so enormously rich that he could leave his tradesmen's bills unpaid for years on end. He sat in the House of Commons for forty years and was a noted dealer in rotten boroughs – considered to have gone too far even for pre-Reform Bill days. In 1810 he conferred a borough on Trelawny's father – he is said to have pulled down half the houses to reduce the electorate to the manageable number of five – and Colonel Brereton too became a Member of Parliament.

Trelawny apparently was fond of his mother and she did what she could to protect her children from their father, but she evidently shared many of her husband's characteristics. She was a snob and a flatterer, and devoted much of her life to a prolonged attempt to secure the inheritance of Sir Christopher Hawkins. Her frenzied efforts to find suitable rich husbands for her daughters later caused her to be publicly caricatured as Mrs Brawney-Be-at-Em, and she seems to have spent her life in touching ignorance of what her son John was really like, accepting unquestioningly whatever fanciful stories he cared to tell her about himself. When in 1929 a portrait of Mrs Brereton was opened for cleaning, it was found that someone had written 'a very disagreeable old woman' on the back of the canvas.[7]

There were six children who grew to adulthood in this unhappy family and others died in infancy. As Trelawny said of his father, 'Every succeeding year he reluctantly registered in the family bible the birth of a living burden. He cursed my mother's fertility and the butcher's and baker's bills.'[8] The elder son, Harry, was born in the same year as Trelawny so they, the only two boys, were very close in age. The girls of the family were later to grow tall and awkward like their mother. The eldest, who reached the huge height in those days of six feet one inch, was known as 'the grenadier'.[9] All the children disliked, feared, and despised their father.

Trelawny's earliest recollection of his boyhood was when he and his brother were five and he was later to entertain Shelley and his friends at Pisa with the story. Trelawny and a little girl are playing in his father's orchard, probably at Shotwick in Cheshire, when the old grey raven which his father kept as a pet makes a peck at the girl. Trelawny, enraged, seizes the bird and succeeds in tying the girl's sash round its neck and hanging it from a tree. Harry and he then throw stones at it and hit it on the head with sticks, but suddenly when they think the bird is dead, it springs up, covered in blood and with one eye hanging loose from its head, and attacks them again. After a long struggle, the two boys, though bleeding from innumerable cuts, overpower it again and sink it in a duckpond with a stone tied round its neck.[10]

Trelawny loved to tell this story and he told it well. He saw it as the first manifestation of a characteristic of which he was curiously proud. He was prepared to endure annoyance and oppression up to a certain point, he said, but when provoked beyond that point he was ruthless. He would be seized by a blind desire for revenge and would destroy without mercy. It was a grievous fault and grievously did he repent it, he would say, echoing Mark Antony, but his disingenuousness is transparent. Far from being ashamed of his revengeful and violent nature, he gloried in it.

Already in boyhood he had developed that contrariness which was to stay with him all his life. If forced to do something, he would stubbornly do the opposite. Forbidden to play on the grass in his own garden, he would climb into the neighbours' orchards and steal the fruit. If his parents were mean, he would be extravagant. One day he gave a pigeon pie to a beggar woman, and when she conscientiously came back later with the dish and the fact was discovered, his father flew into a rage and Trelawny was cuffed and kicked. In relating this story years later, Trelawny remarked 'I hated her honesty and never afterwards could endure old women'.[11] It was her weakness that he hated, not her honesty. Always ready to accept violence and give violence freely in return, he was disgusted when others allowed themselves to be oppressed.

No boy born into such a background could be indifferent to the past. Trelawny and Hawkins had been among the great families of Cornwall, of England, for hundreds of years. Generation after generation of men and women bearing these names had been involved in wars and rebellions, foreign conquests, and voyages into the unknown.

Tales of love and elopement, murder and revenge, were part of the folk history of the entire region.

A few miles from Trewithen was Trelawne, the great house from which the Trelawnys had originally taken their name, inhabited by the senior branch of the Trelawny family.[12] There was nothing here of the studied meanness of Trewithen. The extensive woods and fine lawns were tended with loving care, and the rambling old house teemed with devoted servants. The house revealed in every aspect the results of hundreds of years of ancestral wealth. Even the tombs in the crypt were hung with velvet and fastened with silver nails and gilt plates. Visitors would be shown the ancient vellum scroll, prepared by the antiquary Camden himself, which traced the genealogy of the Trelawny family to Domesday Book and beyond. They would see the relics of the Trelawny who was at Agincourt with Henry V, and the military baton given to another Trelawny by Queen Elizabeth.

The portrait which every visitor paused to admire was of a tall frank soldierly man with long hair and moustaches, wearing a white satin coat and carrying a black cap with a white plume. It was labelled 'John Trelawny, born 1592'. Did the unhappy awkward boy John Trelawny, born 1792, ever gaze at that portrait and see himself as he would like to be? There was a tapestry which, it was said, the Emperor of China had presented to a member of the Trelawny family for some forgotten service. It was of brilliant colours, dazzling with gold and silver thread, and represented a crowded scene of exotic birds, tigers, elephants, and dragons, and a procession of noblemen following the Chinese Emperor. Then there was a tapestry which had been worked by an unhappy Trelawny lady in mourning for a dead child. The scene is of a cemetery with a pyramid and cypress trees; a woman in mourning sits nearby holding a book. It resembles the Protestant Cemetery at Rome which was to play such an important part in Trelawny's life, and where the ashes of Shelley, Keats, and Trelawny himself now lie.

In later years, he liked to boast that the blood of kings ran in his veins. He never shook off a certain arrogance of superior birth and an accompanying contempt for those not so fortunate. But at the same time he was always an outsider. He had been born into the system but he could never be part of it. Short of accident he had no hope of inheriting the lands and income and the associated political power which made country life so agreeable to his stolid relations. As a younger son the system required that he should leave home and make his own way in the world. It was on Harry and on Harry's children that the hopes of the family were fastened. Harry would perhaps be the Sir Christopher Hawkins of the new generation, and what an uninspiring ambition that was to any boy of the smallest sensibility.

When they were eight, the two brothers were sent to school. The family were then living in Bristol and the school selected was a private establishment run by the Reverend Samuel Seyer which catered for the sons of prominent local families. According to Trelawny, the decision to send them was precipitated by one of their father's periodic rages. One day he surprised them stealing apples in the orchard, angrily ordered them to come out, and without even going back into the house led them for two miles through the streets of Bristol to the gate of a high building. The bell was rung, they were admitted, and the schoolmaster appeared. Brereton spoke as follows:

> Well, sir, will you undertake the charge of these ungovernable vagabonds? I can do nothing with them. Why, Sir, this fellow does more mischief in my house than your sixty boys can possibly commit in years. . . . He is savage, incorrigible! Sir he will come to the gallows if you do not scourge the devil out of him. I have this morning detected him in an act of felony for which he deserves a halter. My elder son, Sir, was instigated by him to be an accomplice; for naturally he is of a better disposition.

With this Brereton made the necessary arrangements with Seyer, and without a further word to his two boys, he left.

Trelawny's account of the miseries of his first days at school could apply to generations of schoolboys before and since. His experience is normal among the more expensive English boarding schools. Many men survive unscathed from the system and some thrive on it, and even Seyer's school has its roll of distinguished alumni who made good. It is almost obligatory, almost part of the conventions of autobiography, for famous men to claim later that they were miserable at school, that they were badly treated, and that they learned nothing. Yet the Reverend Samuel Seyer's establishment was run with a severity remarkable even for the time. It was situated on a hill inside an old military fort with high windowless walls all around like a prison. Many of the rooms had iron bars on the windows, the food was disgusting and inadequate, and the punishments were frequent and severe.[13] 'I was flogged seldom more than once a day or caned more than once an hour,' Trelawny wrote. One of his contemporaries, recalling the same years, said that he was caned upon an average three times a day for seven years though not flogged.[14] The difference is not significant.

The schoolmaster was a dapper little man with sharp cruel eyes and a cold formal manner. The large bright silver buckles in his shoes, the stock tied tightly round his neck, and the powdered wig indicated a man old-fashioned in his dress and in his views. He was a passionate antiquarian and for thirty years was vice president of the local literary club, assiduously collecting material relating to the history and antiquities of his native city, and he had also published sundry sermons and books on Latin grammar. He was a pedant.

He held right-wing political views to the point of fanaticism, detesting all liberal causes, all ideals of the French Revolution, and all things French. During the wars, when hatred could pass for patriotism, he published a treatise which advocated suppressing the French language in England.[15] The dissemination of hateful French revolutionary ideas, he declared, was made easier by the use of French as the language of diplomacy. French books or plays should be heavily taxed or prohibited by law, and all French 'tutors, servants, and courtezans' expelled. Instead, Latin should be revived as a working language, an idea almost as bizarre in his day as it is now.

As with his father, so with his schoolmaster, Trelawny's reaction was total. The more they beat and punished him to make him conform to their own values, the more obstinate he became in his determination to be different. As soon as he had any awareness he unhesitatingly proclaimed himself an atheist, a republican, and a sympathiser with the French Revolution. Priests and Christianity were forever to be associated in his mind with misery, oppression, and self-righteous injustice.

According to his own account, Trelawny spent two years at the Seyer School, but then his endurance was at an end. He decided to organise the other boys into a conspiracy. One day when Seyer's assistant was taking them on a country walk he seized him, held him down and – remembering maybe his victory over the raven – twisted his cravat round his neck until he could hardly breathe, 'till the sweat dropped from his brow like rain from the eaves of a pig's sty'. Then the boys flogged him. When they got back to the school, Seyer determined to make an example of Trelawny by flogging him in front of the assembled school, but on the first stroke, Trelawny seized the schoolmaster by the legs so that he fell heavily on the back of his head.

Trelawny was overpowered and put in solitary confinement with a bread and water diet, but he still refused to submit. On the second night he set fire to the bed clothes with his candle and caused considerable damage to the building before the fire was put out. The next day, on Seyer's orders, he was despatched home under guard.[16]

Trelawny's father was mercifully away and apparently Trelawny was not punished. A return to school was, however, out of the question and Brereton looked around for some other way of dealing with his violent, ungovernable, rebellious son.

2

The Navy

These are to certify the principal Officers and Commissions of His Majesty's Navy that Mr Edward Jno. Trelawny served as volunteer of the 1st Class on board His Majesty's Ship Colossus under my Command from the 20 November 1805 to the date hereof, during which time he behaved with diligence and sobriety and was always obedient to command. Given under my hand this 29th December 1805.

J. N. Morris, Captain[1]

At the age of twelve Trelawny joined the Royal Navy, a profession to which younger sons of the gentry were traditionally assigned. He was entered in the books of H.M.S. *Superb* at Portsmouth on 15 October 1805 as 'volunteer first class' and set sail at once to join Admiral Nelson's squadron off Trafalgar. A few days later the *Superb* put in near Plymouth to take on board Admiral Duckworth and a consignment of stores, and then sailed south.

On 3 November at sea off the Scilly Isles she encountered the schooner H.M.S. *Pickle* that brought the news of the great victory at Trafalgar and the death of Lord Nelson a few days before. And so, to his everlasting regret, Trelawny missed his chance to participate in the most famous naval battle in history. Shortly afterwards the *Superb* met the survivors of the battle on their way back to England, and Trelawny spent a few days in the *Temeraire* before being drafted into his own ship, the *Colossus*. Both vessels had suffered heavily in the battle, losing their masts and sustaining many casualties, so that one of Trelawny's first experiences of naval life was to hear the screams of the wounded and the dying in the filthy holds of the ship as she made her way home through a violent storm in the Bay of Biscay. Another was the invasion of the ship by the doxies of Portsmouth when she arrived (it was normal for women to be allowed to stay in all messes when a ship was in port) and the traders who swarmed over the fleet to strip poor Jack of his hard-earned pay and prize money.

The *Colossus* could not go to sea for some time, so Captain Morris wrote to Colonel Brereton asking what to do about his son. They decided to send him to a naval school near Portsmouth, where his name appears in the account books, until a new appointment could be found for him.

Life on board a man-of-war was dangerous and uncomfortable. In the age of sail, ships could and did remain at sea for months on end without the need to return to port. At all times danger was near, as much from the perils of the sea as the violence of the enemy. More ships and lives were lost through storms and wrecks than fell to French guns. The food was coarse and stale; the drinking water polluted; washing was rarely possible. Sailors were liable to numerous deficiency diseases ranging from scurvy to loss of teeth, and in the East and West Indies entire squadrons would sometimes be devastated by typhus or yellow fever. The sailors lived, ate, and slept in a small confined space beneath decks only a few feet above a bilge where the accumulated filth and detritus of the voyage slewed about in a disgusting cesspool. Even on the most uneventful voyage men would frequently be killed or mutilated by falling from the yards on to the deck, and if someone fell overboard the chances of rescue were small. Drunkenness was rife, normal in fact, in all parts of the ship, with nearly every man taking his half pint of spirits a day. Associated with drunkenness was a high incidence of mental disorders as men sober or drunk stumbled about knocking their heads and damaging their brains against the timbers. The Admiralty maintained its own bedlams so great was the problem.

It was a violent age and its coarseness was undisguised. The hypocrisy of the Victorians was yet to come. Naval boys were not the curly-haired cherubs dressed in neat sailor suits beloved by later generations, but apprentices for a rough life and the cruel trade of war. The youngest boys lived in the gun room where the gunner was expected to keep an avuncular eye on them, but before long they were moved to the after cockpit, the midshipmen's mess, which was notorious for riot and drunkenness. Trelawny had numerous stories about his early days in the navy, the cruelties and thievery, the bullying and victimisation. He used to tell how he had been forced to swallow liquor for the first time; how an older man, the master's mate, took him on his first all-night run ashore; and how he had surprised his commanding officer in a brothel in India.[2]

At sea, scarcely a week went past without a man being flogged, stripped to the waist, tied to a mast, and his back beaten with a rope and then salt water thrown over the bleeding flesh, but violence was also an intrinsic part of social life on board a man of war. The proper response to any insult intended or not was a challenge. Quarrels were resolved by bare-fist fighting; the loser usually lost a few teeth, if he had any left, in the process; and it was socially acceptable to laugh if a comrade broke a few ribs. It was a rough code but one with which Trelawny was familiar from his time at school. He thrived on it and he never felt any inclination to rebel against it. All his life whatever company he moved in, however gentle, he remained quarrelsome and combative, quick to take offence and eager to start fighting at the slightest provocation. He lived his life according to the manners of the after cockpit.

Colonel Brereton thought that he had chosen well for his recalcitrant son. And, in fact, despite all the dangers and disadvantages, the navy was an attractive profession. For an ambitious man without the prospect of an independent fortune it offered a more promising career than any other. There was no buying or selling of commissions as in the army, so wealth was not strictly necessary for promotion. On the other hand an influential and well-connected family, such as the Breretons were, could ensure by political interest that its less-well-off members would be looked after. In war-time it was possible to become rich, even immensely rich, through the system of dividing the proceeds of the sale of captured enemy vessels among the crews. The chances were not high but, in the opinion of many men, they were worth running huge risks for, and the advantages of being an admiral or a captain over a commander or lieutenant, let alone a man on the lower deck, were vast.

For the successful naval officer the sky was the limit – riches, honours, perhaps a peerage, a position in the government, a stately house and country estate and the prospect of founding a new aristocratic family. The crucial step was promotion to post-captain. Once an officer had reached that rank a comfortable future was assured, even without prize money, whether he was afloat or retired. The pay was adequate and even if he was never given active employment, the so-called 'half-pay', which was more than half in fact, was also adequate. Once on the post-captains' list, advancement was entirely by seniority and a man had only to stay alive to be sure in time of becoming admiral of the fleet. Families were therefore anxious that their naval sons should pass through the lower commissioned ranks of lieutenant and

The British invasion forces landing at Mauritius, 29 November 1810.
Trelawny was probably in command of one of the boats

Midshipman under punishment at the masthead

Privateer Schooner attacking and sinking an East Indiaman

Port Louis, Mauritius, after the surrender, 1810. Surcouf's privateer, the *Revenant* and her prizes lie at anchor with units of the British fleet

commander as quickly as possible, and in particular that they be commissioned as lieutenants at the earliest possible age.

There was a minimum age for entry to the navy of thirteen; and for promotion to lieutenant of nineteen; but at a time of inadequate records these requirements were difficult to enforce, and provided a candidate for a commission looked reasonably mature, the examining board would not enquire too closely. For five shillings the porter at the Navy Office would supply him with a piece of paper certifying him to be whatever age he wished to be. To obtain a lieutenant's commission, however, it was necessary to present captains' certificates showing six years' satisfactory naval service and this condition was harder to evade. It therefore became the practice to put boys into the navy as young as possible so that, if nothing else, they could gather the necessary documents. Sometimes boys were entered on the books of ships without being aboard so as to gather credit for sea-time, but even by the loose standards of official morality of the time, this was considered cheating.

Many of the most successful admirals of the time owed their success, in part, to their parents' foresight in putting them afloat when they were very young and thus giving them a good start on the seniority lists. The Breretons, by putting Trelawny into the navy before he had reached his thirteenth birthday, although breaking the regulations, were not breaking the conventions. With reasonable luck and some pull and push from influential friends he was likely to be commissioned as a lieutenant by the age of eighteen at the latest. If the war went on, as seemed likely, he might be set for a very successful career. They gave him all the help they could. Sir Christopher Hawkins wrote letters on his behalf to Sir Edward Pellew, the admiral (from Cornwall) who was Commander-in-Chief in the East Indies during Trelawny's service there; and the Breretons cultivated the friendship of the various naval captains who agreed to take their son in their ships, on occasion having them come to stay at one or other of their homes.

A boy volunteer like Trelawny was in one of the most privileged positions in the navy. Not for him the lash which kept the lower deck loyal to their duty. He would from the beginning have the status of a gentleman. The captain would always be conscious that the influence of a man's family could affect his own career. He would want him to be successful and would be tempted to gloss over any failures. He might transfer a difficult young man to another ship if he got the chance, but he would do his best to turn him into an acceptable naval officer.

From the muster records of the ships in which he served we can follow Trelawny's career and watch him playing the normal game of exaggerating his age. In H.M.S. *Woolwich* in 1807, he was rightly entered as aged fourteen, but just over a year later in 1808 he was entered as nineteen. In April 1810 when he was still only seventeen he was entered as aged twenty two and thereafter during his naval career, although he sometimes slipped back to twenty one, he was always officially above the minimum age for appointment as lieutenant.

At the beginning of 1806 he joined the frigate H.M.S. *Woolwich* in which he was to make his first long voyages, under the command of Captain Francis Beaufort, the famous hydrographer, a short man, who according to Trelawny, 'used to twist and screw his head aside to look up at me and snarl'.[3] The *Woolwich* sailed to Bombay and Madras by way of the Cape and escorted home a convoy of merchant vessels, the East India Company's China fleet, which had been assembled off Ceylon. She then sailed to the mouth of the River Plate where she remained for six weeks making a survey for an Admiralty chart, returning by way of the Cape and St. Helena. Apart from a few weeks in Plymouth when Trelawny made a brief visit home she was away from England for nearly two years.

Within two months Trelawny was at sea again, this time in the frigate *Resistance*, cruising in the Channel and the Bay of Biscay, and again, when he reached England after eight months, he was by his father's request, immediately transferred to the frigate *Cornelia* bound for Bombay and the East Indies, and spent much of 1809 cruising in the Indian Ocean. He was on board when she was sent to explore the virtually unknown archipelago of Diego Garcia, which was being considered as a possible assembly place for an attack on Mauritius, and then in December 1810, while serving in the *Cornwallis*, he took part in the invasion itself.

A huge force of ships and men had been assembled, for it was not known how strong the French were and the commander-in-chief was determined to take no chances. On 29 November, the invasion fleet appeared off Mapou Bay and forty-seven boats were got ready to lead the invasion force. Trelawny, as a midshipman, was probably in command of one of these boats. An eye witness described the sight as the invading boats approached the unknown shore:

The bay was undefended, as far as could be ascertained, by works; and an opening in the reef promised to admit as many boats abreast as would suffice to land the first division of the army . . . The arrangements were such that, in little more than an hour, two thousand men had been embarked, the boats placed in their proper stations and preceded and flanked by gun boats: the whole of the division now moved towards the shore, presenting a most magnificent and interesting spectacle . . . While pulling to the beach, we on board could not but feel the most lively anxiety for the event, and continued gazing intently till we saw the troops land, form, and advance, without a musket being fired.[4]

The French offered token resistance later, but Trelawny probably stayed on board ship and would not have seen any fighting. When the French capitulated soon afterwards, honours were exchanged, and a grand ball was held in Port Louis for all the British officers. In the days that followed there were opportunities to explore the island and Trelawny was to remember Mauritius vividly and affectionately for the rest of his life. Within three weeks of the invasion, however, the *Cornwallis*, with Trelawny on board, had set sail on the long voyage back to India.

For two months she refitted at Madras, during which time she was renamed H.M.S. *Akbar*, and then, with the commander-in-chief Sir Samuel Auchmuty on board, she sailed to join a new fleet which had been assembled to invade Java. It consisted of four line-of-battle ships, fourteen frigates, seven sloops, eight East India Company cruisers and fifty-seven transport vessels crammed with 12,000 soldiers, their guns and horses. On 19 April 1811, the first day out from Madras, the fleet was struck by a tremendous hurricane but no ships were lost. In July when the ships reassembled at Malacca, an ammunition ship blew up, but again they were lucky, and the invasion force was still near full strength on 4 August when they started to disembark on the coast of Java about ten miles from Batavia.

The defenders of Java were not content with a token resistance like their comrades in Mauritius. When a British officer was taken blindfold through the Dutch and French lines to demand the surrender of the island, the governor told him that his forces would fight to the last extremity. After a good deal of skirmishing the Dutch and French retired behind fortified lines and the British prepared for an assault. Guns from the warships were landed and dragged to the scene by detachments of seamen, and it was probably on 22 or 23 August 1811 that Trelawny was wounded – a ball lodged in his knee and he was slashed in the face – when a party of French made a sortie from the jungle and attacked the naval guns. On 26 August the British army assault went in, and although over 500 men were killed or wounded, the defenders were overwhelmed and the island capitulated soon afterwards.

The navy had suffered few casualties in the fighting and Trelawny was one of only twenty-nine men reported wounded, but soon after the surrender the terrible *cholera morbus* which had been lurking among the British forces before the invasion burst into an epidemic. Over two hundred seamen died in unspeakable misery and hundreds more, including Trelawny, suffered severely. In October, presumably invalided, he returned to India, where he was transferred to H.M.S. *Piedmontaise* and immediately set sail for the long voyage back to England. On 12 August 1812 she reached Woolwich docks. Trelawny was then under orders to transfer to another ship, the *Armide*, but she had sailed before the *Piedmontaise* reached port, and in any case he was probably still too ill to go to sea. His family took him down to Cornwall and nursed him back to health with fresh food and clean air.[5] By Christmas 1812 he was again quite well.

And here the authenticated record of Trelawny's naval career comes to an end. He never went to sea again, and a final settlement of pay was made in 1815. At the time he left the service he was nineteen, having been at sea almost continuously for seven years. He had gone as a small boy: now he was a grown man.

3

At the Masthead

I was torn away, not seeing my mother or brother or sisters, or
one familiar face; no voice to speak a word of comfort, or to inspire me with the smallest hope that anything human took an
interest in me. Had a servant of our house, nay, had the old
mastiff, the companion of my childhood, come to me for one
hour, I could have hugged him for joy, and my breast would have
been softened to parental love instead of hardening indifference.
Trelawny's later account of going to sea.[1]

During these years when Trelawny was in the Navy, Colonel and Mrs
Brereton thought they were doing well by their son, for they had done
everything possible to advance his career. In particular they had
ensured that he earned the maximum sea-time – no wasting time on
shore when he could be collecting those valuable certificates so necessary for advancement in the profession. John seemed to like the
service – just what a rough, tough boy needed.

In fact Trelawny was desperately unhappy. His family's haste to
get him to sea and keep him there looked to him like deliberate re-
jection. As he returned from each voyage having seen exotic lands,
battles, storms, and strange beasts, all that his family seemed interested
in was to get him to sea again as soon as possible. Sometimes he never
even went home but hung around Portsmouth or Plymouth waiting to
be posted. He was an unattractive boy. As his uncle wrote after seeing
him in 1808 when he was home on leave: 'He is much grown but
improved I cannot say for in all my life I never saw such a lout of a
boy. His health too is not good.'[2] His father too made no secret of his
continuing disgust with his younger son.

Trelawny grew to hate the navy with a deep loathing which was to
persist for the rest of his life. He proved incapable of submitting to the
discipline which the service demanded. Despite all his advantages, he
was always in trouble; in modern parlance his behaviour was 'disturbed'. Some of his captains, conscious of the influential connexions
of their exasperating protégé transferred him on the first opportunity

to another ship, and few midshipmen in so short a naval career can have been moved so swiftly round the fleet. And he was always being punished.

The commonest method was to send him to the masthead for four or five hours at a stretch. There he would sit clinging to the rigging high above the ship, swaying with every wave and breeze, cut off from all human contact. It is easy to picture him there, hour after hour, nursing a sense of grievance, planning more disobedience and indulging a secret longing for revenge. The masthead was one of the few places which gave any sense of privacy, a place where a withdrawn boy would withdraw further into himself with nothing to entertain him but his own thoughts.

Or sometimes he would read. Marryat, who was a midshipman in the navy at about the same time as Trelawny, says that he acquired most of his education while at the masthead under punishment.[3] We may imagine Trelawny on high, avidly reading the few books available on a man-of-war, the latest voyages and travels full of adventures in remote unknown lands. One such was William Bligh's famous account of the mutiny on the *Bounty*. Bligh had been the captain of the *Bounty* when the mutiny occurred and it is difficult not to admire the courage and resource of a man who sailed the loyal members of the crew to safety over thousands of miles of ocean in an open boat. But to Trelawny, smarting under his own humiliation, it was the mutineers who were the heroes and especially Fletcher Christian who struck the first blow against the hated captain.

At the masthead the sickly teenage lout would undergo a secret transformation:

> Though not one of these granite pillars I gave token not artificially of belonging to their hardy breed for at this period of my life I had attained the attributes of perfect manhood. I was six feet in stature, robust, and bony, almost to gauntness; and with the strength of maturity, I had the flexibility of limb which youth alone can give. Naturally of a dark hue, my complexion readily taking a darker from the sun, I was now completely bronzed. My hair was black and my features perfectly Arab. At seventeen I looked to be seven and twenty.[4]

Then again, in the loneliness of the night when all was quiet, Trelawny and the other boys on watch would talk. They would dream of deserting, of making a new life in India where fortune awaited the brave adventurer. And they would spin elaborate dreams of mutiny and vengeance against their cruel officers.

Trelawny's own account of his life in the navy, written much later, is a catalogue of violent assaults on his superiors. In one ship, he says, the captain's clerk tried to steal his books. A fight developed and Trelawny wounded the man severely by stabbing him with a pen knife. He was taken before the captain, and spat in his face. In the *Cornelia*, it was the second lieutenant who, according to his story, brought out his violent obstinacy. In a brawl in a billiard room at Bombay Trelawny drew his sword and struck the lieutenant on the mouth with the hilt. He kicked him, tore his coat open, and beat him with the sword until it broke. He then thrashed him with a billiard cue until the blood was running from his mouth and some of his teeth were jammed in. If Trelawny's friends had not intervened, the lieutenant would have been killed. As it was, he was left in a heap on the floor 'blubbering like a boy'. But as with so many of Trelawny's battles it is difficult to see what was the principle on which he was so proud of having taken a resolute stand. He simply exulted in his own truculence.

If he hated the Royal Navy, he loathed the Honourable East India Company. In an age unashamed of economic exploitation, profit was everything, and the objective of every Englishman was to make enough money to retire in comfort to England. Although the Company had already assumed responsibility for governing parts of India, and was putting up magnificent buildings with the confidence of men who were sure the Company was there to stay, there was little sense of responsibility towards the native population. To Trelawny, the Europeans in India, arrogant and grasping, bloated with overeating and overdrinking, were contemptible, to be classed with the other objects of his hate, hereditary landowners like his father, schoolmasters, naval officers, and his other childhood oppressors. But at the same time his own attitude to the natives was as unenlightened as any nabob. When he saw the slaves at Mauritius labouring in the tropical sun, their bare backs long since broken by the lash into festering sores, he was shocked and disgusted. But pity was not in his nature.

The merchants of Bombay and Calcutta were forever complaining that the navy was not doing enough to protect them. Although the British had an overwhelming superiority in numbers, French warships and privateers roamed the Ocean from their base in Mauritius attacking the local shipping and the commerce of the East India Company.

Usually there was only a handful of raiders, but they exerted an influence and a terror out of all proportion to their numbers. They would appear suddenly, capture or sink a few merchant vessels and send their prizes back to Mauritius. Before the British forces could contemplate pursuit they would be attacking other shipping hundreds of miles away.

To the boy Trelawny, sulky and defiant under the latest assault on his pride, these French ships were allies, perhaps his only allies. Seldom seen yet always present in men's thoughts, these ships alone, it seemed, could shake the intolerable complacency of the Royal Navy and the Honourable East India Company. They alone could inflict the pain and humiliation on his oppressors which he longed to inflict himself. They were the enemies of Trelawny's enemies; therefore they were his friends. What is more they were heroes, gallant, courageous, fighting men acknowledged as such even by their enemies.

One man above all others terrified the British merchants in the Eastern seas. Robert Surcouf was one of the great corsairs of France.[5] For nearly twenty years he scoured the Indian Ocean. He knew its harbours, tides, and islands as well as any man of his day, and he had friends in every port from the time when he had been a slave trader. Surcouf was a privateer: a *lettre de marque* from the French Government gave him the privileges of an officer in the French navy, but for much of the time he was a simple pirate. His strength was in speed and cunning rather than fire power, and, if it came to fighting, he much preferred a hand-to-hand encounter with cutlasses to any cannonade. That way the captured ship and its cargo would not be damaged.

In 1796 he boldly took his small ship alongside the huge British East Indiaman *Triton* as she lay at anchor. With only eighteen men he stormed on board armed with cutlasses and battleaxes, killed the captain and two other men who stood in their way, and captured the ship. The loss and humiliation to the Company were intense – East Indiamen were heavily armed and regarded as virtually the equivalent of naval frigates; and the *Triton*, it was said, had over 450 men on board. In October 1800 he captured another East Indiaman, the *Kent*, by coming up under false colours and sending an armed boarding party into the ship before anyone was fully aware of what was happening, killing the captain and taking over the vessel. Soon afterwards Surcouf returned to France where he was fêted by the Government and enrolled in the Legion of Honour. He was personally presented to Napoleon to give his advice on the best way of conducting the naval war against England, and various tempting offers were made to France's sole naval hero of the war.

Then in 1807, at the time when Trelawny first arrived in the East, Surcouf suddenly reappeared in the Indian Ocean in a newly fitted out privateer, the *Revenant*. The result was dramatic. He made straight for the Bay of Bengal, which the British had regarded as safe, and captured five ships. He then sailed west and captured another seven, all of which were, despite the British blockade, successfully sent back to Mauritius, and since many of them were laden with rice, the effect was to relieve the siege.

A feeling of despair seized the British merchant colonies in India. A price was offered for Surcouf dead or alive, but his enemies had no real idea of what they were looking for. One of the Calcutta newspapers declared 'We hope that Surcouf will soon be captured by one of our cruisers. When he is we will put him in an iron cage and exhibit him to the people.'[6] The merchants of Bengal turned on the commander-in-chief for his failure to provide adequate naval protection. They prepared a long petition to the Lords of the Admiralty explaining how the whole situation in India had been transformed by the arrival of one French privateer. Marine insurance was now impossible to obtain, and trade was virtually at a standstill. The note of panic in their voices rings through the bureaucratic prose of their petition:

> All the captures . . . were made in the Bay of Bengal by two French Frigates and a Privateer named the *Revenant* of sixteen guns. It was the lot of this privateer to make the greater part of these captures, and his depredations were committed chiefly in view of the coast of Coromandel, where he had remained upwards of three months, distant little more than four hundred miles from Calcutta and within one hundred leagues of Madras roads, the principal station of His Majesty's ships, and where at the same time the Flag of a British Rear Admiral and several of His Majesty's pennants were displayed. It will scarcely be believed, or rather it will be believed with surprize and indignation that the privateer in which the Enemy has thus successfully extended his depredations along our defenceless shore, still continues on his station, and notwithstanding the extent of the British naval force in this country, such is the unprotected state of our seaboard, that this single privateer already so destructive to our commerce, and though of a force contemptible when compared with the smallest of His Majesty's ships, continues to spread consternation throughout the ports of India, creating alarm for the

safety of the ships that are at sea, deterring the outward bound from proceeding on their voyages, and inducing Government as a means of produce, to lay an embargo on the Trade.[7]

By October 1807 Surcouf had captured so many ships that he could not spare the hands to guard his prisoners, so instead he provided boats to send them back to India. His reputation rose higher still. Soon the British settlements in India were full of released prisoners singing the praises of their amazing captor. The *Revenant* sailed so fast, they declared, that no British frigate would ever catch her. Even the Company merchants could not withhold a grudging admiration when Surcouf generously arranged for the luggage of a certain Mr Nicoll, one of his prisoners who had escaped, to be sent on to him.[8]

Trelawny never met or saw Robert Surcouf. Often while in H.M.S. *Woolwich* or on his other voyages, they would sight a strange sail, there would be a chase, and the vessel would be brought to or she would throw off her pursuers. In the mounting excitement of these long chases the sailors would speculate and bet on the possibility that this time they might encounter the legendary corsair. Stories of the man, true or fantastic, flew about, how he had run away from school as a boy and by the time he was twenty-one was already rich and famous, captain of the most successful privateer in the Indian Ocean, how he had disobeyed and humiliated the Governor of Mauritius. But neither the *Woolwich* nor any other of the British naval vessels in the Indian Ocean ever found him. He was everywhere and nowhere, real enough to his victims but more terrifying to those who only knew his reputation. When in 1810 the British authorities finally decided to mount a full-scale invasion of Mauritius, this was largely because they could see no other solution to the problem of the French privateers.

By the time the island was conquered, Surcouf had returned to France but there were reminders of him everywhere. He had a fine house in Port Louis befitting a merchant prince, and everyone in Mauritius knew him. In the harbour stood his greatest monument, a mass of shipping, prize vessels of all types and sizes which Surcouf had brought in. Among them lay the *Revenant* herself, the famous ship in which Surcouf had won his latest triumphs. Did the young Trelawny, on shore leave from the invasion fleet after the surrender, have the opportunity to inspect this ship? Anyone who saw her, surrounded by all the shipping she had captured must have been amazed. Could this single vessel have caused such destruction? Was it possible that with this one ship Surcouf and his handful of followers had terrified and humiliated the Royal Navy and the whole of the British establishment in India? Was it to catch this ship that the British had assembled an invasion force of tens of thousands of men and a fleet of warships? And where was her captain now? Back in France? or capturing more British ships in the Channel, or the West Indies, or the Mediterranean?

Here was a real hero with whom the young Trelawny could identify. Here was a man who had compelled the world to take notice of him, a man who got what he wanted. Perhaps Trelawny too might become such a man? In reality he might be a despised midshipman, a clumsy teenager, an easy victim to be punished and humiliated by any officious junior officer. But alone at the masthead or in the long watches of the night, it could be different. He could dream. He too could be a Surcouf.

After a wounding snub from the lieutenant he would creep away and silently indulge his secret hatred in some quiet corner of the ship. He would find a way of punishing these petty dictators who held him in their power. He would join the legendary Surcouf, and become one of the chosen band of supermen of the *Revenant* – the second-in-command. With his hero in command he would capture their fine ships, burn their proud forts, steal their silks and spices and cargoes of tea, he would wipe the smile of superiority off their fat faces. As naval life became more intolerable, so Trelawny increasingly withdrew into his fantasy world.

4

Rejected

There are more helpless beings in the world than orphans . . .
Far more cruel is the lot of those who have hard-hearted and un-
feeling parents; or still worse, those who are selfish and indifferent,
exacting from their helpless and dependent offspring, duty and
obedience without giving in return a single glance of kindness
. . . The pride of my nature impelled me to shake off the bondage.
I did so. I could not endure the weight of slavery; but I cheerfully
put on the heaviest chains the foes of liberty have to impose –
and they are heavy. I walked with an elevated front. Alone I
withstood a fate that would have overpowered thousands, often
defeated, it is true, but ever, in losing, I have still won. In this hard
struggle, I had little refreshment but from the fountains of my
own soul.

Trelawny's view of his life struggle.[1]

In 1812, the year he left the naval service, Trelawny had been
formally qualified for at least a year to be considered for a lieutenant's
commission. Many of his contemporaries had already outstripped him,
for in the East Indies station, from where it took many months to
exchange a letter with the Admiralty, the rules were often set aside by
the commander-in-chief. Promotion could be accelerated and prize
money was plentiful. But although Trelawny had been personally
commended to the commander-in-chief it had done no good. This was
not due to excessive scruples on the part of Sir Edward Pellew, for he
had seen to it that his own sons were post-captains by the time they
were Trelawny's age and were earning thousands of pounds in prize
money. He himself earned – if that is the correct word – over £100,000
during his few months of command. Trelawny was simply not the kind
of boy who could be turned into a successful naval officer.

He never obtained his commission. By 1812, the year he returned
from India, a waiting list of qualified candidates had developed, and
commissions were being awarded at the rate of about twenty a month.
Then in 1815 the long war with France which had gone on almost
continuously since 1793 came at last to an end, the navy was drastically

cut back, and as a generous gesture by the Admiralty and the Treasury before the long days of peace began, no less than 833 lieutenants' commissions were authorised in the months of February and March. The men concerned had no careers to look forward to; their chances of being appointed to a ship, let alone of being promoted or winning prize money, were minimal; but at least with their commissions they would draw half-pay and be able to maintain a show of gentility. Those who were not in the lists, like Trelawny, got nothing. In the National Maritime Museum there is a picture of a 'midshipman on half-pay' a man no longer young, blacking shoes on Tower Hill – the point is of course that a midshipman had no half-pay. It was about this time that Trelawny began to refer to himself as Lieutenant Trelawny.[2] Perhaps it eased his humiliation. Perhaps this was his first successful lie.

In any case, very soon after he returned to England in 1812 an event occurred which put all thought of returning to the navy out of his head. Trelawny fell in love. He was nineteen when he met Caroline Addison and she was younger, and although neither family approved, they were married soon afterwards in May 1813.

She is described as beautiful and well educated, with the usual accomplishments of a lady of her time, who read French, drew, embroidered, and played the piano. Trelawny was still enough of a conformist to try to justify his choice according to his father's own standards. Caroline's family was 'fully the equal' of his own, he insisted, one of her sisters was married to a general and the other was engaged to someone 'much my superior'.[3] But his father was beyond reason. His son had disobeyed yet again and that was enough. He refused to accept the marriage or to increase Trelawny's allowance.

The young couple took cheap lodgings first in London then in Bristol, and after their first child, a daughter, was born in 1814, they lived very quietly. Plans were made to move to Wales to avoid expense and for a while it was intended that Trelawny would take a job with a merchant house in Germany. But all these schemes fell through, Trelawny fell into debt, and he was at last driven to the humiliation of seeking help from his father. Brereton, it seems, paid up, but we can imagine the cries of 'I told you so' with which this gesture was accompanied. He also altered his will.

Worse was to follow. The marriage was a disaster. Within a short time of the wedding Trelawny took to going off for long periods by himself, staying with friends in the country or on shooting expeditions and even when he was at home, he would frequently go out to the theatre by himself. In 1816, when Caroline was pregnant with a second child, the family were living in lodgings in Bristol kept by a Mrs Prout, and it was there that the maid, looking through the keyhole, discovered that Caroline was having an affair with another of Mrs Prout's lodgers, a certain Captain Coleman who was twenty or thirty years her senior. Some systematic spying revealed the whole business to Mrs Prout, and one day she waylaid Caroline on the staircase as she emerged from Coleman's room with her shoes in her hand. The couple were given notice to quit, but Caroline persuaded Mrs Prout to say nothing to Trelawny, and although his suspicions were aroused shortly afterwards, he seems not to have known fully what was going on until shortly before his wife suddenly eloped with Captain Coleman in December 1816. Soon the whole humiliating business was laid bare including the fact that everyone but himself had known about it.

As the law stood at the time, if he wanted a divorce he had first to bring a civil suit for 'criminal conversation' against Coleman, then go to a church court, and finally promote a private Act of Parliament. But there was no alternative, although Trelawny characteristically tried to challenge Coleman to a duel, and he embarked on a painful litigation which was to make his life miserable for years to come. The case was heard in July 1817 among much public interest. Besides newspaper reports there was the usual pamphleteer on hand ready to rush out his account of the family's disgrace to catch the market. After an embarrassing succession of servants and chambermaids had exposed Caroline's behaviour in vivid detail, Trelawny won the case but the damages awarded were put at only £500 and anyway Coleman escaped paying.

To whom could Trelawny now turn for the help and sympathy he so clearly needed? Certainly not to his family. Brereton's only idea was to bundle his son off to the army by buying him a commission, and when that offer was refused, his anger became fanatical. The name of John Trelawny, he declared, must never be mentioned in his presence again. Mrs Brereton and his daughters were to break off all contact with him, and he was no longer to be regarded as his son.[4] Soon afterwards when Trelawny's brother Harry also defied his father by marrying against his wishes, he too was disowned, and the whole Brereton family was thrown into further misery. But as a letter of Trelawny's mother reveals, they missed Harry more than Edward John:

Our sufferings have been dreadful. I told [Harry] in our last interview
that he was about to stab his parents who could not endure disgrace. The
loss of children we have survived but these horrors we could not. All his
answers to me have lately been 'I know you are prejudiced and will
prejudice my Father against me' What an accusation! I think I shall never
get over it from a son, so intensely beloved as was this man. It seemed so
natural to love him, the elder and future protector of his sisters and a
person that we expected to serve his family, without vices, & I thought
of a most affectionate [disposition] to his family although a reserved man
in general . . . His Father told him he would not receive him now we
are without sons . . . My poor daughters have all been ill by their
sufferings. You can hardly suppose how sincerely Kitty has lamented her
brother; she has fainted from want of rest and is as pale as death.[5]

The rest of the family were equally unhelpful. In 1812 when he first got
back to England from India, Trelawny stayed for a while with his
mother's brother, John Hawkins, at his country house, Bignor Park,
Sussex. Cut off from his nearest family he now turned to his uncle without hesitation. 'My dear Uncle' he began his friendly letter which asked
if he could pay a visit.[6] But Hawkins was apparently no different from
the other members of his family. He scented that his nephew was going
to ask for money and snubbed him and so, frozen with yet another
humiliation, Trelawny addressed his uncle for the last time:

Sir,
    Till your letter reached me, I did not suppose my miseries could bear
augmentation. The conscientious conviction of *never* having overleaped
the boundaries of honor – and the idea that I had been more sinned
against than sinning with the undiminished respect of the major part of
my famely, caused me so *uncautiously* addressing you – that I should have
been answered by so unjustified a rebuke had altogether escaped my
mind and this is the *last* time I shall ever take the *liberty* to trespass on
your time.[7]

Alone in London, cut off from his family, his only friend was the
daughter of his former landlady, who was herself undergoing a crisis
at this time, Augusta White. They had met while Trelawny and his wife
were staying with Captain and Mrs White at Bath in 1816, after they
had been given notice to quit by Mrs Prout in Bristol. Trelawny's
second child had been born at the Whites and it was there that Caroline's
involvement with Captain Coleman was finally exposed. He wrote to

Crim. Con.

THE
TRIAL
BETWEEN

LIEUT. TRELAWNEY,
PLAINTIFF,
AND

CAPT. COLEMAN,
DEFENDANT,
FOR

CRIMINAL CONVERSATION
WITH THE

PLAINTIFF'S WIFE,
INCLUDING THE

Amorous Love Letters,
&c. &c.

Tried in the Court of King's Bench, Westminster, before Mr. Justice Holroyd, and a Special Jury, July 9, 1817.

TAKEN IN SHORT-HAND.

LONDON:

Marchant, Printer, Ingram-court, London.
Published by JOHN FAIRBURN, 2, Broadway, Ludgate-Hill.
(Price Three-pence.)

Augusta of his anguish and of his determination to fight Coleman in a letter written a few days after Caroline eloped:

My dearest Crusta,

I send for my Cloathes – would to God I could see you once again but God Grant we may meet in happier hours – on Sunday pray for me – that day decides my life or death. I will trust to providence and the rest of my days shall compensate to my poor orphans for the wretchedness drawn on them by your Sincier and affectionate Friend – Last Wednesday, Augusta, will never leave your memory. Let my anguish there remind you of what *I* must endure and pity *even* while you must condemn. God bless you all adieu adieu . . .[8]

The White family were entirely on Trelawny's side, and Mrs White treated him as if he were her own son. But in February 1817, within two months of Caroline's elopement, they were themselves struck by a tragedy of their own. Captain White, who had long been unhappy and bowed down with money troubles, committed suicide and Mrs White and her daughters were left without a protector. Now it was Trelawny's turn to rise to the occasion. The White family had treated him like a son when his crisis struck; and he would be that same son in their hour of need. He wrote to Augusta without sentimentality:

After so dreadful a castrophe most of your friends would write lamentation at your Father's rash fate – but as I differ and am not swayed by opinions of other men – I shall commence with rejoicing that your unfortunate Father has at last ended his miseries – religious men would say – fool – his miseries are but commenced; for those of this world are but trivial to those in the next – but my soul tels me tis no such thing – A God of such infinate mercy – could not be more pityless than this hard hearted miserable world – God knows your Father's errors were most amply attoned for heare, – his faults weare many – his attonement *ample*, and his peace will last *for ever*. . . . .

tell your Mother to command me in every way. I would have come to you on the moment – but – that on reflection I have considered it was better not. . . . If I can be of the most *trivial* service *command* me and *I will fly* down to my *loved Sisters* – hasten to Town and as far as the most unremitting attention and participation comfort. Your Mother shall find in me a *Son*, you a *Brother*, and your Brothers a *Father* . . .[9]

Together Trelawny and the White family set about repairing their shattered lives. Some relations of the Whites called Johnson who lived in the Channel Islands agreed to take charge of Trelawny's younger daughter (the elder stayed with Caroline); arrangements were made for the schooling of the younger White children; and one of the daughters went out to work. As for Augusta, although for a while there was a suggestion that she and Trelawny might eventually be married, they drew back and went their separate ways, although their friendship was to last for the rest of their lives. In 1822 Augusta emigrated to Canada where she married.

For Trelawny, the years following the crisis of 1817 were probably the most difficult of his life. They are also among the most obscure and, for long intervals, we do not know where he was living or what he was doing. But it is clear that during this period his life was transformed. Like the victim of an accident who has lost part of his brain and has to learn the simple skills of life for a second time, his personality was permanently altered. He refused to accept failure. He refused to accept the judgement of his elders and betters. His family might regard him as ignorant, wilful, disobedient – a black sheep who had contemptuously resisted all their well-meaning schemes to set him up in one of the respectable professions open to a younger son, and brought failure and disgrace to everything he touched. Well, now that he was free of his family he could also shake himself free of his reputation. He could flaunt the characteristics which they had tried to beat out of him.

But to change the future, he had to change the past. The failures had to be exorcised, the disagreeable events suppressed, and in place of the painful reality, an acceptable myth had to be created. Many people edit their memories and censor their pasts, but with Trelawny the operation was drastic. The past had to be blotted out in its entirety. As a first step, as if to symbolise that he was a new person, he decided that he should now be called Edward Trelawny. To his family and to Caroline he had been John. From now onwards he would have his own name and live his own life.

5

Books

Trelawny would be a good fellow if he could spell and speak the truth.

Remark attributed to Lord Byron[1]

To all appearances Trelawny had reached adulthood without the rudiments of education necessary to pass as a gentleman. For example he could not spell. No wonder his famely and freinds were deseived with rgard to his abelety. It was hardly posseble to cumminicate with him; his spelling was a veretable proff of his indolense. They did not kno that he would one day be admiered and, in his oppinion, imortalized. It must surly not allways have loked resonable to see his retched spelling as an ingaging aspect of his magneficent and indefagetable emagination. Weare the sacrifieses they weare obllidged to make in sending him to shoole and to sea quight superfluas? What could they do to alevate the expense of theare extrordinary son and find him a disierable carer?[2]

His parents were of course wrong about this as in everything else about their younger son. Bad spelling is not illiteracy any more than good spelling is good literature. Only pedants and pedagogues confuse the two as Trelawny might himself have forthrightly declared. In fact, Trelawny's eccentric spelling has a value of its own,for when he writes abought his helth and strenth, of his uncezing amasement, of his persuit of plaseures, of being happy and contended, of souring above the clouds, of being sigened by ilness at prseant, or even his favourite cry from *Othello* 'who can controul his fate?' do we not hear a hint of a Cornish accent? And even while his parents were despairing that he would ever learn anything useful, Trelawny was giving himself an intense literary self-education

Within a few years his spelling had greatly improved although every letter has an ocasional error, and by the time he met Byron and Shelley in 1822 he was quite capable of writing orthographically if he chose. In later years he appears to have deliberately misspelt as a contribution to the personality picture of himself which he was building and he was especially careless or careful about the names of his friends. Anyone can be forgiven for Liegh Hunt and maybe even Daniel Robers[3] and Gane Williams[4] are understandable. But what about Bironic?[5] At a time when he had long established himself as Lord Byron's closest friend? And could a man signing himself John Trelawny unknowingly refer in the same letter and on the same page to his friends the Jhonsons and to Sir Jhon St Aubyn? The answer is that he could, for even when he was twenty-nine, he sometimes thought his own name was Jhon Trelawny.[6]

During his years in London he was reading voraciously, making up for the wasted years which he had spent confined in warships. And night after night he would be at his place in Covent Garden or Drury Lane to see the great players of the day – Mrs Siddons, Kean, the Kembles, Mathews – in their famous Shakespearean roles. On one such occasion he is said to have been at the centre of a disturbance and made such a spectacle of himself that he was obliged to make a public apology in the newspapers.[7]

He loved especially the great tragedies, *Othello, Hamlet, Macbeth*, and *King Lear*, which he saw performed again and again in that highly melodramatic style which was then the fashion, and he could recite long passages by heart. His letters are full of Shakespearean quotations, not carefully looked up in a book but thrown down on the page as he remembered them, full of errors – a sure sign of spontaneity.

He wrote to Augusta White, who had asked about the portrait of him which she was keeping:

> Should any other eye ever peruse it and wonder what could tempt you to preserve or admier such an object, answer in the words of Desdemona!
>
> > I saw Othello's visage in his mind
> > And to his honors and his valient parts
> > Did I my soul and fortunes consecrate
>
> As to the fitness of the quotation in regard to me, never mind that, no acasion to anaylise these things, – I have latterly spent much time with some of the most sensible of the actors – I do not court their society as is often the case for pleasuere & fun – but for instruction and mental intercourse, as many of them are extreme well red, & clever, and men of talent are always disierable companions, be their rank in life what it may.[8]

He began to see his life in tragic and dramatic terms. Poetry gave a grandeur to misfortune and his own failures were ennobled and made tolerable by clothing them in Shakespearean language. He took the faults which his family saw, and with the aid of words, turned them into virtues. Yet, therapeutic value apart, what did his friends think when they received letters such as the following written to Augusta White in 1817, in which he refers in typical style to the decision of her sister to take paid employment and his own uncertainties about going abroad?

> Thank all good stars that your sister is so fortunately situated. I hear she is quight happy & contended – and it joys me to think tis so. Would the same humble way of life serve you – I fear me not – would to heaven I could better speak my love and interest for you – my wishes always outstrip my means and even bankrupt my emagination fertile as it is in coining – the giddy phantoms of the mind – I form a thousand differant plans to dispose of myself – one suceeds another in quick succession – but till released for ever from the chains which still bends my spirit downwards, and till shaken of must mar every aspiering hope – let that golden dream be realized – let me hear that what I have long dreampt is true and more I ask not – I shall then like the lark when first uncaged after a tedious bondage – wing my weigh on high, and sour above those clouds which have long kept me in darkness,

> > I hope though young and rose liped cherubim
> > Bright as the reinbow's hues – which to
> > the soul of lead, does dart thy sunbeams,
> > melts the o'er, extracting all its drossy heaveness
> > and bids it live they votary. –

> but tis time to desend from these cloud clapt towers, those airy nothings, and take another glimpse of this bare earth.[9]

One wonders whether Augusta picked up the references to *Othello, The Tempest, A Midsummer Night's Dream,* and *Richard II.*

A list survives of the books which Trelawny owned about this time and it is revealing of the kind of man he was.[10] The works of Lord Byron were at the head of his list, and he had copies of Shakespeare and Milton, and a virtually complete library of the most successful romantic literature of the day, Sir Walter Scott, Samuel Rogers, Thomas Moore (although no Lake poets). But he had no classics, no history, no biography, no science, no philosophy, no travel, except, prophetically, a book about Greece to which his uncle John Hawkins had contributed. The view of the human world which a sociologist would form if he had to rely on Trelawny's library for his picture would be a strange one. It was however this strange world which Trelawny increasingly tried to inhabit, a world of war, love, treachery, passion, fate, mystery, revenge.

The first cantos of *Childe Harold's Pilgrimage*, which made Byron famous, came out in 1812, the year of Trelawny's release from the navy, and the book had gone through ten editions by 1815. *The Giaour*, published in 1813, sold 12,500 copies within a few months. *The Corsair*, which appeared in 1814, sold 10,000 copies on the day of publication and more than 25,000 within a year. *Lara* appeared in 1814, *The Siege of Corinth* in 1816, *Manfred* in 1816. On the day a new poem was published, the streets near John Murray's at 50 Albemarle Street were jammed with carriages, as lords and ladies, gentlemen and footmen jostled at the sales windows in their eagerness to buy.[11] Trelawny, we may guess, was among those crowds and on his visits to Drury Lane he may have caught a distant glimpse of the famous poet in person in his private box.

To the young Trelawny, the effect of Byron's poems can hardly be exaggerated. Conrad the Corsair, the Giaour, and Lara, overwhelmed his imagination. Here, he felt, was life as it should be lived, on the grand scale. How like himself they seemed. Was he not a man of strong passions like Conrad or Lara? Had he not been forced into a harsh and violent world while still a child? Did he not have a taste for quarrelling and revenge, a reputation for truculence?

These qualities had hitherto brought him only failure and disgrace but that, surely, was the fault of his narrow-minded family and their allies, the Seyer School and the navy, who were too mean-spirited to appreciate the magnificence of it all. Now he had a justification. He need not feel ashamed of his character and apologise for it, he would be proud. It was he who was right and they who were wrong. Among his books he preserved a single back number of the *Monthly Review*, the issue which contained a long review of *The Corsair* when it first appeared: 'The Corsair . . . is possessed of great merit; and in this respect it must rank before any other effort of the author's pen, that it contains one whole character drawn with uncommon force and discrimination. Conrad is stained with all sorts of crimes; he is (as we are to presume) an outlaw from society; he is a pirate, and a murderer, but with all this, he loves truth and feeling . . .'[12] This is how Trelawny increasingly liked to imagine himself. He even looked like a Byronic hero. In the navy he had been a clumsy unattractive adolescent, but by the time he was twenty a remarkable change had occurred. The gangling youth was now tall, with thick hair and fine sharp features, dark in complexion, interesting, mysterious, handsome. In this respect at least his masthead dreams had come true.

About this time his friends started to call him 'The Turk' or 'The Grand Turk', a significant detail.[13] The popular image of a Turk in those days was derived from pictures, and especially from the engraved pictures of Turks which illustrated the works of Lord Byron. Trelawny was called 'The Turk' because he looked like the pictures of Conrad and Selim. Perhaps it started as a joke, but the idea stuck.

6

Switzerland

As to pecuniary affairs, but that you have, I should not mention them. My father's allowance since my connection with Mrs T has been three hundred per annum which sum I have *never exceeded*, or ever applied to *any individual* of my friends for pecuniary aid, although *burthened* with an extravagant wife and two children – it needs no comments, I state only facts.

From a letter to his rich uncle
John Hawkins 6 May 1817[1]

Without friends or family, England held nothing for him and he needed to start afresh. He intended for a while to go to Buenos Aires which he had visited in the navy, and where he had friends, and join a new colony – perhaps with Augusta White. But with the law's delay it was not until 1819 that the final act of divorce was obtained, and by that time the idea of South America had been abandoned, and he decided instead to go to the Continent. Life was cheaper there and for a man in Trelawny's position, that was a very important consideration. The allowance of £300 a year from his father – which continued to be paid despite their quarrel – was adequate but only if he watched every penny. He had his daughter to maintain – at a cost of perhaps £50 per annum – and books and hunting, his two chief interests, were expensive.

A useful indicator of what Trelawny's allowance was worth is the level of half-pay in the armed forces, for although retired officers usually had other sources of income and might even occasionally work, the customs of the day allowed that they should, if necessary, be able to subsist on their half-pay alone. We may take the following as official indicators of the amounts considered sufficient to maintain minimal gentility in Trelawny's day:

Senior Captain RN	£265 per annum
Senior Commander RN	£183 per annum
Senior Lieutenant RN	£128 per annum
Junior Lieutenant RN	£ 91 per annum

Obviously he was well above the distress level.

However, readers in the 1970's do not need to be reminded of the insecurity of an income fixed in money terms: anyone dependent on a fixed income is bound to be influenced by fear of inflation. Between 1790 and 1813 during the long wars with France, the price level in England almost doubled, and although after the peace in 1814/1815 it fell a little, there was a further spurt in 1817 and 1818 which seemed to indicate that prices were going to start rising again. In fact the inflation was short-lived. The economy was already settling down to a long period of unprecedented growth, and prices were beginning the steady fall which was to last right through the century. Trelawny was to be one of a fortunate economic élite who enjoyed an unearned income rising in real terms, paid for out of taxation, but of course no one could be sure, when prices started to rise in 1817, that another long inflation was not on the way. The decision to live abroad, although obviously a result of many other factors, was good economic sense. On the rates of exchange which were available on British currency, a pound would buy one sixth more in France and Switzerland than in England. In Tuscany a pound would buy more than twice what it bought in England.[2]

In the autumn of 1819 Mrs Brereton decided to take her daughters to Paris and Trelawny accompanied them. Maria Edgeworth gives a tantalising glimpse of him at a party there in May 1820 at the house of the famous scientist Baron Cuvier. She probably knew him as one of the midshipmen of Captain Francis Beaufort with whom she was connected, for Trelawny had no claim to distinction at this time: 'Then Cuvier presented Prince Czartoninski, a Pole, and many compliments passed; and then we went to a table to look at Prince Maximilian de Neufchatel's *Journey to Brazil*, magnificently printed in Germany, and all tongues began to clatter, and it became wondrously agreeable; and behind me I heard English well spoken, and this was Mr Trelawny, and I heard from him a panegyric on the Abbe Edgeworth whom he knew well.'[3]

By the summer Mrs Brereton and her daughters had gone back to England, but Trelawny had moved on to Switzerland. His life was aimless. He was a young man in search of entertainment. Geneva, he complained, had not much to offer, no dice, no cards, only occasional theatres and opera, and little in the way of society. Most of his time was spent on hunting and fishing expeditions, in company with a retired naval officer called Daniel Roberts, whom he had known in England.

For Roberts, hunting was the only activity that made life worth while, and he was to spend the rest of his days (fifty years' worth as it turned out) slaughtering chamois in the Alps, woodcocks in the swamps of Italy, and trout in Wales. He had had a distinguished career in the Royal Navy during the war and, like Trelawny, served in the fleet which captured Java, but on a visit to Paris in 1815 immediately after the peace, he was involved in a violent incident with a French officer and his career was at an end. In 1820 Trelawny was content to follow him and much of his attention was taken up with dogs, horses, and guns, on which he spent lavishly – one favourite dog cost £20. Sport was noble and manly and exciting and, occasionally, dangerous. It was the violent man's substitute for war, but it hardly satisfied the romantic appetites which had been aroused in Trelawny by literature.

It was at Ouchy on the Lake of Geneva he wrote later, that he first became interested in Shelley. One day he met a bookseller friend seated on the terrace in front of the house where Gibbon had written the *Decline and Fall*. 'I am trying to sharpen my wits in this pungent air which gave such a keen edge to the great historian so that I may fathom this book,' the bookseller said. 'Your modern poets Byron, Scott, and Moore, I can read and understand as I walk along, but I have got hold of a book by one now that makes me stop to take breath and think.' It was Shelley's *Queen Mab*. Trelawny asked how he got the volume. 'With a lot of new books in English which I took in exchange for old French ones,' he replied. 'Not knowing the names of the authors I might not have looked into them had not a pampered prying priest smelt this one in my lumber room and, after a brief glance at the notes, exploded in wrath, shouting aloud "Infidel, jacobin, leveller; nothing can stop this spread of blasphemy but the stake and the faggot; the world is retrograding into accursed heathenism and universal anarchy!" ' The bookseller, when the priest had gone, took up the book saying to himself that surely it must be something worth tasting . . . 'The fruit is crude but well-flavoured; it requires a strong stomach to digest it; the writer is an enthusiast and has the true spirit of a poet. . . . They say he is but a boy, and this his first offering: if that be true, we shall hear of him again and again.'

Here it seemed was another author with whom Trelawny could identify fully. Not only was *Queen Mab* written in the rich romantic exaggerated style which was to his taste, but it articulated his own personal, political, and economic grievances.[4]

Soon afterwards, Trelawny heard the name of Shelley again. In the summer of 1820 he was a frequent guest at the country house near Geneva of Sir John St Aubyn, a rich old Cornish baronet who kept open house for his friends and acquaintances including his fifteen illegitimate children. Trelawny knew him as a neighbour and friend of the family both in Cornwall and in London, and one of the sons, John Humphrey St Aubyn, who was almost the same age as Trelawny had probably been at the Seyer School at the same time. It was at Sir John's house that he met Edward Ellerker Williams and Thomas Medwin, retired officers recently returned from India who were also living near Geneva.[5]

Williams who was born in 1793 in India, the son of an officer in the East India Company's army, was almost exactly the same age as Trelawny. He had spent some time at Eton, where he did not know Shelley, and was then entered in the navy at the age of eleven, but he hated it so much that he transferred to the army and went to India. A few years later he returned to Europe with Jane, the wife of another officer, and he was now living with Jane as 'Mr & Mrs Williams'.

As for Thomas Medwin, the most important fact of his life was that he was Shelley's cousin and had been at school with him. He was about three years older than Trelawny and Williams, and he too had served in India in the armed forces. Like Williams, he was now a lieutenant on half-pay, yet another of that army of down-at-heel retired officers whose careers had been cut off by the coming of peace and who were living abroad to avoid expense.

Trelawny's new friends shared his taste for romantic literature. Williams had ambitions to write a play and soon afterwards composed *The Promise, or a Year, a Month and a Day* which was turned down by Covent Garden. He tried again with *Gonzaga, Duke of Mantua* but he had little talent and probably knew it. Medwin on the contrary could regard himself as on the road to success. He had already published two books of poems, *Oswald and Edwin* and *Sketches in Hindoostan*, besides contributing a long article to a learned journal on certain cave temples he had seen in India. John Humphrey St Aubyn was writing *Mazza, a tale in three cantos*, a poem in imitation of *The Corsair*.[6]

Medwin has gone down in literary history as the prince of toadies, a man who wormed his way into the confidence of Byron and Shelley and made money by writing up their conversations. He was regarded by almost all of his friends as something of a bore, a view which the evidence of his literary works tends to confirm. Yet in 1820 Medwin had no need to feel inferior to his young cousin. Medwin, Williams, Shelley, St Aubyn, whatever their ultimate fame, all had in 1820 much the same precarious status as far as literature was concerned.

When Trelawny met Medwin in the summer of 1820, Shelley had just sent him a copy of his own new tragedy *The Cenci* and the two cousins were exchanging eager letters of criticism of each other's literary works. Shelley, who at the time was trying to establish a colony of like-minded friends, began to send Medwin pressing invitations to visit him at Pisa. And so, in response to Shelley's invitation to Medwin, the three rootless retired officers, Trelawny, Medwin, and Williams were drawn into the orbit of Shelley himself, and the idea began to take shape that they might all three go to Italy together to live near the man whose poetry and life they admired.

Trelawny immediately became wildly enthusiastic about *The Cenci*, as earlier he had passionately admired the verse tales of Lord Byron. On 20 September 1820 when he and Daniel Roberts were staying at an hotel in Lausanne, Roberts fortuitously made the acquaintance of two English ladies when he was sketching in the town. When introductions were made, it turned out that they were Mary and Dorothy Wordsworth and soon afterwards the famous Wordsworth himself appeared. Since they were all clearly preparing to leave in their carriage at once, Trelawny saw that there was no time to be lost. As he wrote later: 'I asked him abruptly what he thought of Shelley as a poet. "Nothing," he replied as abruptly. Seeing my surprise, he added, "A poet who has not produced a good poem before he is twenty-five, we may conclude cannot and never will do so." "The Cenci!" I said eagerly. "Won't do," he replied, shaking his head as he got into his carriage.'[7] At this time Wordsworth had probably never heard either of Shelley or of *The Cenci* which he was later to declare to be 'the greatest tragedy of the age'.

When Trelawny returned to Geneva after this excursion to Lausanne, news had arrived that his father had died in England a few weeks before, and he set off at once for home. Since Edward and Jane Williams intended to spend the winter in a French provincial town – to save money – they accompanied him to Chalons in his carriage. Medwin remained in Switzerland but shortly afterwards crossed to Italy to meet Shelley at Pisa. However, before the three friends went their separate ways, it was agreed that they would all meet again the following spring in Italy and go on a boating holiday with Shelley whom at this stage only Medwin knew personally.

Trelawny, it seems, was under the impression that the death of his father would make him a rich man, and made extravagant offers to his friends, for it may be Trelawny who is referred to in a letter Shelley wrote shortly after Medwin's arrival in Pisa: 'We have also been talking of a plan to be accomplished by a friend of [Medwin], a man of large fortune who will be in Leghorn next spring, and who designs to visit Greece, Syria, and Egypt in his own ship. This man has conceived a great admiration for my verses and wishes above all things that I could be induced to join his expedition.'[8]

Shelley, who had been toying with the idea of going to the East for some time, took this plan sufficiently seriously to begin learning Arabic in preparation, but it was soon dropped and the outbreak of the Greek Revolution in the spring of 1821 put it finally out of the question. But in any case, if Trelawny had hopes that his money troubles were over, his father's will must have come as a great disappointment. He was left no money or property at all to call his own, but a life income, on certain conditions, on £10,000 of 3% gilt-edged stocks; in other words, an income of £300 per annum.[9] He was destined to live on that for most of his life, and bitterness at being a younger son never left him. As he wrote later to Mary Shelley, when she too was in money difficulties, with his favourite cry from *Othello*:

I sympathise in your distresses. I have mine too, on the same score – a bountiful will and confined means are a curse, and often I have execrated my fortunes so ill corresponding with my wishes. But who can control his fate? Old age and poverty is a frightful prospect; it makes the heart sick to contemplate. Even in the mind's eye – he readily would wring a generous nature till the heart burst. Poverty is the vampyre that lives on human blood and haunts its victims to destruction. Hell can fable no torment exceeding it, and all the other calamities of human life – war, pestilence, fire cannot compete with it. It is the climax of human ill.[10]

The situation was unalterable. Trelawny stayed a few months in England, but as soon as Brereton's estate had been settled, Mrs Brereton and her daughters decided to move permanently to Paris apparently in the belief that potential husbands were easier to catch there. Trelawny himself returned to Switzerland and met Roberts at Geneva in early June 1821.

Hunting was still the passion of his life, and for three months he and Roberts pursued the unfortunate wild life of the Grisons. In his treks through the mountains he saw himself as Byron's *Manfred*. 'A hunter of the hills' he called himself, echoing *The Prisoner of Chillon*. 'The sport is tolerably good', he wrote to England. Fortune had been kind, although there had been 'trifling drawbacks' – their guide was killed by falling off a precipice and so was an expensive dog. 1822 was to be Italy's turn. Trelawny and Roberts laid plans to go on an extended expedition in the marshlands of Tuscany to kill snipe and woodcock; and horses and dogs were specially shipped to Leghorn to await his arrival.[11]

It was still the same aimless, useless, and wasteful way of life and Trelawny knew it. For all the high-flown grandiloquence of his language with its Shakespearean imagery and Byronic sentiments, Trelawny was a retired naval hearty. His new friends, Williams and Medwin, were also hunters. Both were fond of telling stories about lion and tiger shooting in India, and Williams joined Trelawny on some of his hunting expeditions in Switzerland. But though they were retired from the armed forces like himself, they were literary men too. They seemed to be making more of their lives.

No doubt Trelawny intended eventually to join them at Pisa as he had promised the previous year, but he was in no hurry, although letters from Williams began to point up the contrast in their lives. While Trelawny was preparing to waste his time and money chasing birds through the malarial swamps of Italy, Williams and Medwin were taking strides in their literary careers. They were all living at Pisa with Shelley and his friends and were at work on their books. Then suddenly towards the end of the year news arrived from Williams of an exciting new development. Through their connexion with Shelley, Williams and Medwin found themselves on friendly terms with the greatest literary celebrity of the day, for they had managed to make the acquaintance of Lord Byron who had arrived at Pisa at the end of October. The man whom, above all others, Trelawny admired! The author of *The Corsair*! The greatest Byronic hero of them all!

Trelawny wrote at once to ask Williams if he thought it would be possible for him to make the acquaintance of Lord Byron and he decided to leave Geneva for Genoa. At first Williams was guarded in his reply, but then on 26 December he wrote again. He was now on much closer terms with the poet than previously, he explained, and he was sure that an introduction could be arranged if Trelawny wanted it, although Byron normally refused absolutely to meet English visitors. In fact everyone at Pisa was now eager for Trelawny to come. The talk was all of the boats for the planned holiday in the spring. Byron wanted to join in the scheme and he was going to build a boat of his own. But they needed advice for everybody at Pisa was a landlubber. Would Roberts be able to help? What did Trelawny think?

He did not hesitate. Abandoning his plans for the hunting expedition with Roberts, he set out immediately for Pisa. He arrived on the evening of 14 January 1822.

7

Bamming the Blues

Towards the beginning of January Mr Trelawny arrived at Pisa. He was a friend of Williams through whom he met Shelley – and he was presented by Shelley to Lord Byron. The same evening LB visiting Madame Guiccioli as was his habit, opened a book which was lying on the table. It was a volume of his works. 'These are bad things to read, (said Lord Byron) 'I had believed up to the present time that these elucubrations, the fruit of solitude and a remedy against not doing anything worse, were at least not dangerous, but since this morning, I am afraid that I have been wrong. For I met an Englishman so eccentric that since his adolescence he has tried to realise the type of my Corsair. He keeps the poem under his pillow and they say that in the seas of India he aimed at creating such a personality by his deeds and behaviour.'

'Has he got a Medora too,' asked Teresa

'She must be dead,' replied Byron 'for it is claimed
that he leaves a Gulnare in every country he passes through.'

'I would be curious to see him; said the Countess.

'You won't like him,' replied Lord Byron.

Teresa Guiccioli writing much later.[1]

Percy Bysshe Shelley and his wife Mary had been living in Italy for nearly four years, having been driven to leave England in March 1818 by a succession of misfortunes. But their exile had brought little relief. In September 1818 one of their two children died, and when the other also died in June 1819, it seemed doubtful for a long time if Mary would ever fully recover. And everywhere they went they seemed to be pursued by money troubles, ill health, and misrepresentation.

Shelley had little public success as a poet, although many of his greatest works had already been published. The world was mainly interested in him as an object of scandal. It seemed incredible to his uncomprehending father that his son and heir, who could without effort have had fortune, position, and a seat in Parliament, should grow up to be a revolutionary and an atheist; and as for his views on 'free love', they were too painful to contemplate. Then Shelley had left his wife Harriet and their children – Harriet had later committed suicide –

to run away with Mary Godwin when she was still only sixteen, and he had taken along with him Claire Clairmont, Mary's step-sister, as part of his new *ménage*.

And certainly Shelley's household in Italy was a most unusual one, if not the 'League of Incest' or the 'Academy of Blasphemy' of contemporary comment. Mary – as befitted the only daughter of William Godwin and Mary Wollstonecraft – was highly educated, intellectual, and independent. She had been scarcely nineteen when she wrote *Frankenstein*, which achieved an immediate popular success, and she was determined to establish herself as a novelist. At the time of Trelawny's arrival in January 1822, she was mainly taken up with the care of her two-year-old baby son, Percy Florence Shelley, who had been born after the deaths of her earlier children.

Claire was a very different type of woman. She had joined Shelley and Mary when they first eloped as there was nowhere else for her to go, and she had lived with them off and on ever since. She too had an intense relationship with Shelley, the exact nature of which is still a matter for scholarly curiosity, and it was widely believed that she had borne him a child. What was beyond doubt was that the father of her daughter, called Allegra, who was being cared for in a neighbouring convent, was Lord Byron, whom she had contrived to meet and then to seduce – there is no doubt who was the initiator – before Byron left England. Claire was not living at Pisa when Trelawny arrived, but he met her not long afterwards.

The Williamses, Edward and Jane, with their two young children lived in the same large house as the Shelleys – it was divided into apartments – and the two families had become very close. Shelley, true to his principles, was ethereally in love with Jane, and Williams had become his best friend. For the first time for many years the strains of life had begun to ease. Shelley spent untold hours with Williams – whom he greatly preferred to his cousin Medwin – at his new craze, exploring the rivers and canals in their little boat and making plans for a more ambitious sailing expedition the following summer. Mary had begun at last to emerge from her long depression. In many ways the last months at Pisa were the happiest they had experienced in all their time in Italy.

They now had a circle of friends among the English colony. Mr and Mrs Mason, like the Shelleys and the Williamses, were living in Italy as a result of scandal. Mrs Mason whose real name was Lady

Mountcashell (her husband, an Irish peer, was still alive somewhere) was a strong-minded intellectual woman who had known Mary Shelley's mother, Mary Wollstonecraft, when she was a governess in the household in Ireland. She had been living with George William Tighe, 'Mr Mason', for years, and they had two daughters. She had written a book of stories and in 1823 was to publish her *Advice to Young Mothers on the Physical Education of Children by a Grandmother*. Tighe was an expert on the horticulture of potatoes on which he wrote articles and was known as Tatty Tighe.

John Taaffe, another of the Shelleys' friends also had a colourful background. While a student at Edinburgh University, he was involved in a love affair with an older married woman which ended abruptly when she tried to murder him with a razor as he lay asleep. To bring him to his senses, his father cut him off from his expected inheritance and sent him on a long voyage abroad and he had finally settled in Italy. While living at Pisa, Taaffe made a secret marriage in an English ship out of sight of land but his wife died in 1819, and he was now totally absorbed in compiling a gigantic commentary on Dante. Few people had read his earlier published work, *Padilla, a Tale of Palestine*.

Dominating the Pisa circle, 'the very spirit of the place' as Williams said, was the great Lord Byron himself. His palace across the Arno within sight of the apartments where the Shelleys and the Williamses lived was filled with servants, animals, carriages, wine, books, and all the other impedimenta which he found indispensable for his comfort. Teresa, the Countess Guiccioli, his acknowledged mistress, lived in another palazzo nearby and her brother, Count Gamba, acted as Byron's secretary.

Byron was at the height of his artistic powers. He had long since given up writing the romantic verse tales which had swept the world in his early years and which had so enchanted Trelawny. He was at work on *Don Juan* turning out brilliant canto after brilliant canto late at night with a bottle of wine at his elbow. It had been planned that he and Shelley with the help of Leigh Hunt, who was to come from England for the purpose, should co-operate in producing a new journal, *The Liberal*, and this was the main reason for his being at Pisa. Meanwhile he lived somewhat apart from the others, and when he gave a dinner party, it was an event.

The talk of the Pisa circle was all of books, of books read, of books to be written, and of the continuing inability of publishers to recognise or reward talent. Medwin, Williams, and Taaffe liked to bring their manuscripts and fish for compliments, but even their best friends had difficulty in finding encouraging things to say. Byron disdained literary chatter except with Shelley whom he greatly admired, and he had a keen nose for any suspicion of pretentiousness.

Shelley himself was not writing much. Overawed by the presence of Lord Byron, he was perhaps a little jealous, and he seems to have lost much of his confidence that he would himself ever be successful. He was more interested in the progress of the poems which he had already written. A few copies of *Adonais*, his marvellous elegy on the death of John Keats, had been printed at Pisa and Shelley was looking forward to seeing how it would be received in England. He was also awaiting copies of his poem on the Greek War of Independence, *Hellas*, which had just been published.

This then was the extraordinary group of people among whom Trelawny arrived in January 1822, invited by Williams to advise them about boats and boating. Whatever he said later, he was out of place among them. The members of the Pisa circle, almost to a man (and woman), were engaged in literature. Those few who had not yet had books published had high hopes of doing so, and others knew that their literary immortality had already been secured. Trelawny, although he knew Shakespeare and early Byron by the yard, was barely literate, and the drafts of verses which he confided to his notebook show little sign of latent talent.

He felt uncomfortable too about money. Although his new friends were forever complaining about shortage of cash, they were, compared with him, extremely wealthy men. Byron, in particular, kept a huge establishment at the Palazzo Lanfranchi – the weekly bill for his horses and animals alone was over ten times Trelawny's total living expenses.[2] Shelley too, although frequently embarrassed for ready cash, was heir to a vast fortune and his father could do nothing about it since the estate was entailed. Shelley and Byron could cheerfully make a wager that the first who came into his inheritance would pay the other £1,000 knowing that, when their expectations were realised, a sum like £1,000 would never be missed.*

Trelawny came from the same class as Byron and Shelley. It was the English system of property and the accidents of birth and death that had led to such an uneven pattern – in Byron's case a series of lucky

* The table at the foot of the next page gives some estimated indication of the differences.

deaths, in Trelawny's the unfortunate fact of being born a younger son.
In such company, despite their common origins, Trelawny the naval
adviser would have to be on his guard if he were not to be regarded as
a mere servant.

Then again they had led such interesting lives. Apart from Medwin,
they all had at least one magnificent scandal to their credit and some
had several. They had carried their principles into action and defied the
censure of the world. Trelawny had been expelled from the Seyer
School for insubordination – how drab that must have seemed compared with Shelley's departure from Oxford for publishing *The Necessity
of Atheism*. Trelawny had written nothing and done nothing. He was
simply an unsuccessful naval midshipman obliged by a low income to
live abroad. True, he had been in the East and seen many strange things,
he had taken part in several battles and been wounded. But so had
thousands of young men. Williams and Medwin were full of stories of
India which they knew far better than Trelawny.

However, if Trelawny was apprehensive at meeting the great Lord
Byron and his friends, he was determined not to show it. Byron,
he had heard, was himself a Byronic hero and Shelley a rebel. Trelawny would show these men that he was one of them. He described
later his first meeting with Shelley on the evening of his arrival at
Pisa:

> The Williamses received me in their earnest cordial manner; we had a
> great deal to communicate to each other, and were in loud and animated
> conversation, when I was rather put out by observing in the passage near
> the open door, opposite to where I sat, a pair of glittering eyes steadily
> fixed on mine; it was too dark to make out whom they belonged to.
> With the acuteness of a woman, Mrs Williams's eyes followed the direc-
> tion of mine, and going to the doorway, she laughingly said 'Come in
> Shelley, it's only our friend Tre just arrived.' Swiftly gliding in, blushing
> like a girl, a tall thin stripling held out both his hands; and although I

	Income	Capital	Expectations
Trelawny	£300	£500	Some, but small and remote.
Shelley	£1,000	None	Heir to a fortune worth over £100,000 yielding an expected income of £5,000 to £7,000 per annum
Byron	£8,000 to £10,000	Estates and bonds worth over £100,000	Expected to inherit part of the huge Milbanke fortune.

could hardly believe as I looked at his flushed, feminine and artless face that it could be the poet, I returned his warm pressure, After the ordinary greetings and courtesies he sat down and listened. I was silent from astonishment; was it possible that this mild-looking beardless boy could be the veritable monster at war with all the world?[3]

The next day Trelawny was taken to meet Lord Byron to talk about his proposed boat, and he was received with the charm, friendliness, and courtesy which so many people found irresistible. Byron chatted about this and that and then he suggested a game of billiards. Within a few minutes he was treating Trelawny, as he tended to treat all strangers, like a life-long friend. He was amusing and delightful company with an unending stream of anecdotes. His conversation was sharp and witty, and darted from topic to topic. He was sophisticated and slightly mocking, satirising himself as often as other people, and confidentially passing on scandal about his closest friends. Most people who had the good fortune to meet him found his conversation enchanting, but to the humourless, lightness is triviality, and Trelawny was an unusually humourless person.

He was mortified. 'I had come prepared to see a solemn mystery', he wrote later, 'and so far as I could judge from the first act it seemed to me very like a solemn farce. I forgot that great actors when off the stage are dull dogs.'[4] For no-one could have been further from the Byronic hero he had expected to meet than the Byron of 1822. His congenital foot deformity made him limp and he was beginning to stoop. The curly auburn hair so beloved by the engravers was receding fast, his knuckles were covered with fat, and he had a noticeable paunch. It was not simply that Byron was suffering from the onset of middle age, it was clear that he never could have been the hero that Trelawny imagined. Far from being a bronzed hero immune to wind and weather, Byron was something of a fop, forever fussing over his dress, taking elaborate care to show off his white neck against his black clothes. He lay in bed till noon and Trelawny discovered from his valet that he had done that all his life.

Trelawny by contrast had grown his hair long and he sported long curling moustaches. He had a deep resonant voice and a swagger in his step, and his conversation was studded with grandiloquent phrases. It was Trelawny who was the Byronic hero not Byron. He had come to Pisa expecting to meet the Corsair in person but instead he had become the Corsair himself.

Trelawny was ridiculous. With even a spark of fun, he would not have attempted the role he had now assumed, let alone carried it off successfully. The world will only accept a man at his own estimation if he carries off the part with conviction and with a part so unconvincing as Trelawny's, panache approaching genius was needed. But that was what he had. Trelawny was determined to show these sophisticated people that, if he could not match them in sophistication, yet he was no ordinary man, nor was he just another retired officer with a few war stories from India like Medwin or Williams.[5] The Pisa circle might write poetry and novels and plays about hideous violence and dark irresistible passions. They might conjure up visions of dungeons and torturings, of battlefields awash with blood, of monsters, poisonings, incest, murder. But it was all imagination. They had never actually met characters like the Corsair, only read about them and written about them. Their lives were words, not deeds. He, Trelawny, was different. He had seen these things with his own eyes, and done those things with his own hands.

It may have begun as a piece of bamming, and here a word of explanation is required. Bamming was a kind of joke, a tease much practised at the time. It consists of telling a tall story to see how far the listener can be taken in. It is a ponderous form of entertainment which appeals to those who prefer wet humour – if wet humour is the opposite of dry humour. It is the humour that a new boy at school has to endure, or the juniors in an officers' mess. The Prince Regent was bamming when he described in front of a party of foreigners at dinner how he had personally commanded the British army at Waterloo. Byron was bamming Samuel Rogers when he told him, as they passed an Italian peasant girl carrying a baby, that he was the father. This was a successful bam, for Rogers believed everything and solemnly repeated the story years later.[6] Trelawny's humour was of the wet variety. Practical jokes he enjoyed, especially if they involved a dash of cruelty, but gentler humour or sympathetic irony was alien to him. The Byron of *Beppo* or *Don Juan* was incomprehensible. Bamming was the nearest he got to wit.

The ladies of the Pisa circle were an ideal target. They were young, attractive, and earnest. They were intellectual and proud of their advanced ideas and sophistication. They were blue-stockings – the 'blues' as they were called in the slang of the day. Mary Shelley was instantly attracted to Trelawny. He came nearly every day to the

Shelleys' house, and while Shelley and Williams were boating, Trelawny would entertain the ladies. He escorted Mary to a ball, he escorted her to the Carnival. The ladies were all eager to dance, eager to listen, eager to be impressed. Years later Trelawny drafted a description of how he bammed the blues, which might refer to one of the balls which Mrs Beauclerc was accustomed to give at Pisa for her seven unmarried daughters:

I was struck at first with the drilled and regimental like sameness of all the people I saw of the high cast . . . Every appearance of manhood was declared vulgar – every one complained of some malady or other either real or imaginary – and to look and lisp like a sick girl was considered the higth of ton – chins nicely mown – and tallowy hands and complexion – I say nothing of the fashionable Ladys for they never said anything and the men had so closely and abominably imitated them that had they been plucked of their feathers a naturalist would have had some difficulty without being well versed in phisiology of classing them – they looked like a box of butterflies stuck in the box like room with pins. They I mean the men gazed at me not with their eyes for they seemed to be all blind but with glasses and certainly must have thought me a monster. My face and hands were almost blackened by the exposure to the elements – and rough as the bark of an oak – my black thick hair curling in mopes over my face – with the stride and voice of a lyon. I stood amongst them – however – the gentler sex who doate on lyons – and monsters – thought it would be an interesting thing to tame me – and what so savage they cannot tame – they thought I was worth reclaiming from my wild habits – and that was enough – a coterie of Saint like blues determined forthwith to take me in hand – the first query put to me was if I was a christian – to which I simply replied I did not know – what have you never been christened – I dont know – perhaps my mother does – have you never read the bible – no – there was a parley then – if they should not give me up as hopeless – or what would have been more hopeless turn me over to the Bible or Church Missionary Society – they declared however that that would not do – for we had Missionaries in the South Seas – did you never see any of them – one deeply embued in travels and voyages said to me – I said yes – I keel hauled one of the black vermin for giving my men tracts – those that read them were never worth a damn after – and we never had a fair wind till I threw them overboard – they looked with unutterable horror at this – but on closer inquiry discovering that he was not of their church but an anabaptist they were in some sort pacefied and agreed I did well not to listen to him – but I did very bad to drown him – I said they are like the horned Devil fish – they never sink.[7]

It this was the kind of story he told, it certainly made an impression on the ladies. Five days after Trelawny's arrival at Pisa, Mary Shelley wrote a description of him in her diary:

> Trelawny is extravagant – un giovane stravagante – though not as the Venetian Godoliere meant* – partly natural and partly perhaps put on, but it suits him well, and if his abrupt but not unpolished manners be assumed, they are nevertheless in unison with his Moorish face (for he looks Oriental yet not Asiatic) his dark hair, his Herculean form, and then there is an air of extreme good nature which pervades his whole countenance, specially when he smiles, which assures me that his heart is good. He tells strange stories of himself, horrific ones, so that they harrow one up, while with his emphatic but unmodulated voice, his simple yet strong language, he pourtrays the most frightful situations; then all these adventures took place between the age of 13 and 20. I believe them now I see the man, and, tired with the everyday sleepiness of human intercourse, I am glad to meet with one who, among other valuable qualities has the rare merit of interesting my imagination.[8]

But if it began as bamming, it soon became something very different. Trelawny had a gift for story-telling and his audience were delighted. They liked his stories, they pressed him to tell more. Surely he must have some interesting tales to tell about life in the great wide world beyond their experience?

His real past was unknown. None of his new friends knew anything about him beyond what he chose to tell. The oldest acquaintance was with Williams but that only went back to Geneva less than two years before. Daniel Roberts had known him longer but he lived in Genoa. Trelawny, having failed to win promotion to lieutenant, did not even have the tenuous link with the past that Roberts, Williams, and Medwin had, of drawing half pay from London.

He told the story of his unhappy childhood and his unloving parents. He described how he and his brother had killed their father's raven, and told them of his early experiences in the navy; how he was sent to serve in the East Indies fleet; how he had visited strange lands in many parts of the world and seen strange sights. He told of sea battles and land battles, and he showed the scars of wounds on his body.[9] But it was not enough. His story did not match the personality

* This may mean that the words 'un giovane stravagante' were applied to Trelawny by Tita Falcieri, Byron's gondolier, himself not a colourless figure.

he had now assumed, or live up to the promise of his physical appearance. It was a hero they wanted, a corsair, not a failed midshipman.

And so Trelawny embarked on a deception. His years in the navy were recast to fit the model of himself which he had now assumed and which his new friends were only too eager to accept. He had the appearance of a corsair, he had the style, the way of speech, the knowledge, the character – all that was lacking was a past full of suitable experiences and adventures. There flooded back into Trelawny's mind the secret life he had led in the navy, the fantasies at the masthead, his encounter with the great Surcouf, the vengeful blows struck against authority, their triumphs together against the British in India. The Pisa circle wanted a corsair with a dark mysterious past marked by crime. Well, if that was what they wanted, he could supply.

8

Trelawny's Story

My bosom swelled with the free beatings of my heart; to roam
at liberty, unchecked by churlish superiors, was exstacy. I had
thrown off my cap, though the sun looked like molten gold or
brass; and was proceeding to tear off my clothes though the white
sand sparkled fiercely, and pierced the soles of my feet like fire,
so abhorrent to me was every vestige or sign of slavery – or
which was the same thing at that moment, of civilization.

Trelawny's description of tearing off
his naval uniform.[1]

The story begins in Bombay. Trelawny, the young, proud, rebellious
midshipman, hates the navy and despises his officers. He has lived a
life of insult and injury, particularly from his lieutenant, a Scotsman,
and at Bombay he decides he will take no more. One evening he picks
a fight in a billiard saloon and would have killed him if a friendly hand
had not taken his sword and substituted a billiard cue at a critical
moment. As it is, the lieutenant is severely wounded, a hue and cry is
raised, and Trelawny has to flee from the town. He escapes. He is a
fugitive but he is also a free man.

The friend with a billiard cue introduces himself as de Witt, but he
is travelling under an *alias*. His real name is de Ruyter. He explains
confidentially that although he is travelling disguised as a merchant, he
has a French *lettre de marque* commissioning him as a privateer, permitted to wage war with his own ship on all the enemies of France.
When de Ruyter proposes to Trelawny that, since he clearly cannot go
back to the Royal Navy, he should join his own band of followers, he
immediately agrees and sets sail in de Ruyter's ship soon afterwards.
Without a second thought he deserts from the British navy and takes
service with the enemy. He is a traitor. What right has his own country
to call on his loyalty he asks. The British in India are tyrants, imperialists, conquerors, enslaving free peoples for the profit of the Honourable
East India Company Trelawny is soon given the command of his own
ship, with a crew of Arabs stiffened by a few desperate European

adventurers. With de Ruyter in company, they sail off to see what fortune war will bring.

It is hardly necessary to repeat that none of this is true. De Ruyter never existed. Commendable efforts to find traces of him in the official archives of several countries have met with no success, for de Ruyter is a character who existed only in Trelawny's imagination. Insofar as there was a model, it was Robert Surcouf the French privateer whom Trelawny had pursued in vain over the Indian Ocean in 1807 and 1808, and de Ruyter was given as many of the characteristics of the real Robert Surcouf as Trelawny knew – which was not much. Like Surcouf, de Ruyter had formerly been in trouble with the French colonial authorities for attacking shipping without proper authority. Like Surcouf, de Ruyter had a fine house in Mauritius. And, like Surcouf, de Ruyter on his return to Europe had several audiences with Napoleon in which he advised him to devote more resources to cruisers to attack British shipping. But the correspondence is far from exact. De Ruyter's character is built up with a miscellany of other attributes which Trelawny personally happened to admire. He is a voracious reader of Shakespeare, he hates the usual Trelawnian targets, kings, priests, imperialists, East India Companies, Scotsmen, blue-stockings; like Trelawny he thinks that Europe is finished and that the future of the world lies with the United States and he has become an American citizen although born a Dutchman, having also with splendid disregard for the constraints of chronology, fought alongside George Washington.

De Ruyter is also the Corsair. The word was used at the time to describe the French privateers, and Robert Surcouf was the most famous corsair of the Napoleonic wars. But de Ruyter in Trelawny's imagination was also a manifestation of the Byronic corsair, Conrad taken from the Aegean and resettled in the Indian Ocean.

It is difficult to describe, even in summary form, the varied adventures which befell Trelawny and de Ruyter in their voyages. Those who wish to follow them in detail will have to read the *Adventures of a Younger Son*. They hunted lions in jungles amid the ruins of lost civilizations; they rescued princesses from distress; they found buried treasure; they attacked and destroyed nests of pirates; they were trapped by seductive enchantresses; attempts were made to poison them; they were betrayed by inscrutable oriental potentates, and time and again were only rescued in the nick of time. In the few cases where

Trelawny is not himself the central figure in the action, minor characters fill the gaps, the solitary white man on a remote island lording it over the natives, survivors dying of thirst in an open boat after a shipwreck, eloping lovers disguised as brothers.

There is a good deal of casual violence. Most incidents involve the death or mutilation of a few members of the crew or of hapless natives who happen to be caught up in the drama. Trelawny himself has few scruples about killing with his own hands, and boasts about the ferocity of his anger and the joy of revenge. Quick to wrath, quick to strike, but when calm again, magnanimous and even tender to the survivors (insofar as there are any), but even by the liberal conventions of privateering, some of his killings are simply murders. At Penang for example, after a bout of drinking, he picks a quarrel with a jeweller in the bazaar over the price of some article, and in the subsequent turmoil, the jeweller's shop is destroyed, his brother stabbed, and a policeman strangled. The jeweller seeks out Trelawny and follows him, hiding a poisoned dagger in his cloak, but just as he is about to strike, Trelawny sees the shadow of his uplifted arm on a wall and escapes the blow. There is then a chase (which includes Trelawny's pistol misfiring and his throwing it away) and the pair finally confront one another, as in the culmination of all good chases, on a narrow plank stretched over a deep chasm. The jeweller lunges forward and comes within a scratch of his target, but it is he who falls into a dock choked with the accumulated stinking filth of a public slaughter-house, and as Trelawny watches, he gurgles to his death in this grotesque quicksand. Trelawny, who started the affair and is decidedly in the wrong even by his own curious standards of behaviour, feels a 'pang of regret' and moves on to the next adventure.

Every masthead adventure was found a place. Trelawny imagined himself playing the part of Fletcher Christian in the mutiny on the *Bounty*. He imagined himself as the young John Paul Jones, abandoning home at an early age and leading his country's enemies against his native land in the name of liberty. He took real incidents which he had witnessed and recast them in such a way that he was the hero. In his stories he was always the captain of the ship, always the bravest and the most resourceful. Dangerous situations were made more perilous. Backgrounds were transferred to more exotic locations, and liberally decorated with romantic furniture such as sunless jungles, venomous serpents, lurking wild beasts, and shifty oriental princes.

Corsairs of the Byronic type are attached to Gulnares, Medoras, and Leilas, women scarcely more credible than their dark mysterious menfolk. They are beautiful, young, loving, pure, obedient and patient. They are sexless, devoid of any recognisable individuality, and boring. They inspire indefatigable love in their corsairs, who are usually true to them despite provocations and temptations. Often they are princesses and sometimes they are taken as slaves by monstrous pashas.

Trelawny's fantasy would not have been complete without such a heroine at his side. Her name is Zela,[2] and she is acquired when Trelawny and de Ruyter, in company with a French squadron, attack a notorious city of Maratti pirates in Madagascar. The expedition is divided into three parties with the French Commander, de Ruyter, and Trelawny ('Well done, my lad! always the first in danger') commanding one party each. They land at night and are thus able to surround the city and block the main exits before they put in their assault. The slaughter is terrible, of men, women, and children: 'A great many were butchered, and no prisoners made; for blood is like wine, the more we have the more we crave, till excited to madness, one excess leads to another; and it is easier to persuade a drunken man to desist from drinking whilst he can hold his glass, than a man whose hands are reeking with blood, to desist from shedding more.' At last de Ruyter calls for a halt to the killing. 'Call our people off, and let the poor devils go. Seize what prisoners you can, but take no more lives.'

But when Trelawny goes to release the prisoners he finds that the Maratti women are going round killing them as they lie bound hand and foot. Trelawny seizes one old woman and 'dashed her down with such force that she never stirred more, but lay sprawling like a crushed toad, the faint sparks of life being extinguished without even a groan escaping her'. But the man whom she had been hacking with her knife is already dying. In his last minutes he takes a ring from his own hand and places it on Trelawny's finger, as a symbol that he wishes him to take responsibility for his young daughter Zela who is at this moment 'kissing his incrimsoned hands and eyes, bent over him in speechless and indescribable anguish.' It turns out later that the ceremony is, by Arab custom, a solemn marriage and Zela henceforth regards herself as Trelawny's wife.

Although at first they have no language in common, Trelawny and Zela soon fall deeply in love. On their subsequent adventures together Zela is ever at hand to save his life from beasts, storms, and enemies.

But their happiness is short-lived. One day she is attacked by a shark, and a jealous widow, who has amorous designs on Trelawny, in revenge puts poison in her wound and she dies.

Nearly a month passes with Trelawny sunk in grief until one day de Ruyter tells that he must sail at once to Europe to take important despatches to Napoleon in Paris. The crew is discharged, the booty sold, and de Ruyter and Trelawny speed round the Cape and up the Atlantic to land at St Malo. Napoleon has long discussions with de Ruyter and makes him many tempting offers – promotion in the navy, a colonial governorship, command of a department of France on the Channel coast, but all are declined. Soon after, when on a secret mission to the Barbary coast, his small ship meets an English frigate. De Ruyter sinks his despatches over the stern as a hundred balls from the frigate's cannonades crash around him, and when the battle at last is over, his body is found wrapped in the tricolour under which he had long fought so victoriously.

With the deaths of Zela and de Ruyter, Trelawny has lost everything that made life worth living. Though scarcely in his twenties he has drunk life to the lees and nothing remains. Sunk in despair, he arranges to be taken to England by an old Guernsey smuggler and landed at some secret cove. Wrapping himself in the boat's sail, he lies down to sleep on a solitary rock in the sea, the fit resting place, he reflects, for an outcast.

And so Trelawny's story brings him back to a point where reality can again resume. Up until the incident in the billiard room in Bombay it was largely true; from the time he arrived back in England it was also largely true. Between Bombay and that solitary rock it was fantasy. Trelawny had acquired a past appropriate to a contemporary corsair. Now he had his years of wandering, his thousand crimes, his load of guilt. Now when his new friends at Pisa saw the occasional melancholy in those ever-changing eyes they would know that he was thinking of de Ruyter or Zela, and they would marvel at the amazing strength of the man who could have endured so much.

9

The Pisa Circle

He was so awful, yet
So beautiful in mystery and terror,
Calming me as the loveliness of heaven
Smoothes the unquiet sea: – and yet not so,
For he seemed stormy, and would often seem
A quenchless sun masked in portentous clouds,
For such his thoughts, and even his actions were;
But he was not of them, nor they of him,
But as they hid his splendour from the earth.
Some said he was a man of blood and peril,
And steeped in bitter infamy to the lips.
From Shelley's unfinished drama about Trelawny

In retrospect, the months that Trelawny spent with Shelley and his friends in Italy were the happiest of his life. As he wrote later to Jane Williams: 'Our Pisa circle is one not to be forgotten – their was no other such in the wide world – such hearts as ours united under the sunny clime of Italy – such scenes and events no time can fade – their glowing colours – can never be dimmed – to try even to forget them is as vain as to expect their return.' [1] They were all young – only Byron had passed his thirtieth birthday – the world and its prizes still stretched out before them, and they enjoyed themselves.

On a typical day the men would practise boxing or fencing or shooting. Byron would travel the 400 yards to the city gate in his carriage to avoid being stared at, and then mount his horse and ride a couple of miles with the others to Cisanello where they were permitted to shoot in the grounds of a villa. They would stick a silver coin on a split cane and shoot at it from fifteen paces. Trelawny says that Byron and Shelley as well as himself were good marksmen and they all usually hit the target.

The evenings would be spent in visiting or at the theatre. The members of the circle had a keen professional interest, although the plays even of Byron and Shelley, whatever their other merits, are unperformable. On one occasion Byron proposed that they should themselves act *Othello* in the great hall of his palace.

Who shall be our audience?
All Pisa.

Byron was to be Iago, Williams to be Cassio, and Medwin to be Roderigo. The part of Desdemona was given to Mary, and Jane was to be Emilia. The Moor himself, of course, was Trelawny who already knew much of the part by heart. But the project was laid aside after a few rehearsals apparently under pressure from Teresa who, not speaking English, could not be given a part.

There were occasional quarrels and bouts of bad temper. Byron's social arrogance, irritating to all his friends, caused a good deal of annoyance in a group whose shared ideals were supposed to include an overthrow of the existing order. But despite the occasional strains, the Pisa circle felt a strong sense of community and like other expatriates they clung together for mutual security against the natives.

On Sunday 24 March, Byron, Shelley, Trelawny, Count Gamba and a visitor, Captain Hay, set out for their usual ride and pistol practice. Williams was too absorbed in writing his tragedy to join them that day. On their way back in the evening they were joined by Mary Shelley and Teresa Guiccioli, who had gone out for a drive in Teresa's carriage, and by Taaffe. They were riding slowly along the road deep in conversation when suddenly a man in uniform rode at a gallop between Taaffe and the kerb, causing Taaffe's horse to rear out of control and the others to suffer a nasty fright. Since the man was wearing a bright uniform and epaulettes, they assumed that he was an officer, although in fact he was a sergeant-major called Masi, slightly drunk, who was in a hurry to get back to his unit for the roll call. Had they known he was not an officer there would have been no incident since only officers were socially required to have good manners. Byron, Shelley and Trelawny all spurred their horses in pursuit and caught up with him just outside the city gate where, amid much mutual abuse, Byron and Trelawny challenged him to a duel.

By this time a crowd had gathered and the guards at the city gate naturally tended to take the part of their own countryman, and when the English party decided to ride on home through the city gate they found their way barred. Trelawny tried to push his way past and an affray broke out. Masi drew his sabre and started striking him with the

Trelawny the Byronic hero, Italy 1822–3, from a portrait by W. E. West

Trelawny the Corsair, Italy 1822–3,
from a portrait by Joseph Severn

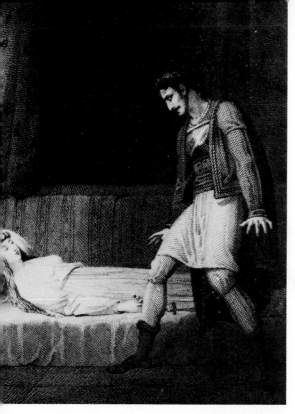

Illustrations by Richard
 Westall for Byron's
 Corsair, first published
 in 1819

That man of loneliness and
 mystery,
Scarce seen to smile and
 seldom heard to sigh;

. . . . .

He left a Corsair's name
 to other times,
Link'd with one virtue,
 and a thousand crimes.

Sunburnt his cheek – his
 forehead high and pale
The sable curls in wild
 profusion veil;
And oft perforce his
 rising lip reveals
The haughtier thought it
 curbs but scarce conceals.

Trelawny and the
jeweller's brother
at Penang

Trelawny and
Zella with
the orang
outang in
the Borneo
jungle

flat edge, and at the same time, two of the guards tried to seize the bridle of his horse, but Trelawny with characteristic bravado forced his horse on through the gate and, although hit, he escaped unwounded. Shelley however was struck on the back of the head and knocked sense-less from his horse. Hay suffered a severe sabre cut across his nose and one of Byron's servants received a blow in the chest which caused internal injury. Outside the Palazzo Lanfranchi where Byron was staying, Byron met Masi again and there was another altercation. Suddenly an unknown figure charged out from the house with a long pitchfork and Masi fell bleeding from his horse, badly wounded.

It was never established for certain who the attacker was. It was generally believed – probably wrongly – to have been one of Byron's servants, and two of them were arrested on suspicion, but the affair now became much more serious. It was learnt the next day that Masi's injuries were expected to be fatal and that extreme unction was being administered. Anti-English feeling in Pisa ran high. Teresa had to be given tranquilising medicine and Taaffe fussed around emphasising his own courage in the affair. False Taaffe, Jane Williams called him, giving sharpness to a joke which had surely been made before, but Trelawny and the others defiantly continued their habit of riding outside the town for pistol practice, taking good care to be armed.

In the end the affair blew over. Masi recovered. The British Consul was brought in. Judges were appointed and after a long investigation, the English were vindicated and Masi was dismissed from his regiment. Trelawny's fearlessness and pugnacity were remarked on and admired and his reputation continued to rise.

As events were to turn out, however, the Masi affair was the begin-ning of the end of the Pisa circle. The Government took fright and expelled the Gambas and Byron felt he must follow them to another place of exile in Italy. At the same time, as spring broke, the Shelleys and the Williamses began to look for a house near the sea a day's journey from Pisa where they hoped to spend the summer boating. With the death of Allegra, Claire's daughter by Byron in April, Shelley and Byron were no longer bound together as they had been before, and neither any longer had much faith in the proposed new review on which they were supposed to be co-operating. The news that Leigh Hunt, the third member of the proposed team, was on his way made little difference to their failing enthusiasm.

During his first weeks at Pisa Trelawny met Shelley nearly every day. The more he got to know him the more he liked him, and he began to feel that they had a good deal in common. They had been born in the same year, they had both broken with their fathers. Shelley's father had wanted to put him in the army, Trelawny's father had put him in the navy. Shelley had started to call himself Percy, rather than his family name of Bysshe when he rebelled. Had not John become Edward? And far from being the effeminate that he appeared at first, Shelley loved guns. He loved boats. He loved women. Shelley talked incessantly about the rights of man, about the evil of organised religion, about the oppression of governments confined to rich hereditary landowners. He would talk and laugh and shriek his opinions in an interminable flow of irresistible enthusiasm. He was an intellectual and a political theorist. He was one of the unacknowledged legislators of the world.

In his admiration for Shelley, Trelawny began to see his own life in a new light. His disobedience at school was obviously, in retrospect, a manifestation of his early love of liberty. His dislike of being a younger son was obviously, in retrospect, a protest against the power of parasitical landowners. His dislike of the Reverend Samuel Seyer, of his officers in the Royal Navy, and of the East India merchants was obviously, in retrospect, part of his lifelong struggle against priestcraft, imperialism, exploitation, and oppression.

He started to copy Shelley in his attitudes. Trelawny had an un-predictable temper – had not Shelley? – well then, Trelawny need not bother to control it, he could glory in it. Shelley was extravagantly generous in contrast to his mean father – was not Trelawny the same? Had he not as a boy given a whole pigeon pie to a beggar woman? The model of the Byronic hero, which hitherto had been at the centre of his conception of himself, was given a graft of Shelleyan political principles and Shelleyan behaviour patterns.

And all the time, Trelawny would be telling his stories and charm-ing the blues of Pisa with his fantasies. Night after night de Ruyter would scud across the Indian Ocean in quest of pirates or princesses. Night after night Zela would rescue her man from certain death at the hands of treacherous natives or the claws of ferocious beasts. It is easy to imagine these occasions – Mary and Jane chatting about the books they had been reading during the day – Hope's *Anastasius*, Martin's *Account of the Natives of the Tonga Islands*, Scott's *The Pirate* – and Tre-lawny capping their literary stories with 'true' experiences of his own.

In February Pisa celebrated the Veglione, the masked carnival, and each evening for three days Trelawny and Williams took Mary and Jane out in the town and afterwards to the theatre where there was feasting and dancing until three o'clock in the morning. The Lung Arno was crowded with masqueraders in fancy clothes and grotesque disguises; Mary wore Turkish costume, Jane a Hindustani dress. Did Jane's marvellously extravagant head-dress, one wonders, spark off stories from Williams and Jane about their time in India which Trelawny, with Mary to impress, felt obliged to outdo? More prosaic people than Trelawny lose their grip on reality at carnival time.[2]

If he had been merely bamming, and Trelawny and Byron both enjoyed a good bam, then surely his secret would not have lasted long. Even the suspicion of a smile or a wink would have brought down the whole edifice. Or again, if he had been merely acting, he could not have kept up day after day in front of such a critical audience. Trelawny was only able to convince people with his stories because when he was telling them he was convincing himself. He imagined himself into them. Having already for so many years repressed his real memories of the navy in favour of the masthead fantasies, the process was easy, and the more he talked and elaborated, the more coherent the stories became.

Mary Shelley above all the rest was fascinated by this strange man who had swept into her life, so unlike the others whom she knew, and Trelawny was conscious of his success. He came oftener and oftener and stayed later and later. During his first month at Pisa he met her on twenty-eight out of thirty-one days. From her journal, we can see the personality which he was putting over, at first perhaps with a hesitation which touched off a slight suspicion, but soon with complete confidence and conviction. After a month's acquaintanceship she tried to describe her friend in a letter:

> Trelawny – a kind of half-Arab Englishman – whose life has been as changeful as that of Anastasius and who recounts the adventures of his youth as eloquently and well as the imagined Greek – he is clever – for his moral qualities I am yet in the dark – he is a strange web which I am endeavouring to unravel – I would fain learn if generosity is united to impetuousness – nobility of spirit to his assumption of singularity and independence – he is six feet high – raven black hair which curls thickly and shortly like a Moor's – dark grey – expressive eyes – overhanging brows – upturned lips and a smile which expresses good nature and kindheartedness – his shoulders are high like an Orientalist – his voice is

monotonous yet emphatic and his language as he relates the events of his life energetic and simple – whether the tale be one of blood and horror or of irresistable comedy. His company is delightful for he excites me to think, and if any evil shade the intercourse, that time will unveil – the sun will shine or night darken all.[3]

Shelley himself also appears to have had little difficulty in accepting Trelawny for what he claimed to be: 'A wild but kind-hearted seaman',[4] he described him when introducing him to Leigh Hunt. 'Our Pirate' he called him in another letter, with only a touch of irony.[5] Shelley found Trelawny a trying companion at times – who would not? but he seems to have liked him well enough. As Mary was to write later, describing how she and Shelley had agreed fully in their assessment of him 'We heard people speak against him on account of his vagaries, we said to one another "Still we like him – we believe him to be good"'.[6]

In February 1822, Shelley began a new drama, intended for Trelawny, based on one of his stories, that of the Widow of Yug who falls in love with a pirate and offers to make him a prince of her oriental kingdom.[7] The pirate is of course Trelawny himself as Mary Shelley herself confirmed when she published the fragments after Shelley's death. In the play he remains loyal, despite some backsliding, to his true love who is presumably Zela. De Ruyter too had a role to play, but Shelley gave up after writing a few hundred lines and we do not know how the story would have developed.

With Byron the situation was different. He had had more experience of life than the others; he knew human nature in its weaknesses while Shelley concentrated on its strengths. Without ever saying to his face that Trelawny was a liar, he saw through him. He teased him without Trelawny realising that he was being teased: 'He one day suddenly interrupted the description of a hurricane I was narrating [Trelawny himself wrote later] and said abruptly putting his hand on my horse's mane "T. have you ever written a book?" I answered, no! "I am glad of that" he replied "for then it is possible we may be friends!" '[8] Another remark was noted by Dr James Kennedy who recorded some of Byron's conversations later at Cephalonia: 'Dr – when on board one evening, was narrating to his lordship some wonderful act of legerdemain which he witnessed at Paris; Lord B. smiled "you look incredulous, my lord" said the Doctor. "Not at all," replied Lord B; "Where is T? I dare say he saw the same thing," '[9]

Byron liked Trelawny – there can be no doubt about that. They got on well together and were friends, although Byron demanded deference. But never in his wildest fits of liberalism did Byron regard Trelawny as his equal.[10] He was a colourful appendage to the Byron entourage – like the huge bearded gondolier Tita that he had picked up in Venice and the bears, monkeys, peacocks, and other living exotica which did so much for the Byron image. It was flattering to be cultivated by someone who so obviously admired his romantic poetry even if he was absurd. Trelawny was an excellent fellow, he used to say, when Trelawny was not present, until he took to imitating my *Lara* and *Corsair*. It was a good joke and people laughed, until eventually a great number of Byron's friends and acquaintances believed they had personally heard him say it.[11]

But the subject which obsessed the Pisa circle during the early part of 1822 was boats, boats, boats. The idea that Shelley, Williams and Trelawny might spend a summer together in a house by the sea and explore the sea coast in their own boat, no doubt with Mary and Jane and the children and perhaps Claire playing a suitable domestic role in the background, had been in their minds since the summer of 1820, a full year and a half before Trelawny ever met Shelley personally. Although the more ambitious versions of the plan, such as sailing to Greece or to Syria, had long since been abandoned, the Shelley dream of a summer colony by the sea had grown ever more urgent.

As Williams wrote to Trelawny at Genoa on the day after Christmas 1821 when Trelawny was on his way to join them at Pisa: 'I shall reserve all that I have to say about the boat until we meet at the Select Committee, which is intended to be held on the subject when you arrive here. Have a boat we must and if we can get Roberts to build her, so much the better.'[12] The Select Committee consisting of Shelley, Williams and Trelawny must have sat late the day Trelawny arrived, for the very next day he wrote to Roberts at Genoa asking him to place the order for the immediate building of the boat. She was to be tailor-made to their specification and built in the naval dockyard – an unusual proceeding, but the admiral-superintendent was a particular friend of Roberts. He was a Liverpool man called Wright who, retired like Roberts from a distinguished service in the Royal Navy, had accepted a flag-officer's commission in the Sardinian Navy.

Trelawny knew exactly what kind of vessel they ought to have – he even brought a model of it with him to Pisa. For the man who had spent so many hours of his boyhood dreaming dreams at the masthead, the choice was obvious. She was to be a schooner built in the American style. She was to be a replica of one of the vessels in which Trelawny the privateer had roamed the Indian Ocean with de Ruyter!

During the endless months which Trelawny had spent chasing the elusive Surcouf in the navy, he had had many opportunities to observe these vessels. Being neutrals, the American privateers had no need to avoid the Royal Navy and their captains and crews had that cocksureness and contempt for Europeans which Trelawny felt was proper to free republicans. They were small, fast, slim, low in the water and marvellously adapted to the privateer's role. As Trelawny wrote later 'America has the merit of having perfected this nautical wonder, as far surpassing all other vessels in exquisite proportion and beauty as the gazelle excels all animated nature'.[13] In 1811 when the nineteen-year-old Trelawny was a midshipman in H.M.S. *Akbar*, they had captured an American privateer schooner sailing under French colours, and it seems likely that Trelawny was second-in-command of the small British naval party which sailed the prize vessel with her American crew to Bombay.[14] It was probably the nearest he ever came to commanding a ship during his naval service, the nearest he came to living out this dream in practice.

The other members of the Select Committee at Pisa – their imaginations set racing by Trelawny's de Ruyter stories – were soon as delighted with the model of the American schooner as Trelawny. Within a few days Mary had renamed the Select Committee – the 'Corsair Crew' and all three were soon scudding across the ocean in their imaginations.

A fortnight later Shelley, Williams, and Trelawny went to the docks at Leghorn to do some window shopping. The harbour was full of vessels of all sizes and rigs from all parts of Europe, an English cutter, a French chasse marée, an American clipper, a Spanish tartan, an Austrian trabacolo, a Genoese felucca, a Sardinian zebeck, a Neapolitan brig, a Sicilian sparanza, a Dutch galleot, a Danish snow, a Russian hermaphrodite, a Turkish sackalever, a Greek bombard – or so Trelawny said later, rolling the exotic names round his mouth with the relish of a practised gourmet wine-taster. They paid a visit to the Greek ship – Shelley wanted to meet some real Hellenes having steeped himself in Greek literature from the earliest age and having recently written *Hellas* – but the high point of the day was a visit to the American schooner, a real-life version of the model which had so delighted them.

They were invited on board and admired her beautiful lines and smart fittings. As good English republicans they insisted – much to the astonishment of the American mate – on drinking a toast to the memory of George Washington. This is said to have been the only occasion when Shelley touched grog. But the mate could not have guessed what fuel he was throwing on their red-hot imaginations when he mentioned to the visitors that the ship has previously been employed in 'neat work' in the Persian Gulf. This meant that she had been a pirate.[15]

That night when the corsair crew got back to Pisa a further letter was sent to Roberts. The boat they wanted, Trelawny wrote, was to be smaller than they had previously indicated – 17 or 18 feet instead of 30 – but to be fast, 'a thorough Varment at *pulling* and sailing!' [16] and, if Roberts agreed, to be fitted with three lugs and a jib.

Roberts and the shipbuilder protested at this proposed design – presumably from doubts about the seaworthiness – and modifications were made. But in essentials the experts were overruled. Shelley, Williams, and Trelawny knew what they wanted and they were paying the piper. Had not Drake sailed round the world in a vessel of 30 tons? Did not Captain Bligh sail half way across the Pacific in an open boat? As the three young friends lay on the beach talking about the boat on which they had so long set their hearts, they would scratch patterns in the sand of the fittings they wanted, and pore over the chart of the Tuscan coast,planning their voyages of exploration with the eagerness of Christopher Columbus or Vasco da Gama.

As she was eventually built the boat was thus basically a scaled-down version of a much larger vessel. Beautiful to look at as was to be expected taken from such a model, but contrary to all principles of naval architecture. The wind and the waves cannot be scaled down along with the hull and the masts and the sails. She was fitted with a heavy iron ballast whereas a larger vessel would have had moveable water barrels which could be jettisoned in emergency. She had no deck. Any water that broke over her would remain on board.[17]

Lord Byron watched the growth of their boyish enthusiasm with a mixture of detachment and envy. When he had arrived at Pisa in the autumn of 1821, plans for the summer boating holiday were already far advanced, but he was quickly infected by the excitement and eagerness of his younger friends across the Arno and he too decided to have his own vessel. Trelawny and Roberts – as they were friends of Admiral

Wright – were made responsible for ordering her from Genoa and she too aroused great enthusiam. She was to be a larger vessel than the other, a schooner of conventional design with a professional crew and fitted out as befitted a rich and famous milord:

> It will not be possible will it [Trelawny wrote to Roberts] to have any sort of water closet in so small a vessel as Lord B? Let the cabin be most sumtuously fitted up: with all kinds of conveniences for provisions, wine, books, tables, sofas, hooks for pistols, riffles, beautifully painted, but not gaudily! What think you of blue and white – she is to be named (a damned curious one youl say) GUICCIOLI? It is the name of a favrite mistress of his who is here – and will be at the Bay with him who is certainly a lovely girl?.[18]

In the event Byron's vessel was named rather provocatively the *Bolivar* after the South American liberator, and Byron indulged his sense of drama by having her fitted with a few cannon (for show and noise not for defence) specially cast with his coat of arms and his motto 'Crede Byron', 'Trust Byron'.

The Shelleys and Williamses were a little miffed at the way in which Byron in his grand way could so easily take over their own idea and outshine them. As far as poetry was concerned, Byron enjoyed an apparently effortless superiority which Shelley found all the harder to bear because he could see that the poem of Don Juan on which Byron was working, was indeed a great masterpiece. It seems to have been Trelawny's suggestion that their boat itself should be named the *Don Juan* and,since Williams apparently agreed, Shelley raised no objection. But Shelley's resentment erupted when Byron,contrary to all seamanlike good form, ordered the shipyard to paint the name *Don Juan* in large letters on the main sail and this had to be cut out and a patch inserted. Shelley's boat thus sailed under the name of Byron's greatest poem – she was never in fact called the *Ariel* as Shelley wanted – with the totally misleading implications about Shelley's attitudes to sexual love which the name implied.

Byron's decision to build his own vessel did however solve one potential problem which might otherwise have caused difficulty. The original boating plan had envisaged that Shelley, Williams, and Trelawny should be joint owners, but Shelley, although he was happy enough to share with Williams, understandably felt reluctant to commit himself to the continuous close company of Trelawny which joint ownership would imply, and so he arranged to become the sole owner.[19] Trelawny was thus freed to concentrate on the *Bolivar* and he was taken into employment by Lord Byron to act as captain of the vessel.

At last in June 1822 both the *Don Juan* and the *Bolivar* were ready. Excitement had been mounting as the Shelleys and Williamses awaited the arrival of their long desired toy. In April they had moved to their summer house on the remote and rocky peninsula that juts into the Gulf of Spezia, the Casa Magni at San Terenzo near Lerici, and Williams seems to have spent much of his time for weeks scanning the skyline in hopes of seeing the new boat arriving from Genoa. As delay followed delay, they had even tried sailing their flat-bottomed skiff on the sea but that was not successful. Williams also struggled to make a tiny light boat of canvas and reeds – anything to get out on to the sea.

Whatever their enthusiasms however, neither Shelley nor Williams was a seaman despite Williams's brief service in the Royal Navy. Shelley could not swim and would not give up his habit of having an open book in his hand even when he was steering. 'You will do no good with Shelley', declared Trelawny, 'until you heave his books and papers overboard; shear the wisps of hair that hang over his eyes; and plunge his arms up to the elbows in a tar bucket.'

They were determined that, in sailing, if not in poetry, they would not be outdistanced by Lord Byron. When first indications suggested that the *Bolivar* was comfortably faster, Roberts and Williams started to make further changes to the design of the *Don Juan* to try to give her more speed. Top masts were added to her two masts which were already too long, and she was fitted with no fewer than three foresails.

The *Don Juan* must have been one of the most unseaworthy vessels ever constructed – even if to a lubberly eye she looked worthy of carrying the great de Ruyter himself into battle against John Company's East India Fleet.

The Storyteller Part 1

When his brain is once heated, out of everything that is cast in, it forges something new; not out of willfulness, but from the laws of its nature and kind.

Claire Clairmont writing about Trelawny.[1]

Trelawny did not invent his stories from nothing. He took actual experiences and changed them into something more interesting, decorating the dull world of reality with exotic and colourful ornament, turning untidy situations into neatly rounded dramas, and bringing forward Edward John Trelawny to the centre of the action. Gradually the original ideas were so convoluted with accretions and distortions as to be scarcely recognizable. As Trelawny grew older and the stories were repeated, the imaginative element luxuriated like some great tropical plant, enveloping, crushing, and extinguishing the tender facts.

*　*　*　*　*

In the spring of 1809 Trelawny was serving as a boy volunteer in H.M.S. *Cornelia*. On 29 March the log book records that one of the other boys, John Campbell, who was presumably a messmate and friend of Trelawny's, fell from the main top and was killed.[2] Trelawny later told a story which may owe its origin to this incident. While at the masthead one day, he said, sent there as punishment by a bullying lieutenant, he had an idea on how to escape such treatment in future. He would pretend to fall off but actually dive into the sea – a desperately dangerous plan not only because of the terrific height and the danger of falling on the deck but because even if he fell in the sea, the chances of being picked up were not good. The log books are full of cases of men lost overboard in such circumstances and a seaman was lost from the *Cornelia* in this way a few weeks after the death of John Campbell.

The Trelawny of the story is nothing daunted. He chooses his moment and hurls himself into the sea. A boat is lowered and he is rescued. His lungs are nearly burst but he wins his point against the lieutenant, who is reprimanded for endangering one of the ship's boys.

*　*　*　*　*

In the days of wooden warships a fire on board was one of the greatest hazards of the sea. During the Napoleonic wars more men and ships were lost through accidental fires than through the violence of the enemy. When Trelawny was in H.M.S. *Akbar* off Java in 1811, a fire broke out but it was evidently extinguished before any serious damage could be done. The log for 18 September records: 'Found the Gunners Store Room on fire. Occasioned by Gunners Mates and Gunman. Beat to Quarters. Put the fire out.'[3]

When Trelawny told his story later, the fire breaks out not in the store room but in the powder magazine, an infinitely more dangerous place. Panic seizes officers and men, some rush to the boats, others climb the rigging. Trelawny alone keeps cool and volunteers to go down into the magazine where he discovers, as probably occurred in fact in the *Akbar*, that the signal lights have been ignited accidentally from the pipe of the gunner's mate, who is drunk. He grasps the burning lights in his bare hands and puts out the fire. When he reappears on deck he is begrimed with wet gunpowder; his hands and face are scorched, his hair and eyebrows burnt, and he falls down insensible. But the man who saved the ship is a hero for the rest of the voyage.[4]

* * * * *

During Trelawny's voyage to India in H.M.S. *Woolwich* an incident occurred which he was to recall for the rest of his life. The first reference to it is in a letter from his mother in March 1807: 'Two days since a long and entertaining letter arrived from John who is just returned to Plymouth safe after having been overset in a boat when he saved himself by swimming ashore. Those that could not were drowned.'[5]

Shortly afterwards the *Woolwich* set sail again, this time to conduct a survey of the River Plate off Montevideo. On 3 September 1807 a dangerous incident occurred as the Captain's log records:

At 8 came up a heavy squall with thunder, and lightning. Struck T[op] G[allant] masts . . . At 11 calm, got out boats and sent them for water. At 1.30 pm came on to blow fresh. The boats attempted to get on board but could not fetch. We consequently veered a boat astern with 1200 fathoms of rope but to no purpose as none of them could fetch her. They consequently bore up for the harbour. On hauling the line (there being a very heavy sea) the boat was obliged to cut and make for the harbour.[6]

Clearly this was a nasty day. It must have been terrifying to have been either in the boats that were sent for water or in the boat that was later let out on a rope to try to give them a hand. However, there is no reason to believe that the men concerned suffered more than a fright. There is no mention in the log, either for that day or subsequently, of any of the boats having failed to reach the harbour safely or of any casualties.

In Trelawny's later telling, the episode in which the other men drowned is amalgamated with this incident off Patagonia. But the scene is shifted to a more exotic locale off the coast of Borneo. The shore is still at hand but it is 'the abode of wild elephants, tiger, serpents, and fevers'. From the ship they can see lights on shore – as no doubt Trelawny did off Montevideo – but also 'we thought we heard the roar of tigers'. Suddenly lightning strikes the ship. Trelawny is not now a boy volunteer but the Captain: 'The blow was struck before I had time to turn the hands up for the men were sleeping on deck. We were dismasted. I looked aloft and, by the light of a sheet of lightning, saw nothing standing but two bare poles.'[7]

Some of the crew have been swept overboard by the suddenness of the storm. Panic is everywhere but Trelawny persuades the men that, despite the terrific waves and winds, they must launch a boat. The sea was 'dashing jostling and tumbling about like a river where it empties itself into the sea' (like the River Plate). Some men are picked up but two, the second mate and a Swedish boy, are lost. At last Trelawny's boat is compelled to return to the ship, and unlike at Montevideo, they succeed. 'It was with infinite toil we neared and at last got under the lee of the ship.' But suddenly the boat is swamped and Trelawny and six others are thrown into the water. The ship drifts rapidly away. Then something white is seen on deck. It turns out to be Zela who throws him a rope so that he is just able to catch the end of it, and is rescued.

Many years later, Trelawny described a conversation with Lord Byron which he said took place in 1822. Trelawny has just decisively beaten Byron in a swimming contest. 'How far have you ever swum?' asks Byron. 'Eight knots and I was five hours in the water off the coast of Patagonia. The heave of the sea was in my favour, there was no wind, and the water was tepid. Two others with me were drowned.'[8] In this version the weather has become calm – perhaps as it really was in the original incident when the two men were drowned, but that incident of course did not occur off Patagonia but somewhere in India.

*   *   *   *   *

According to Trelawny, one of his shipmates in the navy was another despised boy volunteer called Walter. His father was a rich nobleman with an income of £40,000 a year, but his mother was a poor peasant girl seduced and abandoned and bundled off from the scene of embarrassment, precautions being taken and money spent to conceal who Walter's father was. He was educated at a charity school and put into the navy by his mother in an attempt to restore his gentility.[9]

One of Trelawny's favourite books was a life of John Paul Jones, the founder of the United States Navy who, though born in Scotland, fought long and successfully against the Royal Navy.[10] Among the numerous untrue stories about him in the books of Trelawny's time, and presumably widely believed, was the condescending presumption that a man of his undoubted abilities could not have been the son of a poor farmer, but must have been the illegitimate son of a nobleman. Did some memory of this story, with its opportunities for a hit at the rich who love their coronets more than their children, occur to Trelawny when he wrote about Walter? Then again Walter, who is Trelawny's closest friend, resigns from the navy and joins the army of the East India Company. When Trelawny later told this story, was he recalling Edward Ellerker Williams, whom he thought of as his closest friend at Pisa, who had done the same?

*   *   *   *   *

Another of Trelawny's friends, Darvell, may perhaps also be disentangled. He is picked up having been found adrift in an open boat, a story that itself owes a good deal to the travel literature of the day such as Trelawny's favourite, Bligh's *Mutiny on the Bounty*, and he and Trelawny instantly become friends for life. But like so many of Trelawny's friends he dies young: 'No sooner was the flag of freedom unfurled in the New World by spirits like his own than he hastened to join their ranks. His bleached bones may still glitter on the yellow sands of Peru where the small vessel he commanded was driven on shore and wrecked in a chivalrous action he fought with a Spanish force ten times his superior.'[11]

Twenty-seven years later, Trelawny returned to the same theme in a letter to Seymour Kirkup: 'He was drowned after shipwreck on the Coast of Patagonia – even now I dream of him often both when I am waking and sleeping. We often talk together very sensibly and then he disappears in a crowd of others. He engages to meet again and I think what a fool I was not to beg from him his address. This sort of dream has often occurred, does continue to haunt me up to a week ago – so you see how truly I loved him.'[12] But it is not now Darvell he is talking about but another shipmate called Aston. If Darvell and Aston ever existed, they have coalesced in Trelawny's mind.

*   *   *   *   *

At Pisa, Edward Ellerker Williams lent Trelawny a notebook in which he had written a piece called *Sporting Sketches in Hindoostan*. After Williams's death in 1822 Trelawny kept the notebook, and despite pleas by Jane Williams, never returned it.[13]

Williams's composition is dull and pedestrian. The main part describes a hunting expedition which he and a few fellow officers went on in March 1814 in the district of Rhotuk, about 80 miles from Delhi. They kill a tiger, then a lioness, then another lioness and her cubs. In between times they practice falconry. Near Rhotuk, says Williams, there was a specially dense area of jungle which the natives said was haunted. Strange noises were said to emanate from the caverns with which the thicket was undermined. 'It is said', noted Williams, 'that this is the site of the old city of Rhotuk which . . . . was many ages since rich populous and flourishing but now, according to the scriptural phrase is become heaps, a dwelling place for lions, a desolation and wilderness'. Williams admits to having 'but little inclination' to enter but when a lioness's tracks are found, they go in, with the elephants breaking a path through the jungle and the lions are duly found and killed. Soon afterwards Williams and his friends leave Rhotuk, having killed in four days, besides a number of other animals, nine lions, one tigress and one leopard.

Like most accounts of big game hunting, Williams's narrative is mainly a sickening recital of predictable slaughter. There is said to be great danger in the sport but in fact only one incident occurs in which the huntsmen are at the least risk. A cornered lion leaps on one of the elephants and attacks the driver (or mahout) in the houdah, but in the event 'he only received a light scratch in the thigh'.

Trelawny probably never killed a lion or a tiger in his life, but that did not prevent him from later describing an expedition which he went on with de Ruyter.[14] He simply took Williams's narrative and livened it up. The scene is transferred to Borneo, although Rhotuk is mentioned, to give it a more exotic flavour, and almost every other feature of Williams's plain narrative is taken over, enlarged, romanticised, made ominous, and clothed in rich descriptive language. The place chosen is 'said to be the ruins of an immense Moorish city, once called the City of Kings, but now the city of the tigers'. The hunters are 'the first for centuries' to disturb 'the hallowed precincts of ogres and spirits confidently reported to reside there'. They force their way through the jungle among 'broken masses of buildings, chasms, and wells'. They see a 'vaulted ruin' and 'a Moorish palace'. Suddenly dozens of tigers leap out. One man is instantly killed, several more are badly mauled. One Malay falls with his spine so badly injured that he dies in great agony. Trelawny himself is knocked down by a tiger but is saved by the presence of mind of de Ruyter.

Suddenly he remembers Zela, whom he has left in the houdah of one of the elephants. He dashes back and sees a monstrous tiger on the back of her elephant, clinging with his huge claws on the houdah, gnashing its teeth, roaring, and foaming with rage. Trelawny leaps wildly at the tiger and plunges his long dagger in its body and Zela is saved.

There is an orgy of tiger killing and a few other hapless bystanders in the drama lose their lives in gruesome circumstances. Trelawny, true to his adopted character of the pitiless avenger, decides to kill the servant who has carelessly put Zela in danger. It is left to her to jog his arm as he pulls the trigger and so spare the man's life. Even Williams's story of the falconry is pressed into service. A battle is being fought overhead between a hawk and a raven, and the death of the raven is loaded with symbolism.

*   *   *   *   *

Once it is known that Trelawny never deserted from the Royal Navy and that de Ruyter is an imaginary character, all his lesser pretensions collapse like punctured balloons, and when we see them hanging wet and limp, it is difficult to believe that they ever soared in the breeze. However, to his contemporaries the picture looked different. In fact, so far from being thought an imposter, Trelawny somehow managed to combine the wildest falsehoods with a developing reputation for personal integrity. SERMONI CONSONA FACTA was the proud inscription on his signet ring, read by his correspondents as they opened his letters – 'deeds to match words'.[15] In the front of his account book he wrote a quotation from Godwin which he no doubt saw as a motto appropriate to his own life: 'Look through the catalogue of vices of mortal defects and deformities that are incident to the heart of man! If you ask me to point out which are worst, their are two that I will cover with my hand as being those that I cannot think of or advert to, but with the most poignant aspect, insinserity and a temper abject and servile.'[16]

Trelawny found no difficulty in tolerating this inherent contradiction; he thrived on it. When he was being sincere, he was convincingly sincere even if his stories did not correspond to the facts, and how could anyone doubt that a man who admitted to such terrible crimes and character defects in himself could be anything but sincere? Byron's quip that 'Trelawny could not even to save his life tell the truth' gained its currency not because it was obviously true – for then it would not have been interesting – but because it seemed a daring and spiteful overstatement. Most people hearing Trelawny talk of his adventures with de Ruyter would probably rather have agreed with the judgement of the mild and earnest missionary James Kennedy, who spent some days in Cephalonia in 1823 trying to convince Byron of the truths of Christianity – Trelawny 'a gentleman who from great vivacity of imagination and thoughtlessness, exaggerated a little.'[17]

11

The Death of Shelley

I feel so deep a gratitude to him that my heart is full but to name him. He supported us in our miseries, my poor Jane & I. But for him, menials would have performed the most sacred of offices – & when I shake his hand I feel to the depth of my soul that those hands collected those ashes – Yes – for I saw them burned & scorched from the office – no fatigue – no sun – or nervous horrors deterred him, as one or the other of these causes deterred all others – he stood on the burning sands for many hours beside the pyre – if he had been permitted by the soldiers, he would have placed him there in his arms – I never – never can forget this.

From a letter of Mary Shelley, November 1822[1]

On 8 July Shelley and Williams with a boy seaman called Charles Vivian set out from Leghorn in the *Don Juan* to return to San Terenzo. They had been to Leghorn to meet Leigh Hunt on his arrival from England and to draw money, but were eager to get back as soon as possible. Trelawny intended to accompany them in the *Bolivar*, but his papers were not in order and he was refused clearance by the port authorities. There had been a squall that morning and when they set sail in the afternoon, there were unmistakeable signs that a storm was on the way. Roberts climbed the port watch tower and saw the *Don Juan* disappear into the mist. Shortly afterwards the whole area was torn by one of the worst storms for years, which lasted all night and most of the next day.

Mary and Jane,who were at San Terenzo waiting for their husbands to arrive from Leghorn,could hardly believe the news when they heard that they had set sail on the 8th,for they had seen the violence of the storm earlier that day as it roared down the coast. Mary was seriously depressed even beforehand,having suffered a miscarriage on 16 June, and they waited anxiously, scanning the sea longingly from the balcony of the Casa Magni,hoping to see the tall masts of the *Don Juan* swing into sight. The post was expected on 16 July and that seemed to promise a limit to their waiting, but when at last it arrived, there was only a letter from Hunt addressed to Shelley which expressed anxiety about his safe arrival and therefore merely renewed and worsened their anxiety.

Unable to bear the suspense any longer the two women set out at once to Pisa in search of news. The journey took nearly all day and when they arrived at Pisa they went straight to Byron's palazzo, the Casa Lanfranchi, tired, haggard, and sick with worry, They were met by the Guiccioli, surprised and smiling, who apparently was not aware of what had happened, having been deeply involved in recent days in her own problems connected with the expulsion of the Gamba family, and Lord Byron himself whom they also met seems not to have realised fully until that moment just how bad the situation was. Mary and Jane, finding no news – and little help – at Pisa, decided though it was after midnight to press on to Leghorn where Trelawny and Roberts were staying but they were taken to the wrong inn. Trelawny and Roberts could not be found and Mary and Jane tried to sleep in their clothes until 6 o'clock next morning.

When Trelawny and Roberts were found, they immediately started to make urgent enquiries. Money was offered for news and word was passed to the troops manning the coastal watch towers to search their areas. The crews of vessels putting in to Leghorn were questioned, and one vessel reported having seen the *Don Juan* trying to take down the top sails when the wind had first risen, but there was no definite news. Roberts sent a letter to Byron asking if he could use the *Bolivar* in the search operations, a request immediately granted.

Mary was now quite ill and she and Jane were persuaded that it would be best if they went back to the Casa Magni. There was still hope, Trelawny and Roberts tried to assure them – the boat might have gone ashore at some remote place on the long beach of the Bay of Spezia or been driven across to Corsica. Trelawny accompanied them on the long drive back,giving them all the support and hope he could, but as they passed near Viareggio on their journey back towards Lerici, information arrived from the watch tower there that a skiff and a barrel which belonged to the *Don Juan* had been washed ashore.

On the 17th a headless body much mutilated and eaten by fish was washed ashore near the mouth of the river Serchio not far from the watch tower of Migliarino.[2] The next day another mutilated body came ashore at Viareggio and another – of a boy – further up the coast at Massa. They were immediately buried in quicklime on the spot by the health authorities. Trelawny who had been patrolling the coast on horseback every day from the Casa Magni apparently saw the body found near Viareggio before it was buried and was able to identify it as that of Shelley from the clothing and from a copy of Keats's poems which was found in the jacket pocket.

His first thought was for the two lonely waiting women and their children, and how the terrible news could be broken to them. He rode straight to the Casa Magni and he went in unannounced. On his previous visits he had been concerned to try to keep up Mary's and Jane's spirits, but this time no word was said. They saw at once by his face that all was over, and when Mary, breaking the silence, asked 'Is there no hope?' he turned and left the room. The news was given, the shock was taken, the anxiety was over, and the long years of sorrow had begun. Trelawny's gentleness and consideration on this occasion were to be remembered with gratitude by the two widows when much else of those unspeakable days had long been forgotten. On the previous evening the inhabitants of San Terenzo had been celebrating a holiday with dancing, laughing, and singing late into the night, but now all was silent except for the ceaseless beating of the waves and the mournful whistle of the wind.

Next day Trelawny escorted Mary and Jane to Pisa, and the survivors of the circle gathered to decide what to do. Jane wanted the body of her beloved Williams to be reburied in the English Protestant Cemetery at Leghorn, and Mary expressed a wish that Shelley might be buried in the Protestant Cemetery at Rome beside the grave of their dead child William – Willmouse – whom they had loved and missed intensely. It was a place that Shelley himself had written about so movingly in *Adonais*, his elegy for John Keats, which was now in-increasingly seen as applying to Shelley himself:

> He has outsoared the shadow of our night;
> Envy and calumny, and hate and pain,
> And that unrest which men miscall delight
> Can touch him not and torture not again;
> From the contagion of the world's slow stain
> He is secure and now can never mourn
> A heart grown cold, a head grown grey in vain;
> Nor when the spirit's self has ceased to burn
> With sparkless ashes load an unlamented urn.

Go thou to Rome – at once the Paradise,
The grave, the city, and the wilderness;
And where its wrecks like shattered mountains rise,
And flowering weeds, and fragrant copses dress
The bones of Desolation's nakedness,
Pass, till the Spirit of the spot shall lead
Thy footsteps to a slope of green access
Where like an infant's smile, over the dead
A light of laughing flowers along the grass is spread.

And grey walls moulder round, on which dull Time
Feeds like slow fire upon a hoary brand;
And one keen pyramid with wedge sublime,
Pavilioning the dust of him who planned
This refuge for his memory, doth stand
Like flame transformed to marble; and beneath
A field is spread, on which a newer band
Have pitched in Heaven's smile their camp of death,
Welcoming him we lose with scarce extinguished breath.

The health and quarantine regulations were very strict. Two governments were involved since Williams's body had come ashore in Tuscany whereas Viareggio, where Shelley's body had been buried, was in Lucca. There was no question of the remains themselves being moved – nobody was even permitted to touch them from the moment they were washed ashore – but the authorities, helped by an intervention by Dawkins, the British *chargé* at Florence, agreed that, provided a month had passed after burial, the bodies could be exhumed under strict supervision and cremated. The ashes might then be collected and moved wherever the families wanted.

Trelawny made himself responsible for the arrangements. An iron furnace was constructed to his order at Leghorn and wine and incense were obtained to add to the pyre. The *Bolivar* was sailed to the mouth of the Serchio and with Byron in attendance, the body of Williams was dug up and cremated on the beach on 15 August. The process took many hours.

Next day they crossed the frontier to Lucca to repeat the ceremony with the body of Shelley. Three white wands, he wrote later, had been stuck in the sand to mark the grave, but the men had to cut a trench thirty yards in length in the line of the sticks to find the exact spot, and it was nearly an hour before they came upon the grave. In the meantime Byron and Leigh Hunt had arrived in a carriage, attended by soldiers and the health officer, as they had done the previous day for Williams's cremation. Trelawny wrote later:

As I thought of the delight Shelley felt in such scenes of loneliness and grandeur whilst living, I felt we were no better than a herd of wolves or a pack of wild dogs, in tearing out his battered and naked body from the pure yellow sand that lay so lightly over it, to drag him back to the light of day; but the dead have no voice, nor had I power to check the sacrilege – the work went on silently in the deep and unresisting sand, not a word was spoken, for the Italians have a touch of sentiment, and their feelings are easily excited into sympathy. Even Byron was silent and thoughtful. We were startled and drawn together by a dull hollow sound that followed the blow of a mattock; the iron had struck a skull, and the body was soon uncovered. Lime had been strewn on it, this, or decomposition, had the effect of staining it of a dark and ghastly indigo colour. Byron asked me to preserve the skull for him; but remembering that he has formerly used one as a drinking cup, I was determined Shelley's should not be so profaned. The limbs did not separate from the trunk, as in the case of Williams's body, so that the corpse was removed entire into the furnace. I had taken the precaution of having more and larger pieces of timber, in consequence of my experience of the day before of the difficulty of consuming a corpse in the open air with our apparatus. After the fire was well kindled we repeated the ceremony of the previous day; and more wine was poured over Shelley's dead body than he had consumed during his life. This with the oil and salt made the yellow flames glisten and quiver. The heat from the sun and fire was so intense that the atmosphere was tremulous and wavy. The corpse fell open and the heart was laid bare. The frontal bone of the skull where it had been struck with the mattock, fell off; and, as the back of the head rested on the red-hot bottom bars of the furnace, the brains literally seethed, bubbled, and boiled as in a cauldron, for a very long time.

Byron could not face this scene, he withdrew to the beach and swam off to the 'Bolivar'. Leigh Hunt remained in the carriage. The fire was so fierce as to produce a white heat on the iron, and to reduce its contents to grey ashes. The only portions that were not consumed were some fragments of bones, the jaw, and the skull, but what surprised us all, was that the heart remained entire. In snatching this relic from the fiery furnace, my hand was severely burned; and had any one seen me do the act I should have been put into quarantine.[3]

When the fire died down, Trelawny cooled the iron machine in the sea, and then carefully collected the human ashes and placed them in a box, which he took on board the *Bolivar*. The heart was taken by Hunt who later, at her insistence, presented it to Mary who apparently did not regard it as in the least gruesome.

Shelley the great pagan had a great pagan funeral. No priest was near. No prayers were said. Trelawny turned what might have been a tiresome and perhaps sordid administrative ordeal into an unforgettable drama. If he added romance, there was never a suspicion of sentimentality. It helped to bring comfort to the bereaved and Trelawny's first consideration during the whole terrible episode was to help Mary and Jane. He understood too the desolation that the bereaved feel after the excitement of the funeral is over, and when others were perhaps put off by the depression of the two women, Trelawny would come and sit with them, months after the tragedy, talking of little else but Shelley and Williams. The only balm they could bear, Mary wrote later, was praise of their lost husbands and this Trelawny supplied in abundance from his sincere love and admiration for his two friends.

Shelley's ashes were sent to Rome and in January 1823 were buried in the Protestant Cemetery in the presence of a few of the English colony, mainly artists, but none of Shelley's close friends. Two Christian priests performed the burial ceremony, a fine example of the tyranny of the living over the dead; and there the matter rested until April 1823 when Trelawny arrived in Rome. He was horrified by what he found. Shelley's remains were 'confusedly mingled in a heap with five or six common vagabonds'. There was no memorial of any kind. The English artists were more interested in the monument to be erected on the grave of John Keats, and a lively argument was in progress led by Keats's friend Joseph Severn who had been with him at his death. Trelawny had never met Keats nor had any contact with him in any way during his lifetime, but he felt he knew him. He had heard Shelley speak of him and had been with Shelley when the first copies of *Adonais* had arrived from England. Now that Shelley himself was buried in that same graveyard about which he had written so hauntingly in *Adonais*, his imagination started to run, and he took charge of the arrangements at Rome as masterfully as he had done at Viareggio.

Severn was amazed and annoyed at the arrival of this strange character who presumed to know exactly what should be done, and wrote to a friend to find out who he was:

There is a Mad Chap come here – whose name is Trelawny I do not know what to make of him further than his queer and I was near saying shabby behaviour to me. He comes on the friend of Shelly – great – glowing and rich in romance – of course I showed all my paint pot politeness to him – to the very brim – assisted him to remove the Ashes of Shelly to a spot where he himself (when this world has done with his body) will lie. He wished me to think, myself, and consult my friends about a Monument to Shelly – the situation is beautiful and one and all thought a little Basso-relievo would be best suited. – I was telling him the subject I had proposed for Keats – and he was struck with the propriety of it for Shelly – and my friend Mr Gott – (whom I mentioned to you) was to be the doer of it. – I made the drawing which cost us some trouble – yet after expressing the greatest liking for it – this pair of Mustachios has shirk'd off from it without giving us the Yea or No – without even the why or wherefore. – I am sorry at this most on Mr Gotts account – but I ought to have seen that this Lord Byron's Jackall was rather weak in all the points I could judge – though strong enough in Stiletto's – we have not had any open rupture – nor shall we – for I have no doubt that this "Cockney Corsair" fancies he has greatly obliged us by all this trouble we have had. – But tell me who is this odd fish? They talk of him here as a camelion who went mad on reading Ld. Byrons Corsair – that he sailed as one – and has since made both ends meet – I told him this – and to my surprise – he laughed and said it was true.[4]

That laugh was surely one of delight that his reputation as a corsair was now so secure that it had preceded him to Rome.

At Trelawny's direction Shelley's ashes were reburied by the old city wall of Rome near the huge pyramid of Caius Cestius, and he planted six young cypresses and four laurels by the tomb. On the gravestone itself it had been agreed to inscribe Leigh Hunt's suggested epitaph COR CORDIUM 'Heart of Hearts' – although Shelley's heart having been taken from the flames was not there – but Trelawny added the lines from *The Tempest*:

> Nothing of him that doth fade
> But doth suffer a sea change
> Into something rich and strange.

As he explained to Mary in a letter describing what he had done:

This quotation by its double meaning alludes both to the manner of his death and his genius, and I think the element on which his soul took wing and the subtle essence of his being mingled, may still retain in him some other shape. The waters may keep the dead, as the earth may, and fire and air. His passionate fondness might have been from some secret sympathy in their natures. Then the fascination which so forcibly attracted him, without fear or caution, to trust an element almost all others hold in superstitious dread, and venture as cautiously on as they would in a lair of lions.[5]

Not far away was raised a stone on the grave of John Keats. Below the incomplete lyre symbolising his unripened genius were carved the now famous words:

This Grave
Contains all that was Mortal
of a
YOUNG ENGLISH POET
Who
on his Death-Bed,
in the Bitterness of his Heart,
at the Malicious Power of his Enemies,
Desired
these Words to be engraved on his Tomb Stone
"Here lies One
Whose Name was writ in Water."
Feb 24th 1821

Trelawny helped to turn the final resting place of the two young English romantic poets into a secular shrine to romanticism to which pilgrims still journey in their thousands, and although he was only thirty years old and was to live for more than fifty years longer, he characteristically ensured that Edward John Trelawny would share in their glory. He bought the plot adjoining Shelley's grave, and even had the grave dug and a plain stone laid on it so that, as he told Mary Shelley, 'When I die, there is only to lift the coverlet and roll me into it'.

Sketch of a schooner drawn by Edward Williams when the *Don Juan* was being designed

The Casa Magni, Shelley's house at San Terenzo near Lerici, with the *Don Juan*

The Protestant Cemetery at Rome. Shelley's grave with the trees planted by Trelawny is by the ruined tower, Keats's grave in the foreground.

'John Keats died at Rome of a consumption, in his twenty-fourth year, on the 23rd of February 1821; and was buried in the romantic and lonely cemetery of the Protestants in that City, under the pyramid which is the tomb of Cestius, and the massy walls and towers, now mouldering and desolate, which formed the circuit of ancient Rome. The cemetery is an open space among the ruins, covered in winter with violets and daisies. It might make one in love with death to think that one should be buried in so sweet a place.'

From Shelley's Preface to *Adonais*

12

Mary and Claire

I admire esteem and love him; some excellent qualities he possesses in a degree that is unsurpassed, but then it is exactly in another direction from my centre and my impetus. He likes a turbid and troubled life; I a quiet one; he is full of fine feelings and has no principles; I am full of fine principles but never had a feeling in my life. He receives all his impressions through his heart; I through my head.

From a later letter of Claire Clairmont.[1]

Gradually the group of friends who had formed the Pisa circle drifted apart. The *Liberal,* the new review which Hunt was to edit with Shelley and Byron, and which had been the reason for Byron coming to Pisa in the first place, collapsed after only four issues. Byron was irritated by Leigh Hunt's wife and children who showed no respect either for his rank or for his wallpaper. Co-operation proved impossible, and the expected profits did not occur.

Byron moved to Montenero and then, later, to Albaro near Genoa, but Trelawny continued to be in charge of the *Bolivar* and to sail her on Byron's behalf, living at inns at Leghorn or Genoa when not on board. At Leghorn in August 1822, he challenged an officer of a British warship to a duel over a point of naval etiquette, in which Trelawny was in the wrong, and the affair was reported to the Admiralty. The *Bolivar* brought unending trouble and Trelawny, as the man in charge, suffered as so many had done before from Byron's lofty attitudes to money. Leaving bills unpaid and claims unsettled are luxuries available only to the rich, as the sailors found who applied unsuccessfully for their arrears of pay. Daniel Roberts broke completely with Byron when Byron complained that the sailors had been allowed to keep the uniforms that had been provided. Trelawny, the ship's manager, kept up a steady stream of firm polite business-like letters to Byron (no misspellings here) urging him to pay, though as Byron himself was the first to admit, the richer he felt himself to be, the more tight-fisted he became.[2]

On 13 September the authorities at Viareggio reported to the government that two fishing vessels had caught a sunken vessel, schooner-rigged, in their nets and it was thought to be the boat in which Shelley and Williams had been drowned two months before. After the necessary quarantine clearance, the boat was brought ashore and an inventory was taken. The identification with the *Don Juan* was ascertained, – all Shelley's and Williams's belongings were still on board including clothes, books, a large sum of money, and the seven sails with which she had been so heavily overrigged. The boat was damaged, but apparently not badly, for she was repaired and at sea again shortly afterwards. Daniel Roberts, who inspected the damaged vessel, concluded that she had been run down in the storm by a larger vessel – possibly deliberately for the English milords were known to have money on board – and he persuaded Mary Shelley that this was the cause of the disaster.

Trelawny too apparently shared the view that the *Don Juan* had been run down and this later became something of an obsession. However, the story is intrinsically unlikely and there is no need to look for explanations beyond the vessel's faulty design. Roberts and Trelawny, whether deliberately or unconsciously, needed the ramming theory to save themselves from the consequences of accepting that they carried a part of the responsibility of procuring Shelley and Williams an unseaworthy vessel.

The pleasure had gone out of sailing. In October the *Bolivar* was laid up for the winter in Genoa, then Byron sold her and Trelawny was out of a job. What was he to do now? For the last three months of 1822 he lived in an inn at Genoa, dividing his time between Albaro and the town. Each afternoon he rode with Byron from two till five, then he went to see Mary at the Leigh Hunts'. The evenings were usually spent with Gabrielle Wright, said to be a great beauty, the wife of the builder of the *Don Juan* who was away at the time. In January he went with Roberts on a hunting expedition in the swamps which was the reason he had originally come to Italy in 1821, but a man who had allegedly wrestled with tigers in the Borneo jungles was bound to find shooting marsh ducks rather unexciting.

Mary Shelley, who was his closest friend during this period, had had her life thrown into turmoil by Shelley's death and she never really recovered. She sank into a depression which lasted far longer than normal grief, and took to writing down long analytical descriptions of her own state of mind and addressing letters to her dead husband in her notebooks. She felt uncomfortable, perhaps a little guilty, about Shelley. She had never fully shared his beliefs and ideals – but she was also conscious of having failed to live up to expectations in other ways. Shelley was forever falling in love with other women, more or less platonically, and Mary knew that latterly she had ceased to be the centre of his life. Together they had bravely defied the censure of their families and the world. When his father tried cutting off funds, Shelley had always been able to borrow on his expectations and dare old Sir Tim to do his worst. An allowance of £1,000 a year had been granted to him, partly to prevent him ruining the family fortune by selling *post obit.* bonds at vast discount. Now that Shelley was dead everything changed. Mary had no money of her own apart from what she could earn by writing and she had a baby son to bring up and educate. Soon after Shelley's death, when she moved to Genoa with the Hunts, she began the work of putting together the fragments of Shelley's poetry for a posthumous edition of his works.

Lord Byron discreetly gave her money and much practical help. He also willingly took up her cause with Sir Timothy Shelley when her own direct approach was rebuffed by the Shelley family lawyer. But the answer which arrived in January 1823 simply worsened her misery – financial provision would be made but only on condition that her baby son Percy Florence was handed over to be brought up by foster parents approved by the Shelley family. Sir Tim was determined that his grandson, who in 1826 was to become heir to the Shelley fortune, should be disinfected as far as possible from his father's hateful ideas.

The demand was rejected, and – against the advice of many of her friends – Mary decided to return to England, but she did not have the money. Lord Byron made an offer to help but he could not be pinned down and he declined to pay the £1,000 which was due to Mary as a result of the bet he had made with Shelley.* Mary, perhaps recalling the unfailing generosity towards all comers of the dead Shelley, could never forgive Byron his excess of caution in (some) financial matters and their friendship came to an end. In her desolation she turned to Trelawny, and it was only with his financial help that she was able to

---

* See p. 47. There were many legal formalities to be negotiated before Byron received the Milbanke inheritance which became due on the death of Lady Byron's mother, and Byron may have been prudent to delay paying the debt until the money was actually in his hands. But it was never paid.

pay her fare back to England with her son. In her hour of need, she later told Jane Williams, she found that she had only three friends worthy of the name – Jane herself, soon to be made a social outcast on her return to England; Leigh Hunt, with whose family she stayed at Genoa; and Trelawny – only the poor would help the poor.

As with the funeral arrangements, only Trelawny proved worthy. 'I never bore poverty with patience', he wrote to her, 'and I now curse and execrate my destiny that compels me to leave you so ill-provided for so difficult a situation and the new road you are about to take in life.' 'Will you tell me what sum you want', he wrote on another occasion, 'as I am settling my affairs. You must from time to time let me know your wants that I may do my best to relieve them. You are sure of me, so let us use no more words about it.'[3] It was the kind of thing that Shelley himself would have done, and this was perhaps partly in Trelawny's mind. But it was his own nature insofar as any characteristic of Trelawny can be regarded as entirely his own. He was the same man who had opened himself so generously to Augusta White in 1817, and was to do so to others, both friends and casual acquaintances, many times in a long life.

Mary, more than any other person, accepted him and admired him at his face value. She was a little in love with him, and Trelawny, although he did not yet have the boldness of later years, made offers about sharing their incomes which was probably intended to mean more. Trelawny assured Mary in a letter that she was his best friend in the whole world and she wrote back tenderly that she felt the same about him. But if Mary had thoughts, or hopes, that her relationship with Trelawny might become closer, she quickly put them out of her mind. Trelawny would continue to be one of her closest friends, but no more. For Trelawny had fallen passionately in love with Claire Clairmont.

He was always falling in love in Italy, or pretending to. For a while it was Gabrielle Wright, Trelawny admitted who 'almost subdued his tough and stubborn nature to its former softness', but Trelawny was not in earnest even if Gabrielle was. Everybody knew about Mrs Wright's visits to the *Croix de Malthe* inn, and on one occasion the waiter found one of her letters and read it aloud to the company. When Wright returned, Trelawny's connexion with her was quickly ended.[4]

But Claire was an altogether more serious matter, Trelawny first met her on 22 February 1822 and declared later that he had loved her from the first day ('nay before I saw you'). He saw her hardly at all, a few days in February, a few days in April and then occasionally in the summer after Shelley's death. He implored her to marry him or to live with him and poured out a stream of passionate letters.[5] On 6 September 1822 they apparently had a day together which both were to recall for the rest of their lives, but she firmly refused all his proposals. Like Mary she was left stranded by Shelley's death and she had to earn her bread. On 20 September she left Italy for the hard, lonely life of a governess with an English family first in Vienna then in Russia, thus as Trelawny said, putting 'barriers of eternal ice and snow' between them. However much she might regret her Inwalert as she called her aspiring lover in the privacy of her diary in the simplest code known to cryptography, she was in no doubt about what she must do. Despite his flood of letters she gave him no encouragement to come after her or hope that she would return.[6] And so, a year after Trelawny's dramatic debut at Pisa in January 1822, that wonderful world had collapsed. Shelley was dead, Williams was dead, Claire was gone, Mary was going. Byron had given up the *Bolivar*. What was Trelawny to do? He was back in the situation of 1817, a hero in search of a role.

And now he had his fictitious past to cope with and the personality which had developed to fit it. His assumed character of larger than life extravagance, now second nature, was rapidly becoming first nature. If his conversation resembled his letters, he must have been a tiring companion. A hint of world weariness might add to the charm of a Byronic hero, but Trelawny laid it on with a shovel. The thirty-year-old corsair had seen it all, done it all; life offered nothing new, and the ennui was barely supportable.

He had to find a new life. England had no attractions for him and there was little to keep him in Italy. When his mother discovered his address and started to pester him with letters, he knew he would have to move on. The appearance of his mother and sisters would have exploded, totally and immediately, his carefully constructed imaginary past. For the same reason he told Mary Shelley that he had no friends in England to introduce her to. He still knew his life was a lie. A corsair, especially a fraud corsair, must keep on the move or cease to be a corsair. He had to find a new place where his talents could be put to use, a place perhaps where a blow could be struck for the principles so fervently proclaimed by the dead Shelley?

13

To Greece

My head is full of plans of leading an active life – of doffing these
robes of idleness – and of buckling on the sword in the great
struggle of Liberty – either in Greece or Spain – but long habits
of supine indolence are as enervating to the mind and spirit as is
Egypt's burning clime to the physical body.

From a letter to Claire Clairmont, June 1823.[1]

The Greek Revolution broke out in the spring of 1821. In the first few
weeks the Turkish and other Moslem minorities in the Peloponnese and
elsewhere were exterminated in a riot of massacre, and the revolution-
aries soon gained control of most of Southern Greece and some of the
islands, although a number of fortresses remained in Turkish hands
under siege. Successive attempts by the Turks to reconquer the re-
volted provinces in 1822 and 1823 were decisively repulsed, but the
Ottoman Government remained determined to reassert its authority
and the revolution looked set to become a long-drawn-out war.

Although there was at all times an official Greek government which
claimed jurisdiction over the whole area, it consisted mainly of ex-
patriate Greeks educated in Western Europe or Phanariotes from
Constantinople who had flocked to Greece, a land which most of them
had never previously visited, at the time of the outbreak in hopes of
assuming the leadership of the new state. The real power lay in the
hands of local warlords who had instigated the initial massacres and
established themselves with the aid of their own armies. In the
Peloponnese, Colocotrones, an illiterate warlord, was the master.
In Eastern Greece, Odysseus Androutsos ruled his area with a cruel
hand and the leaders of the islands which supplied the ships were also
virtually independent. Nationalism in the modern sense had as yet
hardly developed.

The picture which Western Europe had of the state of affairs in
Greece was sadly different from the reality. The Greek Revolution was
seen by many as an attempt to restore the glories of Ancient Greece.
Others saw it as an extension of the long battle between Christendom

and the barbarian Asiatics. The news from Greece was shamelessly distorted (and invented) by philhellenic newspapers so that readers in Europe could read of great imaginary victories gained by the Greeks, usually at places with familiar Grecian names. The essentially genocidal nature of the war was suppressed, and the assumption that the Greeks were a united people struggling to assert their right to independence as a nation state was scarcely challenged. Hundreds of volunteers from all over Europe rushed to Greece to offer their services in the Greek army.

Shelley was one of the countless European liberals who had greeted the outbreak of revolution with enthusiasm, and his last great poem, *Hellas*, contains perhaps the classic statement of philhellenism. While at Pisa in 1821, before Trelawny arrived, Shelley and Mary had been on friendly terms with Prince Alexander Mavrocordato, a Constantinople exile, who had gone to Greece at the outbreak and was now one of the leaders of the new country. They probably knew something of the plans for the revolution before it began – Pisa was one of the centres of the conspiracy – and there had been talk that they should emigrate to Greece and settle there once independence was secured.

The name of Byron was also inextricably tied to Greece, the setting of many of his earliest and most famous poems, including *The Corsair*. In Canto III of *Don Juan* published in 1821 he had included the poem *The Isles of Greece* – written long before – which perhaps above all others has influenced European attitudes to Modern Greece:

> The mountains look on Marathon
> And Marathon looks on the sea;
> And musing there an hour alone
> I dreamed that Greece might still be free.

It was therefore natural that when Byron and Trelawny, in their separate ways, were each thinking of leaving Italy in 1823, Greece should be high in their minds.

By a coincidence, just at the same time a committee was being formed in London to send arms, men, money, and (especially) advice to the revolutionary Greeks, and one of their first acts was to send an emissary to Genoa to sound out Lord Byron on whether he would be willing to go to Greece as their official representative. Edward Blaquiere, the emissary, pushed against an open door. Byron wanted to go – all he needed was a little persuasion, and when this was applied, he accepted at once.

Trelawny had already passed the word to Byron that he was ready to go with him. 'Tell him how willingly I will embark on the cause', he wrote to Mary Shelley, 'and stake my all on the cast of the die. Liberty or nothing.'[2] But he was sceptical about whether Byron would ever break out of his comfortable Italian habits. It was almost a ritual game which Byron and his former ship's manager would play together. 'I will buy an island in the South Seas', Byron would suddenly shout in one of his moods of exasperation or exaltation, 'Will you come with me, Tre?' 'Of course', was always the ready answer, and plans of this kind had been made to go and fight or colonise in Spain, South America, Turkey and elsewhere. There was even talk for a while of the two men chartering an armed vessel and going privateering in the Aegean like Conrad the Corsair.

Trelawny was therefore perhaps a little surprised when, on 15 June 1823, Byron wrote to say that he was himself definitely going and to invite his company to Greece. 'I want your aid', he said, 'and am exceedingly anxious to see you.' 'I need not say', he wrote in a subsequent letter, 'I shall like your company of all things.'[3] He had engaged a vessel to take him and his party to Greece and was ready to set sail at once for Genoa. He would pick up Trelawny at Leghorn on the way. Trelawny immediately rode to join him. He had virtually no money and one horse, and his single servant was an American Negro engaged, one need not doubt, because of his colour. He apparently told his mother that he was to have 'the command of the *Hypernea*, a fine ship belonging to Lord Byron'.[4] In fact he was to be a member of Lord Byron's suite in the *Hercules,* an old tub chartered by Byron for a single journey.

Trelawny had now told the stories of his corsair past so often that a plunge into a desperate war looked like a return to normality. 'My ardent love of freedom spurs me on to assist in the struggle for freedom,' he wrote to Claire, implying that he had struggled for liberty many times in the past. 'And without ties – wearied and wretched – melancholy and dissatisfied – What was left me here? I have been dying piecemeal – thin – care-worn – and desponding – Such an excitement as this was necessary to rouse me into energy and life – and it has done so – I am all on fire for action – and ready to endure the worst that may befall, seeking nothing but honour.'[5] The *Hercules* sailed on 21 July 1823. Apart from Trelawny, Byron's staff consisted of Count Gamba, a doctor and eight other servants. The ship carried arms and ammunition, ten thousand Spanish dollars in cash and bills of exchange for forty thousand more. Passage was also being given to a few Greeks and to James Hamilton Browne, a volunteer.

As soon as they had set sail, Byron felt a sense of liberation. He was taken back to the months he had passed in Greece and Turkey in 1809-1811 which had been the inspiration for the poems that made him famous. On board ship he was very much the master, treating Trelawny as his factotum as in the *Bolivar*, giving him errands in the polite, friendly, and unapologetic way that comes from an unquestioning assumption of superiority. Trelawny did not mind, but he was conscious that he was in danger of losing his independence. He was determined not to become a hanger-on or to be treated as less than an equal. As he wrote to Mary Shelley before the *Hercules* sailed: 'The Poet's attention and professed kindness to me is boundless; he leaves everything to my direction; if I had confidence in him this would be well, but I now only see the black side of it; it will eventually rob me of my free agency by so weaving me in with his fortunes that I may have difficulty in separating myself from them.'[6]

On board ship the old friendship was restored. They would practice boxing and fencing together, although Byron's malformed feet made any kind of exercise on foot painful, and in calm weather they would swim from the ship's side. It was just like the old days at Pisa. A live duck in a basket was hung from the mast with its head protruding, and Byron and Trelawny would blaze away at it with their pistols. Sometimes, to the admiration of the onlookers, they would both hit the poor bird with a single shot. The Turkish hordes had better take care.[7]

Byron had bought a collection of scarlet-and-gold uniforms with decorated swords and neo-classical helmets such as are presented to retired conquerors on ceremonial occasions, and grew long military moustaches like Trelawny to give himself a severer look. Byron too, he hinted, could play the corsair like his friend. Byron too could be a Byronic hero.

But Trelawny did not like any of this, and refused stiffly to wear his Homeric helmet. The poet, he increasingly felt, would never make a soldier. Corsairs should not stand before the mirror adjusting their cuffs to show off their soft pale hands. Corsairs should not be afraid of the effect of the sun on their complexions. Corsairs should not be measuring their waist and wrists every morning to see if they have put on weight. If Lord Byron really intended to take a serious part in the Greek war he would have to learn to do without a few of his comforts.

But what appeared as fastidiousness to outsiders was of course minimal cleanliness to Byron himself. For his part Byron was horrified by the tolerance of dirt which Trelawny saw (rightly) as inseparable from the life of a philhellene. 'If we could make Trelawny tell the truth and wash his hands we will make a gentleman of him yet' was one version of the famous Byron quip.[8] Trelawny, the extremist in everything, took his contempt of discomfort so earnestly that he seemed to glory in his filth and boast of his lice, but he was at least playing the corsair game consistently. Byron, by his eclectic approach, was bringing the profession into disrepute.

It had been Lord Byron's intention to sail in the first place to Zante where he had arranged to meet Edward Blaquiere, the energetic representative of the London Greek Committee, and to discuss with him, in the light of his knowledge of the Greek scene, how best to proceed. To Byron's intense annoyance, however, Blaquiere was not there. Carried away by an eagerness to rush into print with a journalistic account of the Greek war he had gone back to England. Instead of sailing to Zante, therefore, Byron ordered the *Hercules* to Cephalonia where the British Resident, Colonel Charles Napier, offered a warm welcome, and he was soon settled in comfortable quarters, cultivated by the officers of the British garrison and sought after by the local British community.

The news from Greece was far from encouraging. The reported Greek victories vanished on closer inspection, and disturbing intelligence was coming through of a new Turkish offensive. The Greek fleet was said to be increasingly ineffective, and civil war had broken out in various parts of the country. Letters began to arrive from the Greek leaders with variations on two simple points, warnings against the other leaders and requests for money. It was not at all what Byron had expected, and he decided to proceed cautiously. He would stay for a while in the Ionian Islands, listen to what Napier and the other experts had to say, and he would consult further with the Greek Committee in London. Meanwhile the life of a celebrity, for all its annoyances, had its compensations. Byron enjoyed being surrounded by admirers, and he enjoyed talking. In fact, as the weeks went by, it became increasingly clear that his enthusiasm to plunge into the Greek war with its likely discomforts and inconveniences – and possibly dangers – was rapidly ebbing away.

Trelawny and Hamilton Browne who were not celebrities became increasingly irritated at his apparent lack of drive. Having finally made the decisive step of leaving Italy, Byron seemed content now to fritter away his time as a tourist. True, he had reason for delay but to Trelawny this seemed to be merely an excuse. He recognized Byron's habitual lapse into lassitude, his unwillingness to pack or move house once he had got himself comfortable in a new place. At last Trelawny and Hamilton Browne decided that they would go to Greece even if this meant splitting away from Byron.

He tried to dissuade them from leaving, but when that failed, another plan was thought of. Byron would remain in the Ionian Islands to await news from the Committee in England and to see how the political situation in Greece developed. Meanwhile Trelawny and Hamilton Browne would cross to Greece, go to the seat of the Government, meet the various Greek leaders and try to assess the situation on the ground. They would carry a letter from Lord Byron to give them any entrée they needed, and in the light of their advice, Byron would decide whether to follow. They were thus in effect to be agents of Lord Byron and hence of the London Greek Committee. They were correctly described as 'two of Lord Byron's secretaries'.[9] On 6 September 1823 they took their farewells and set sail from Cephalonia in an open boat. They were never to see Lord Byron alive again.

14

A Dream Come True

I am habited exactly like Ulysses, in red and gold vest with sheep-
skin *capote*, gun pistols, sabre etc, red cap and a few dollars of
doubloons . . . I am alone and without ties, living a wild, savage,
and unsocial life.

From a letter to Mary Shelley, October 1823.[1]

The next morning Trelawny and Hamilton Browne landed on a remote
beach in the Western Peloponnese near which stood a solitary ruined
watchtower. The garrison, a single soldier who occupied the leaky
upper story of the tower, was welcoming and they asked about the
political situation. The only government he obeyed was his master
Colocotrones, the soldier declared forthrightly. As a lesson in Greek
politics the point was well made. That night they stayed in the house of
a mule owner who had agreed to conduct them to Tripolitsa and he
gave a party in their honour. The guests sat cross-legged on the floor
round a low table and ate their meat and rice with their hands. The
daughters of the house served rose water to perfume the guests'
moustaches and afterwards handed each of them a hubble-bubble pipe.
They had crossed the boundary line between two cultures.

The journey to Tripolitsa took three days over rough mountain
tracks through some of the most beautiful country in the world.
Occasionally they would see a local shepherd with a long-barrelled
musket over his shoulder, and the signs of war were everywhere. As
they climbed into the mountains and the rain and cold became intense,
Hamilton Browne who had spent some years in the Ionian Islands and
knew Greek conditions well, nonchalantly pulled on a black silk
nightcap to give himself some protection against the weather. Trelawny,
the newcomer, knew better what was expected. He tore off his tight
European clothes and put on instead a bright red Albanian jacket with
gold buttons, flowing trousers, and a silk girdle and a turban. On top
he wore the rough cloak made from sheeps' fleeces, the capote, a word
well known to the readers of *Childe Harold's Pilgrimage*:

Oh! who is more brave than a dark Suliote
In his snowy camese and his shaggy capote?
To the wolf and the vulture he leaves his wild flock,
And descends to the plain like the stream from the rock.[2]

Trelawny was magnificent. Tall and dark, with flashing eyes and stern appearance, he out-Sulioted the Suliotes. Levant travellers customarily bought the local dress in Albania and Greece, and some actually wore it on their travels. More usually the traveller stuck to his frock coat and breeches, but had his picture painted wearing Albanian dress on his return to Europe. This looked good as a frontispiece to a book. But Trelawny had no intention of cheating. He would do the thing properly – after all, as he was accustomed to tell his friends, he had often laid down to rest on the bare sand of the desert wrapped only in his Arab baracan.

For some skills, however, literary or imaginative experience is no substitute. It took time to get used to the new dress and to wear the appropriate armoury of yataghan and pistols at a jaunty angle in the girdle. At one village he accidentally dropped a pistol and when they went back to ask for it, the villagers turned their dogs on them and fired a few shots. The Suliote uniform was not the passport in Greece that devotees of Childe Harold might imagine.

At Tripolitsa, which was in ruins, they began their enquiries. Trelawny had been especially keen to introduce himself to Prince Mavrocordato, Finance Minister of Greece, of whom he had heard the Shelleys speak and on whom he placed high hopes. They found him in the ruined seraglio of the Turkish Governor which the Greeks had taken over. Through the coloured glass of the arabesques they could see Greek soldiers with their scimitars and ataghans and richly caparisoned horses standing at the ready in the courtyard. One man they saw was wearing a leather cuirass embossed with silver. Mavrocordato however was not like them. He was fattish, short-sighted, and bespectacled, wearing the dark frock coat of European fashion, rather shabby, with no pistol or sword. He was a modern Greek intent on turning his adopted country into a modern European state.

The two men took an instant dislike to one another. Perhaps the Greek smiled at the pseudo-Greek in his snowy camese and shaggy capote. Perhaps Trelawny recalled the despised baboos and cheechees of India who aped their masters' European clothes. The perfection of the romance was vitiated by such intrusive modernism. When Mavro-cordato explained that in his view Greece would do best to establish a monarchy with the king appointed by the great powers, Trelawny treated him with contempt and thereafter no abuse was too severe or too unfair. He was 'a poor, weak, shuffling, intriguing, cowardly fellow', 'a wooden god'. 'I hope ere long to see his head removed from his worthless and heartless body.'[3]

The warlord Colocotrones, whom they met shortly afterwards, was more like the kind of Greek they expected. He was holding court in the Turkish divan, and received his guests seated cross-legged on cushions of crimson and gold velvet. It was Colocotrones's soldiers and servants who were everywhere, and it was clear who was master at Tripolitsa. Why had they not come straight to him, he demanded, instead of to the intriguing, treacherous, cowardly, Phanariote, his colleague Mavro-cordato?

From Tripolitsa the two envoys went on to Corinth and Salamis where the other members of the Greek Government were installed. On the way across the isthmus, they crossed the pass of the Dervenakia where Colocotrones had annihilated the invading Ottoman army the previous year. The Greeks had blocked the pass with trees, and catching the Turks as they entered a narrow gorge, shot them down from the surrounding heights. The ground was covered with the remains of the destroyed army, men, horses, and camels. Heaps of bones were piled into pyramids as trophies but flocks of scavenging birds were pecking about among the dead and hardly bothered to fly away when shot at by the intruders. Trelawny noticed the skeletons of *delhis* still astride their horses, killed by rolling boulders as they tried to clamber out of the gorge, and the rotting black skins of the Negro boys who had been leading the forage camels, with their harnesses still in their hands. One of the soldiers whom Colocotrones had provided as an escort casually cut off a skull with his ataghan and kicked it about like a football.

At Salamis they were introduced to the other Greek leaders, local warlords like Colocotrones, Phanariotes like Mavrocordato. Every-where they were made welcome. They attended dinners given by the political leaders and gave dinners themselves in their honour. They debated the great issues of the war, whether Greece should concentrate on sea or land, whether a monarchy should be established. Already, after only a few weeks in Greece, Trelawny knew that he was going to enjoy himself. For the first time in his life he was important. People listened to him. His views counted. He was a figure in the land. He was the acknowledged friend and representative of the great Lord Byron on whose limitless money every Greek leader had set his eyes. A word from Trelawny might carry great weight, or so every Greek imagined. He was courted; his friendship was cultivated; favours were shown to him; and his strange habits and tastes were indulged. The English were eccentric and had to be humoured, as every Greek knew, and the Cornish English were an extreme example of the type.

It was, they supposed, a form of flattery that he should adopt their dress although, for Mavrocordato and the other westernised Greeks to put on Albanian dress at that time in Greece's history, would have been like Benjamin Franklin putting on Red Indian feathers. Yet even the Greeks, accustomed though they were to mad Franks, may have felt that he carried imitation too far when he ostentatiously allowed the lice to crawl down his hands and cracked them with his nails. Readers of travel books knew that the Albanians in the absence of other totems for national glorification were proud of being the dirtiest people in Europe.

Trelawny and Hamilton Browne did their best to assess the situation, judging the various leaders on the basis of interviews through interpreters, and comparing numerous conflicting stories they heard about the progress of the war. They urged Lord Byron in separate letters to come at once to Greece, to abandon his support for Mavrocordato and to attend in person the proposed congress of Greek leaders which was being arranged.

They also sent details on various more personal points about which Lord Byron had, it seems, asked to be particularly informed – the cost of food and accommodation and the availability of women – for Byron was apparently intending to resume the way of life he had enjoyed so freely during the first visit to Greece a dozen years before. Hamilton Browne, the ex-bureaucrat, gave the information in matter-of-fact terms in a letter from Tripolitsa: 'Forage is plentiful here and living is cheap. Good horses are also numerous but rather high prices are asked. A harem however might be formed on reasonable terms.'[4] Trelawny was more forthright:

> Provisions in great abundance and excessively cheap, one piaster and a half we pay for a dinner for ourselves and two servants – and good grubbing too – grub for horses cheap – maidenheads as plentiful as blackberries – there is good markating in that way.[5]

He had however by now virtually given up hopes for Lord Byron who was, he felt, all talk and no action. Byron had talked of going to Greece, he had talked of giving his fortune to the cause, but all he did was hang about in the comfort of the Ionian Islands. Trelawny wrote in exasperated terms to tell Mary Shelley of the continued meanness of their friend and of his plans to expose him: 'As a last resource, to induce the CHILD to realise his ostentatious professions and put him to the proof *positive*, we have counselled the Government in their present difficulty, to write discreetly to the *Child* to request he will *lend* on Government *security* the money he talked of giving, offering him good interest. This will either extract the money, send him boot- less back to Italy, or turn him the seamy side without to all the world.'[6]

But despite Trelawny's urgings, Lord Byron did not come and did not hand over his money. He even turned down Trelawny's plan that he should come to Athens where he would be made nominal com- mander of the Acropolis with his headquarters in the ruins of the Parthenon. When he finally decided to move to Greece at the end of 1823, it was, much to Trelawny's disgust, Mavrocordato's territory of Missolonghi that he chose.

At Hydra, Trelawny parted from Hamilton Browne. The Govern- ment had decided, partly as a result of their advice, to send representa- tives to London to make arrangements about a loan which was to be raised on the Stock Exchange, and Hamilton Browne went with them. Trelawny carried on alone. At Corinth when he went to inspect the great fortress of the Acrocorinth where a few hundred miserable Turks were still immured, he was arrested by the Greek soldiers and was in danger of being shot as a spy. He enquired afterwards about taking lessons in modern Greek. At Athens he bought twelve or fifteen women, including a Negress, at the slave markets and established a harem. For a while he was content to lie on his sofa smoking, attended by his patient, frightened women, but, not having the practised fatalism of a real-life pasha, he soon became bored with seraglio life.

In the few weeks since he landed with Hamilton Browne at Pyrgos he had already seen sights more romantic than anything in *Childe Harold* or *The Corsair*. The reality of Greece made his imagined ad- ventures in India look tame by comparison. But he was still only a spectator. Exciting scenes and experiences were all around him but, despite his fancy dress, he was an outsider. He was in his familiar place

Odysseus Androutsos or Ulysses

The world's great age begins anew,
    The golden years return,
The earth doth like a snake renew
    Her winter weeds outworn:
Heaven smiles, and faiths and empires gleam
Like wrecks of a dissolving dream.

A loftier Argo cleaves the main,
    Fraught with a later prize;
Another Orpheus sings again,
    And loves, and weeps and dies.
A new Ulysses leaves once more
Calypso for his native shore.

Another Athens shall arise,
    And to remoter time
Bequeaths, like sunset to the skies,
    The splendour of its prime;
And leave, if nought so bright may live
All earth can take or Heaven can give.

From the final chorus of Shelley's *Hellas*

Odysseus's cave
in Mount
Parnassus, from
a water colour
by Major d'Arcy
Bacon

in the theatre watching the drama on the stage but not a participant. At Athens his chance came. The warlord in whose territory Athens lay, Odysseus Androutsos, was about to go on a raiding expedition into Euboea. Would the Englishman like to accompany him, he asked? There would be good shooting, he promised, of either Turks or wood-cocks. It was an offer that was to have far reaching results and Trelawny accepted it at once. The harem was thankfully put into care and main-tenance, and Trelawny set off.

Now at last he was going to see action. This was what he had come to Greece for – fighting. Politics was all very well and sex too from time to time, but fighting, that was the life for a corsair. At last he was going to see the real thing. The life would be hard he explained in a letter to Mary Shelley. He would have to live rough in the mountains, sleeping in the open air, he would have to put up with dirt, vermin and privation. Of course, this was nothing new. During his years as a privateer with de Ruyter, he had learnt to endure hardships. The life of a mountain warrior in Greece, he declared, was nothing to 'parched desert, dry locusts, and camel's milk'.[7] The only dry locusts and camel's milk that Trelawny had actually eaten or drunk had been in his fantasy life at the masthead – the victuals supplied to H.M. ships were less exotic and less nourishing – but as with the capote, even imagined experience was better than no experience at all.

There was much that was Homeric about Odysseus Androutsos besides his name. His father, after struggling for years against Ali Pasha, was appointed by him as guardian of the passes in the Livadia district of Greece, but after an unsuccessful rising in 1789, he died a slave in the Bagnio at Constantinople, remembered in Greek folk song as the greatest mountain warrior of Roumeli.

Odysseus was a baby when his father disappeared, but Ali Pasha had a great career planned for him. At the age of twelve, he was appointed pipe bearer to the Pasha, then,when he was eighteen, he was appointed to the post in which his father had made his name, the governorship of the passes of Livadia. Stories grew up round the son as round the father. It was said that when he was a boy at Ali's seraglio he successfully challenged his finest horse to an uphill race, to continue until the horse fell dead. After his success he was presented with a bride chosen from the Pasha's harem. He could leap over the backs of seven horses, and we almost expect to read that he could throw boulders so heavy that it would take two men of the present day to lift them.[8]

When Ali's enemies finally started to close in on him in 1820, Odysseus slipped away to the Ionian Islands, but when the Greek Revolution broke out the following year, he gathered together 5,000 of his old comrades and established himself in his old haunts as virtual dictator of the whole area known as Eastern Greece, stretching from Parnassus to Athens.

Odysseus was the most cynical of all the Greeks who came to prominence during the War of Independence. He regarded the revolution as a continuation of the old game of local warfare among rival pashas which he and his father had played for half a century, a game with its own conventions and code of rules. At the end of 1821, when the pattern of the war began to settle, he found himself poised in the border lands between rebellious Greece and the area still under Ottoman control. He could, as he chose, either be a Greek warlord or an Ottoman warlord, depending on the swing of events.

Trelawny worshipped him. 'He is a glorious being', he wrote, 'a noble fellow, a gallant soldier, and a man of most wonderful mind.' Odysseus alone could save Greece. He was the Simon Bolivar of Hellas. He was a new George Washington. He was the de Ruyter of his dreams. He was a new Shelley.[9] Odysseus represented everything that Trelawny thought great and good and noble. Although the two men could only speak haltingly to one another in pidgin Italian, Trelawny was sure they were a Roland and an Oliver. 'I must rise or fall with the man with whom I have united my fortunes', he declared, and surrendered himself to an orgy of hero worship.[10]

In the winter of 1823–24 he accompanied Odysseus into Euboea which was still in Turkish hands. They besieged the towns without success, skirmished with parties of Turkish soldiers, and burned about sixty villages mostly Greek. As a contribution to winning Greek independence, it was minimal or worse. As an introduction to marauding life it was irresistible. Trelawny was undoubtedly brave and undoubtedly hardy, the two qualities which the Greek soldiers valued most. He won their respect and Odysseus gave him some men to command. Before long he was one of the most successful mountain guerilla leaders in Greece. In his new life he began to care less and less about his patron, Lord Byron, who had moved to Missolonghi in Western Greece at the end of 1823 but who seemed to be content to dawdle there as he had done in the Ionian Islands, talking politics instead of fighting.

15

The Death of Byron

Trelawny has great plans and intends to manage the affairs of Greece by himself. The best thing is: the Prince takes not the least notice of what T. speaks. You will remember, Sir, the anecdote of the pearl and the sow.

From a letter from the American philhellene Jarvis, 2 June 1824.[1]

Lord Byron was not a strong man. In Italy he had allowed himself to become grossly fat and subsequently he subjected his body to a sudden and severe slimming régime. He ate unsuitable food and drank immoderately. In the Ionian Islands and at Missolonghi he had warning attacks and fits, but he refused advice to move to a healthier place. The rain, the damp, and the cold brought on illness. His doctors, who were young and self-assured, vied with one another in the violence of their supposed remedies, and by repeated bleeding and drastic purgatives ensured that his illness was fatal. He died on 19 April 1824 at the age of thirty-six and the whole course of the Greek War – and much more – was altered as a result.

Trelawny, who was out on one of his expeditions with Odysseus when the news arrived, went straight to Missolonghi and arrived in time to plant a farewell kiss on the lips of his dead patron. Although the last to arrive on the scene, he immediately assumed charge of the arrangements, boldly presenting himself as the obvious executor. It was almost as if, having made such a success of the arrangements for Shelley and Keats, he felt that he was something of an expert on funerals for romantic poets. Byron's papers were sealed to be sent to the heirs in England, but Trelawny unscrupulously copied out for his own use some important manuscripts, including part of the unfinished Canto XVII of *Don Juan* and Byron's last letter to Augusta Leigh. He had a long conversation with Fletcher, Byron's servant, whom he knew from their days in Italy and in the *Hercules*, extracting from him a detailed account of everything that had happened to Byron since he last saw him in Cephalonia. With his eye as ever on the dramatic detail, he used Byron's coffin as a desk and, he claimed later, when Fletcher was out of the room, he lifted up the cloth which covered the dead Byron to look at his withered feet.[2]

To bury Byron in the Acropolis of Athens, although undoubtedly grand and philhellenic, would have implied an approval of Odysseus in whose petty empire Athens lay. Missolonghi on the other hand was inextricably associated with Mavrocordato besides being a miserable mean place in which to spend eternity. After a good deal of wrangling it was decided to send the body back to England, although the soil of Greece was honoured with some symbolic entrails which had to be extracted in the embalming process.

When the British authorities in the Ionian Islands suggested that Byron's body might instead be buried there, Trelawny gave a characteristic outburst:

> Genl Adam and that gallant young officer Sir Frederick Stoven – plotted together came to the resolution of detaining the remains of the Pilgrim of Eternity* – and intering them at Zant.
>
> Mingling his brave dust with stinking rogues
> (Surfeit slain fools) that rot in winding sheets,
> The common dung of the soil!
>
> Let such beings as those who conceived this rot like rats in the obscene holes and corners in which they die – who are only distinguished from such virmin – by their shape and form which obliges naturalists to class them for distinction sake with the human race.[3]

He had used the same kind of language the previous year against those who had failed to bury Shelley in fitting style, and the crude insult that it would take a naturalist to distinguish his opponents from vermin was one he was rather proud of and was forever repeating.

Within hours of the death, the myth-making had begun. The number of people in whose arms Byron had died grew rapidly. His famous last words became longer and longer and included favourable mention of increasing numbers of friends, relations, and acquaintances. Numerous potential biographers began sorting out their notes. Lord Byron had been one of the most famous men of his day. His poetry, his life, and the manner of his death all greatly influenced the way in which the early nineteenth century viewed the world. Now that the great man was dead, Trelawny had to establish a new relationship. His life had

---

* Byron had been called *The Pilgrim of Eternity* by Shelley in *Adonais*.

been dominated by Lord Byron years before they had ever met, and a
Trelawny without *The Corsair* is as difficult to imagine as a John
Bunyan without the Bible. From time to time he had tugged at the
leash, but he was no more capable of independence than the bear which
Byron used to keep chained by the fireplace in his chambers in Cambridge. When they had separated the previous summer, although they
had not quarrelled, they had not been on good terms. Byron, as with
all his friends, was used to making public fun of Trelawny, although
in the last days at Missolonghi he often said he wished Trelawny would
come back – perhaps the finest and sincerest compliment Trelawny
ever received.[4] Trelawny for his part had fallen into the habit of making
disparaging remarks and he and Mary Shelley egged one another on in
criticising their tight-fisted friend.

After Byron's death, this clearly would not do, although a little of it
remained. For all Byron's faults, Trelawny would say, with the con-
descension with which the living take their revenge on the dead, he
was my best friend and I loved him. He began to enjoy his place in the
glow of Byron's fame and to help promote the legend. He rushed off
his own highly-coloured accounts of Byron's expedition to Greece for
transmission to the English newspapers, shamelessly exaggerating his
own role. Trelawny persuaded Byron to go to Greece, Trelawny took
command of Byron's ship, Trelawny stiffened Byron's failing morale
when he wanted to give up, Trelawny proposed a congress of Greek
leaders, Trelawny was his best friend and his trusted adviser. He was
'the friend and companion of many years', he told Stanhope.[5] 'He is
connected with the most interesting years of my wandering life', he
wrote on another occasion, 'his everyday companion – we lived in
ships, boats and in houses together – we had no secrets – no reserve,
and though we often differed in opinion, never quarrelled.'[6] To John
Cam Hobhouse, who was perhaps Byron's oldest and best friend, he
unashamedly declared 'These last four years I accompanied him everywhere and have been his daily companion.'[7] A copy was sent to Leigh
Hunt for him to make an article of it and the story stuck.

It was in fact just two years and three months on the calendar
between Trelawny's arrival at Pisa in January 1822 and Byron's death
at Missolonghi in April 1824. During the last seven of those twenty-
seven months Trelawny had not seen Byron at all. During the year
between Shelley's death in July 1822 and Byron's decision to go to
Greece, Trelawny had, for three months at Albaro at the end of 1822,

regularly gone riding with him in the afternoons, but otherwise had seen him only intermittently. Even during the first few months at Pisa in 1822, it was a huge exaggeration to suggest that Trelawny was Byron's daily companion. His 'four years' of daily association turns out to be a good deal less than twelve months if the periods when they were generally together are added up. However, as with his corsair stories, there was no going back. Trelawny had staked out his claim to a place in the Byron legend and he was determined to maintain it.

To be a satellite of a great man who is dead is not, however, a role that can be sustained for long. The reflected limelight which Trelawny enjoyed in Italy and now in Greece would quickly fade away. If he was to make an impact he could no longer rely on being listened to out of respect for his great connexions. He would have to earn respect, not spend respect accumulated by other people. As he rushed about Missolonghi in April 1824 he was vaguely aware that this was his chance to establish himself in his own right. He felt a false sense of liberation from the man who had so moulded his life and character. Freed from Byron, Trelawny could at last be Trelawny. He would 'play no second part', he declared to Mary Shelley. He would 'soar above' Byron and 'triumph over his mean spirit'.[8] At last he would take his rightful place as one of the movers of men and shapers of great events. He would assume Byron's mantle, and finish the work which Byron, so incompetently in his view, had set out to do. He would liberate Greece.

With his growing confidence, his stories about his past became wilder and more fantastic, with truth and invention about his sea-going days providing a suitably exciting basis for stories about Lord Byron. Julius Millingen, Byron's doctor, who met him at this time noted the growth of a new cycle of invention. While with the buc-caneers in the East Indies, Trelawny apparently claimed he 'passed his happiest days, meeting continually with the most extraordinary adventures and hair breadth escapes. He might have yet continued to enjoy a life so congenial to his disposition, had not his companions sought to kill him during a dispute about prize money. He satisfied his vengence; but seeing himself closely pursued, the terror he felt was so great that he did not stop in his flight until he found himself in the country of the Wachabees.'[9] There, it seems, Trelawny decided to stay and fight and his adventures in Arabia in the Wahabee Wars became as integral a part of his past as his voyages with de Ruyter.

In July 1824 he was at Nauplia when a British warship, H.M.S.
Alacrity, came in, and James Forrester, the ship's surgeon, wrote an
account in his diary of a chance encounter with a strange philhellene:

While here we met with and saw a good deal of a strangely eccentric
person, an Englishman in the Greek service. He introduced himself to the
officer who went on shore on duty at our arrival and accompanied him on
board to wait upon the Captain. He is a fine looking man of about six
feet, dresses as an Albanian, and his features happening to be of a suitable
cast, is perhaps one of the best specimens of all that is characteristic of
these people I have ever seen. His name is Trelawny, a younger brother
of one of the oldest and most respectable families in Cornwall. As we had
no previous knowledge of him he gave us an outline of his career which
commenced in the navy. This he quitted in India but did not assign
the reason. He was then about 15. After this he appears for several years
to have passed through many vagabondising vicissitudes. He had joined
and fought with some tribe against the Malays. He had lived for a length
of time among the Arabs, adopting their manners and wearing their
dress. He had fought with them in the Wahabee War but I am not certain
on which side but think for the Wahabees. He had been frequently
wounded. One scar appears on his face and a musket ball which lodged
on one occasion in his thigh has now got down to the outer side of the
knee where it remains.

He related many curious anecdotes of his intercourse with these wild
people and some adventures which fell to his lot during his stay with
them. After a considerable absence he made his way to Europe and
served some time as a volunteer in the Peninsular War. Became disgusted
with this and has for some years past lived on the Continent where he
formed an intimacy with Lord Byron whose constant intimate he seems
to have been for the last 3 or 4 years and with whom he came to Greece...

Trelawny remained on board all night but declined the accommodation of a cabin or a bed. He wrapt his capote round his head and reposed
on the deck of the gun room until morning.[10]

When he stepped forward to fill the political vacuum left by Lord
Byron's death, the English and Greeks at Missolonghi were so aston-
ished that initially they let him have his way. His first action was to
urge Stanhope, the sole representative of the London Greek Committee
after Byron's death, to give the support of the Committee to Odysseus.
'I think I can serve the cause of liberty in my attachment to him',
he wrote. 'I love noble men and I have singled him out as conceiving
him one. If you think so, lets give him a range of action worthy his

calibre.'[11] Stanhope took his advice, and soon he too, having been exposed to Odysseus's charm, began to regard him as a champion of liberty.

Trelawny simply ignored the fact that he had no authority from the Committee or from anyone else. He dashed here and there between Missolonghi, the Ionian Islands, and Salona, trying to revive the idea of a congress of Greek leaders. A stream of grandiloquent missives on Greece and her problems issued from his pen. The people, he declared, were for the congress even if their leaders were not. Mavrocordato was conspiring to sell the liberty of Greece to a foreign king. In his political pronouncements as in all his writing, he would intoxicate himself with his own rhetoric. He would begin carefully enough, then he would perhaps recall some quotation; strike the appropriate attitude; the words would carry him away, and in his passion for the effect he would lose all rationality about the substance.

His colleagues were bewildered at his strange behaviour. Was he magnificent or simply ridiculous? When Edward Blaquiere arrived at Missolonghi, he found a typical Trelawny communication awaiting:

Messilonghi
Old stile 19   1824

Dear Blackquire

   I leave only today for Salona – if you come here do what you can for Mavrocordato and then follow me to Argos. If you do this you will serve Greece. But expeditious I pray you. I have no time to say why or wherefore – my horse is at the door and I am ready.

Yours v truly
E Trelawny

P.S. The bearer of this is a good patriot and I believe an honest old fellow.[12]

Soon Greeks and English began to tire. They began to smile at him behind his back and the more he blew himself up the more ineffectual he became. On one occasion he stopped a courier carrying mail and, on the pretence of looking to see if there were any letters for himself, broke the seals. The package contained only newspapers, but no matter, gentlemen do not open other people's mail. The word cad is thought to derive from cadet meaning a younger son, and especially a younger son who has entered the navy or army in hopes of a commission. Trelawny was a cad. Even the Greeks thought so.

Blaquiere felt obliged to write a letter of complaint and warning to the Secretary of the Greek Committee in London:

> Knowing that he is the bosom friend of Mr Ulysses I shall be surprised at nothing he does: it would also be the very height of gullability were I for one instant to imagine that Mr T. does not traduce and abuse me to all his correspondents all over the world. He would belie his character and history if he did not. Now as it is of infinite importance to keep the Committee fully informed of everything I have particularly to request that you will place every letter of Mr T's in which my name appears on its table and be read aloud to all and in silence by each member.[13]

Another Englishman who was in Greece at this time included a caricature of Trelawny in a book which he published not long afterwards about his experiences. The Englishman has just arrived in Greece when he meets a strange figure dressed in Albanian costume with a capote thrown carelessly over his shoulder, who addresses him thus:

> You have just arrived, Sir, in this country, if I be not mistaken and have not been as yet initiated into the manners and privations of these barbarians? . . . God grant you may get on well with them. I myself have been a long time – some twelve month, if I err not . . . I have borne with them better than most others, on account of an excessive spirit of romance, which has been mine since my childhood, and has enabled me to trace, in the pursuits and habits of the wretches, now and then, a species of this latter charm. Had it not been for this, I should long ere now have sunk under an insufferable load of disgust . . . With all this, there is a charm in having sported so long the oriental dress, and in taking a tinge from the languor which the eastern clime inspires, to accompany one home, and excite some interest among the fair sex. My costume, which they assure me becomes me amazingly, though I am not myself capable to judge of the truth, cannot sufficiently have hidden from you, Sir, my fame, as to render you ignorant of who I am . . .
>
> You will cease to hesitate when I remind you that I am the same dark mysterious being whom Byron has designated in the person of Lara. My family name is Simpkins, and it is my intention to send over to Scotland the analysis of many admirable scenes to which I have been witness, which cannot fail to enrol me among the list of heroes of the celebrated author there. . . .
>
> But you are not yet aware, my dear Sir, of the beasts you have got amongst. The vulgarity of all the Europeans here is so strikingly base, that any man of refined taste, like myself, creates, I assure you, by being singular, a vast field of interest and adventure. I should by no means be

surprised if you, Sir, who I know to be of family – rank, and of vast
acquirements, by keeping yourself always aloof from these barbarians,
whom I have mentioned; and being biassed by no other hints than my
own, may eventually lead a career not less than I have done. Our names
will then of course be mingled together in the reminiscences of some
masterly pen – and think of the luxury of being known and quoted as the
heroes of a romance fraught with incident; the inspiration with which
the young beauties of our realms will lisp our names upon every occasion,
fondly hoping that their lovers may be such – and imagine only, what is
far better than all, our not existing merely in fancy but embodying here
delightful ideas by our appearance afterwards amongst them![14]

But Trelawny, humourless himself as always, was unconscious that
people were laughing at him. Just as at Rome, a year before, he had
pressed ahead with his plans despite the mocking bewilderment of
Severn, so now he pursued his political aims regardless.

The military stores that had been sent by the London Greek
Committee to help the Greeks in the war still lay at Missolonghi,
rotting and rusting, and the shops were well stocked with field glasses,
maps, pistols, and surveying instruments, whose origins were all too
clear. By far the most important was a brigade of mountain guns and
howitzers, the gift of the British philhellenes, the most powerful
ordnance available to the Greeks. To the consternation of Mavrocordato, who foresaw that Missolonghi would shortly be under siege
from the Turks and would desperately need those guns, Trelawny
recommended to Stanhope that half the brigade, consisting of three
guns and a howitzer, should be handed over to Odysseus. Quite apart
from the fact of Odysseus's unreliability, it made no kind of military
sense to divide up this armament, but Trelawny had his way and the
guns were dragged over the mountain roads to Odysseus's fortress in
Mount Parnassus.

For Mavrocordato this was perhaps the breaking point. He had
been insulted and slandered by this strange Englishman who claimed
to be the friend of Shelley and of Byron but was so different from both.
That was bad enough. Why could not foreigners keep their fingers out
of Greek politics which they clearly did not understand? But the affair
of the guns was far worse. This absurd boastful philhellene in fancy
dress was actually making the victory of the Turks more likely. He was
transferring heavy armaments to the most unreliable of the Greek
warlords and apparently for no better reason than that he liked his

exotic clothes more than Mavrocordato's frock coat. If Greece was to survive as a reasonably civilised nation state on the European model then its internal enemies such as Odysseus would have to be dealt with, and Odysseus's strange English hanger-on as well.

Mavrocordato was right. Trelawny had no understanding of politics. Analysis was beyond him. Politics was drama and politics was war, a personal combat fought with words instead of weapons. He carried a ragbag of prejudices, incoherent and inconsistent, which he thought of as grand political principles, and his love for humanity was combined with a lively hatred of people. Each phase of his life had left a residue of political attitudes to be covered in time by other layers, and his personality can be laid bare like an archaeological site; the despised younger son who protested against inherited wealth and power; the recalcitrant schoolboy who became an atheist and republican in reaction to the Reverend Samuel Seyer's nationalist and right wing views; the unsuccessful naval cadet who decided that the British armed forces were the instrument of imperialism; the rejected youth who compiled fantasies of imagined supermen who would put the world to rights by a few brilliant strokes of violence.

Volney's *Ruins of Empires* and other such books gave him a philosophical framework into which his views could be fitted and Shelley's *Queen Mab* provided a vocabulary. Every sentiment was dressed in high-flown language of romantic poetry and defiantly thrown down as a challenge and a provocation, and the whole conflation was elevated into a great cause, a cause for which Trelawny would willingly die and, more willingly, kill. Tyrants and priests would be overthrown; liberty would appear in the land; and younger sons of wealthy gentry would inherit more money.

Now that Trelawny, for the first time, had the opportunity to influence events and put his beliefs into practice, his superficiality was exposed. Trelawny repeated like incantations the clichés of his favourite books, but he was unable to rise above himself. His behaviour during these days showed little advance from the customs of the midshipmen's mess. If someone disagrees with you, punch him in the face and then we will see who is right. If someone suggests caution, he is a coward. If opponents coordinate their line of action, they are plotting or conspiring. He did not try to persuade, he bullied. Political opponents were enemies and enemies without rights, vermin, rats, monsters, to be exterminated in the name of liberty and humanity.

16

The Cave

Here I have been in Greece amidst barbarians – not retaining a
single recollection of what they were – more than twelve months
– nevertheless I have prospered amongst them – am united in
strongest bonds with the celebrated Chief Ulysses, governor of
Attica – we are sworn brothers – I am really attached to him – his
family are Dear to me – he is brave, clever, and noble – I am playing a first part here – and have work for all my energies, which are
now awakened from their long torpor – Byron, who was mine as
well as your evil genius has ceased to be so. I am at present commanding for my chief an important Fortress – I have had some
trifling escapes – but at present am well and out of danger – yet
I see no limit to my stay in Greece – I am no changeling and must
rise or fall with the man with whom I have united my fortunes.

From a letter to Claire Clairmont,
September 1824[1]

The cave of Odysseus Androutsos lies high above the pinetree line on
the north side of Mount Parnassus, one of the thousands of caves with
which the area is penetrated. The villagers call it the Mavre Troupa, the
Black Hole. According to one story, Odysseus was the first to find it
and climb up to it, but it has been used as a secret retreat since time
immemorial. When the mist occasionally clears, one of the distant
summits, Lycoura, the wolf mountain, can be seen, crowned with
snow, but to the north and west a huge area of central Greece is laid
out like a map all the way to the sea.

At the bottom of the valley is a gorge which for much of the year is
a foaming torrent, the *Kakoreme*, or evil stream. The remains of a
paved road wind from the ancient walled city of Tithorea over Parnassus to Delphi on the other side. In the foreground is a chapel to St
George, built on the foundations of an ancient shrine, set in the midst
of a grove of oak trees, and you can still hear the oracles whispering their
cryptic messages as the wind blows through the leaves. 'I have been in
India, America, and Europe', Trelawny used to say, 'and I never saw a
more majestic place.' And for once he did not exaggerate.[2]

Odysseus fortified the cave in 1823. He saw that it was a natural fortress, impregnable to any contemporary armament and commanding a view of a tract of land disputed between Greek and Turk over which much of the fighting and skirmishing of the war was taking place. Any party of troops venturing on to the plain from the north or east could be seen at once from the Mavre Troupa.

Springs of icy water, the overspillings of underground rivers, surge and spurt noisily out of the rock at many places and for part of the year there is fresh water in the cave itself. Odysseus built cisterns to store it over the period when the springs were dry, and laid in magazines of corn, oil, wine, cheese, olives, and raki, enough, it was said, to supply hundreds of men for twenty years. He reckoned that in time of need he and his army could retire into the cave and withstand any seige although that would have been intensely uncomfortable with klephtic standards of hygiene. Normally the army lived outside in an encampment by the chapel of St George.

The entrance to the cave is some sixty feet up a sheer precipice which, although pitted with innumerable holes in the sandstone, is smooth and crumbling, and there is no other way in. Odysseus bolted larch trees to the cliff face to make a series of crude ladders. As places to live, caves are usually unattractive – dark, cold, dripping, smelly, and forbidding. The Mavre Troupa is more like the terrace of some fantastic Alpine hotel. As the visitor clambers off the topmost ladder he finds himself on a level piece of ground above which the roof of the cave forms a huge rainbow-shaped arch, light and airy and dry, protected from the wind, warm in winter and cool in summer. Further back, the cave narrows into an inner chamber which can only be reached by another ladder, and there are smaller caves running off in different directions like rooms from a landing. Even in the innermost corners there is daylight.

It was to this magical place that Trelawny, Captain Trelawny as he now called himself, transferred the precious mountain guns from Missolonghi after Lord Byron's death. He arrived on 26 May 1824 at the head of a cavalcade of fifty-five horses with the guns, ammunition, tools, maps, telescopes, and other stores, together with Gill an English military engineer sent by the Committee, and Fenton, a philhellene artillery officer from Lanark who had fought alongside the mountain guerillas in Spain. Under their expert superintendence, the fortification of the cave was made permanent. A parapet with portholes was built round the edge of the terrace and the guns were mounted as from a fortress. Behind the parapet a trapdoor was cut through the living rock which opened on to the top of the ladder on the cliff face. Three metal ladders, securely bolted to the rock, zigzagged up the cliff, but the topmost could, if necessary, be hauled up through the trapdoor. At the foot of the lowest ladder, a small fortification was built in which a permanent sentry guard was maintained.

Houses were built on the terrace with timber and roof tiles dragged up from Tithorea and one of the innermost chambers was set aside as women's quarters. Another chamber was used as a chapel decorated with hangings and even the traditional ostrich eggs, brought from ruined churches on the plains, and a Greek priest was employed to conduct services. Workshops and forges for maintaining and repairing the guns were constructed with the tools brought from Missolonghi so that the cave was transformed into a small self-contained military base.

The eating was good, as anyone who orders *klephtico* in a Greek restaurant will know – roast mutton, roast goat, or roast venison garnished with rigani and the other herbs which grow in profusion on Parnassus, besides fresh and salt-water fish, poultry and game. Wild pigeons lived in profusion in the cave itself and there were beehives for honey. Odysseus lived in high state and only the most important were admitted to his table. Two of his half-brothers who lived in the cave ate with the men.

During the day Odysseus and his army, with Trelawny at his side, would make skirmishing expeditions into the surrounding countryside. The pallikars lived on plunder and pillage and were not particular about who their enemy was. Any Turks caught alive were impaled. According to Trelawny, Odysseus's 5,000 pallikars killed 20,000 men in their brief campaign. In the evenings there would be wine and talk and stories, and the soldiers would sing klephtic ballads. A billiard table from the Ionian Islands had been hauled up the cliff face for the entertainment of the troglodytes, and there were books, including the latest Waverley novel, the three volumes of *St Ronan's Well*. Two small deer which had been caught alive on Parnassus were kept tethered in the cave as pets. Trelawny told visitors that he intended to send them to Abbotsford as a present to Sir Walter, but they were eaten before that could happen.

But before Odysseus had the opportunity to enjoy his cavern fortress, events were occurring elsewhere which would soon make it obsolete despite its undoubted strength. In July 1824 the official Greek

Government took possession of a large sum of money, the first instalment of the loan negotiated for them by the London Greek Committee. For the first time in the history of the revolution the Government had (temporarily) more power than the warlords and they determined to use it.

Whatever Trelawny might think of Odysseus, the members of the Greek Government did not trust him. The money, they decided, was to be spent on the fleet and on establishing a new regular army, not distributed to the warlords. Odysseus waited at Nauplia until it was clear that no money would be forthcoming, and then in July 1824 retired with his army to the Parnassus region, having finally abandoned all hopes of making a career within the Greek State. But now that the Government could offer better terms to his men, they began to drift off and he could see that his power was rapidly slipping away.

One stormy day in February 1825, Odysseus with Trelawny and the remaining army were encamped in the ruins of a Greek church at Talanta when a patrol brought in two prisoners, one of whom turned out to be a travelling English gentleman, Major d'Arcy Bacon on leave from the 19th Light Dragoons. The Major was unperturbed although surprised when a tall 'Suliote', one of the leaders, slipped him a pistol. After he had been given a supper of cold mutton, carved by the help of a yataghan, he prepared for bed as unconcernedly as if he had been staying at an hotel. He unpacked a camp bed and, to the growing horror of the Greek soldiers who regarded it as shameful to expose the body, he carefully undressed, folded each garment neatly by his bed, and then walked across to the fire – apparently stark naked – to light his pipe. 'Pray, gentlemen, keep your seats, don't let me disturb you' he said to the outraged pallikars, but when he bent over, the firelight revealed that he was not naked but dressed in flesh-coloured drawers. Everybody suddenly burst out laughing and all thought of murdering the major disappeared. The next morning the tall pallikar who had given him the pistol followed him out and spoke to him 'How well you speak English, my good fellow', he answered Trelawny, and within a short time all was explained and they became friends.

Trelawny told him about the danger which Odysseus was now in, enemy to Turk and Greek alike, and Bacon agreed to carry a message to the Commander of a British vessel in the Gulf of Corinth asking him to give passage to Odysseus and himself to the Ionian Islands. The message was delivered and the *Maitland* kept the rendezvous but, after waiting a few days, it became clear that Odysseus was not going to take this chance to escape.

Instead he proposed to his old colleague and enemy, the Pasha of Negropont (Euboea), to go back over to the Turkish side in exchange for a guarantee of his local position. As an earnest of his good – or rather his bad – faith, he agreed to permit a party of Turkish troops to pass through his territory into Attica. It was a desperate move. Odysseus knew that Ottoman promises were no more reliable than his own, and his men, undiscriminating though they were on the whole, were confused at having constantly to change sides. In the fourth year of a vicious struggle for survival or independence, it was no longer possible to treat the war as a purely local affair. However, Odysseus reckoned that he had no choice. With the possible exception of one or two blood-relatives there was no longer any Greek whom he could trust or who would trust him.

Odysseus told Trelawny that his decision to make a peace with the Turks did not imply any disloyalty to Greece. It was, he explained, simply a means of putting pressure on the Government to get them to share the money. He had, he said, told the Government that, without money, he could not defend the passes against the Turks; once the Government saw the Turks coming through they would soon change their minds. Meanwhile, since he would have to go on an expedition, he needed someone to take command of the cave. Trelawny was to be appointed commander of the cavern fortress of Mount Parnassus.

Trelawny apparently accepted Odysseus's explanations and proposals without question for he had long since lost his judgement as far as Odysseus was concerned. Addicted to the romance which Odysseus supplied, he was happy to surrender his judgement totally to ensure continued injections of the spurious excitement. He refused to believe that the man he worshipped had turned traitor, and whatever the evidence that was later produced, he would never accept it. Trelawny went to his grave believing that Odysseus was a great, if misunderstood, Greek patriot.

There were important matters to be dealt with before the cave was handed over to Trelawny. Odysseus had a collection of antiquities, statues, and objects of value from ancient sites and ruined churches in his area. With Trelawny and two pallikars, he transported these antiquities to Thebes (which was in ruins and deserted) and hid them in a cellar. According to Trelawny, he chose 'an unclean place' just outside the town where no Theban would be likely to linger any longer than nature demanded, and if the story is true, the place was well chosen, for Odysseus's antiquities have never been found. The town of Thebes has long since spread outwards and the local customs before the days of piped sanitation are not recorded, but one day perhaps a Greek bulldozer will uncover Odysseus's hoard and probably destroy it at the same time.

Then there was the treasure. Odysseus like the other mountain chieftains of Greece was credited with possessing a vast store of gold and silver, the fruits of two generations of plunder. Unlike Coloco-trones he could not keep his money in a British bank in the Ionian Islands, for it had to be on the spot. Usually it was kept in the cave, but now that he was about to leave he decided to bury it too. It con-sisted, according to Trelawny, of £15,000 in Austrian double florins, stored in the tins which had contained the English gunpowder brought from Missolonghi. One night Odysseus, Trelawny, and a few pallikars took the tins to Thebes and buried them in a hole three feet deep. They put a layer of earth on top, then a layer of stones, then another layer of earth. This was the best way Odysseus explained, since the place would not sound hollow under foot. One half-expects to hear that, like Captain Flint, Odysseus then killed off the trusty pallikars who helped bury the treasure. He had not read *Treasure Island,* but a few days later he went back alone to the spot and removed the various indicators. Odysseus's treasure, like his antiquities, has never been found.

There was one more thing to do before he could entrust his cave to his English second-in-command. He must formalise the obligation. As ever, Odysseus's aim was unerring and he read Trelawny's character and emotional needs exactly. He offered to tie Trelawny to him in one of the most sacred bonds in Greece. Trelawny would marry Odysseus's half-sister Tersitsa, who was living in the cave, and become a member of his family.

Odysseus, who had already provided so much emotional fulfilment, was now offering Trelawny the realisation of the final Byronic fantasy. Tersitsa was the perfect Byronic heroine. She was exotic, beautiful, and loving with dark hazel eyes and, according to one writer, 'an innocently wild expression like a gazelle'. Her exact age is uncertain – the writers of the time were coy about making her appear too young – but she herself reckoned that she was thirteen. She was a fearless horsewomen and 'galloped like a very spirit'. The marriage was solemnised in the little chapel in the cave, and shortly afterwards Tersitsa became pregnant.

Few people achieve their ambitions. Fewer still have the opportunity to indulge their secret fantasies. For a few months in 1825 Trelawny did both. All his life he had wanted to be a Byronic corsair. He had imagined himself a corsair, he had lied about being a corsair, he had contorted himself into the image of a corsair. Now at last it had come true. Trelawny really was a corsair. But he could also see himself as Torquil, the mutineer from the *Bounty*, who lives in eternal bliss with 'the gentle savage of the wild', his child-lover Neuha, in a secret cave in a South Sea Island in Byron's last great dream romance *The Island*. That poem had been written at Genoa early in 1823 inspired by Trelawny's favourite books which the Pisa circle had been reading and, we may guess, by Trelawny's own stories.

He could also imagine himself in Prometheus's cave in the Caucasus as imagined in Shelley's *Prometheus Unbound*:

> There is a cave
> All overgrown with trailing odorous plants
> Which curtain-out the day with leaves and flowers
> And paved with veined emerald; and a fountain
> Leaps in the midst with an awakening sound
> From its curved roof the mountain's frozen tears,
> Like snow or silver or long diamond spires,
> Hanging downward, raining forth a doubtful light . . .
> Where we will sit and talk of time and change
> As the world ebbs and flows, ourselves unchanged.

Above all, Trelawny could imagine himself in that Greek island 'beautiful as a wreck of paradise' to which he had planned to take Medwin and Williams and Shelley (whom he had not yet met) in his own ship in the summer of 1820. Shelley never saw Greece but in his *Epipsychidion* he had imagined himself and his lover wandering over the mountains and abandoning themselves to sexual passion in an idyllic cavern, cut off forever from the world's cares:

> Our breath shall intermix, our bosoms bound
> And our veins beat together; and our lips
> With other eloquence than words, eclipse
> The soul that burns between them, and the wells
> Which boil under our being's inmost cells
> The fountains of our deepest life, shall be

Confused in passion's golden purity,
As mountain springs under the morning Sun.
We shall become the same, we shall be one
Spirit within two frames, oh! wherefore two?
One passion in twin-hearts, which grows and grew
Till like two meteors of expanding flame,
Those spheres, instinct with it become the same
Touch, mingle, are transfigured; ever still
Burning, yet ever inconsumable.[2]

Trelawny had achieved the impossible. He had taken Byron's fictions and turned them into facts. He had made a reality of Shelley's romantic dreams. At last life had the perfection of literature, the grandeur of art, the excitement of poetry. Trelawny surrendered himself to sensation, soaking in the rich colourful experience, mindless of content or purpose. If in the past he had found it difficult to keep separate his real life and his fantasy life, henceforth it would be totally impossible.

17

The Assassination Attempt

Odysseus: Trelawny! My presence is requisite on the eastern coast.
The Pasha of Negropont has threatened that, unless I lay down
my arms, he will bring such a force against me as shall crush me
instantly.
  Trelawny: Threats are useful only to the threatened: the wise
man has no will for them, and the strong man no occasion.
  Odysseus: Rightly spoken. Our enemy is only our sentinal when he
challenges as the Pasha does. I depart this night. To thy science
I commit the fortification of the cavern, to thy courage its defence.
Whatever else is dear to me in the world I entrust to thee with
the same confidence. Not least in the precious charge is thy own
good name.
    Walter Savage Landor: Imaginary Conversations.[1]

In his cavern fortress, Trelawny had only a vague idea of what his
master Odysseus was planning. Occasionally a messenger would come
with news and occasionally Trelawny would himself go out on an
expedition, but he was more concerned about enjoying the cave and
Tersitsa than in following the political or military situation. He was
with Odysseus when his army circumspectly escorted a Turkish force,
their new allies, through his territory and he even dined with the
Turkish commander, but no one is more blind than the man who has
no wish to see.

Newspapers in Austria, France and England carried the news that
Odysseus had turned traitor taking with him his brother-in-law,
Captain Trelawny, the friend and companion of Lord Byron.[2] The
word even penetrated to Claire Clairmont in Russia,[3] but Trelawny
himself remained unconscious of his new fame. In fact for Odysseus
the gamble had failed. It became clear that this time the Ottomans were
not going to give Odysseus the support he needed. If he stayed with
them, he would in all probability repeat the grand exit of his mentor
Ali Pasha with his head at the top of a pole at Constantinople. In
desperation he abandoned his own men and threw himself on the mercy

of his old henchman Ghouras who was a Greek warlord of the Athens region. He was imprisoned in the Acropolis of Athens to await developments.

The succession to Odysseus's empire now in theory devolved on Trelawny. All eyes turned on the fabulous fortress with its store of provisions, its powerful battery of guns, its magazines of powder, and its reputed treasure. Ghouras was determined to take possession of it for himself, and a complex series of negotiations was set in motion. Word was passed to Trelawny that Odysseus would be released if the cave were surrendered, and one of Odysseus's half-brothers acted as go-between. Many a cup of coffee was drunk and many a hooka was smoked under the whispering oaks by the Chapel of St George below the cave where the long negotiations took place.

Trelawny was adamant. He would not surrender the cave to anyone except to his master Odysseus himself, and would if necessary fight. Cameron, his Hungarian second-in-command – his name scotticised from Komarones – supported him eagerly, but the others in the tiny garrison were not so sure. On one occasion Ghouras arrived at the foot of the ladder with a considerable force to demand surrender, and sent up a letter from Odysseus which appeared to recommend acceptance. But Trelawny said no. The letter had been written under duress, he said. If Odysseus was really willing to hand over his cave to Ghouras, let him be released and allowed up the ladder – he could then hand over the cave himself. The bluff was called and Ghouras retired.

There was now only a handful of people in the cave itself; Trelawny and his wife Tersitsa, Odysseus's mother Acrive and his boy Leonidas, Cameron the second-in-command, Achmet the Turk next in succession, Trelawny's Italian servant, and a few pallikars with their women. There were also two other philhellenes.

Thomas Fenton the artillery officer who had come from Missolonghi with the guns and helped to fortify the cave, was strong and tough and could run over the mountains like any pallikar. There was much of a Trelawny about him. He carried Shakespeare and Burns in his knapsack, wore the Albanian dress, and told impressive stories of past achievement whose relationship with the truth was obscure. Whitcombe, the other philhellene, was English. He was very young – less than eighteen – and he claimed to have been in the navy. Those who met him in Greece said he was simple-minded. Trelawny said his head was full of romantic notions about exotic clothes, treasure, and eastern women, and if Trelawny thought this, his romanticism must indeed have been extreme.

One day in June 1825 Trelawny and the two philhellenes were practising shooting on the terrace of the cave. When Trelawny's back was turned, he was suddenly shot at and two balls hit him at point blank range. Amazingly neither shot touched his spine or penetrated any vital organ. He did not fall but turned calmly round towards his assailants with blood pouring from his wounds. Fenton murmured something about an accident, but there was no mistaking that the attack had been a deliberate one, although Fenton's gun had failed to go off and only Whitcombe had fired. Cameron, rushing out to see what had happened, without hesitation shot Fenton through the head and hurled his body out of the cave over the cliff – 'to the eagles', as Trelawny said. In the confusion Whitcombe managed to escape down the ladder – using his turban as a rope to let himself over the parapet, but he was soon recaptured and for him a harsher punishment was planned. A noose was tied round his ankles and he was hoisted out over the cliff on the crane used for hauling up stores, when Trelawny called a halt.

Trelawny's life hung in the balance for three weeks. He sat on the rock on the open terrace and refused to be bandaged, plastered, poulticed, or even washed. His dress was cut away to expose the wounds, and since his mouth was shattered and his jaw locked, he was kept alive with water and yolks of egg. Meanwhile Whitcombe lay chained deep inside the cave screaming and weeping incessantly, almost to the point of madness. He was told that, if Trelawny should die, he would be put to death by being slowly roasted over an open fire, and he knew enough of Greece to take the threat seriously. By the end of twenty days, however, it was plain that Trelawny was going to survive. With immense pain he forced his jaw to open enough to eat a piece of wild boar meat the size of a shilling, and very slowly his strength started to return. With characteristic generosity he ordered Whitcombe to be set free without further punishment of any kind and he scampered off to Hydra nearly deranged by his experience.

Soon the whole story of the assassination attempt was revealed. Fenton and Whitcombe had been bribed by Mavrocordato to kill Trelawny and hand over the cave. Fenton had apparently been reporting on Trelawny for months, and a number of other prominent Greeks and philhellenes were involved in the conspiracy. The attack was part of a concerted scheme to break the power of Odysseus once and for all, and soon news arrived that, despite the failure to kill Trelawny, the rest of the scheme had gone according to plan. On 17 June, a few days before the attempt on Trelawny, the dead body of Odysseus was found at the foot of the Frankish Tower that stood on the Acropolis of Athens. It was said that Odysseus had been trying to escape from the tower where he was imprisoned when the rope on which he was lowering himself broke, but nobody believed that tale. He had been strangled.

For five weeks after the assassination attempt Trelawny lay in the cave. It was thought at first he was dead, but when it was learnt that he was still alive, his fame spread far and wide. Back in England his uncle Sir Christopher Hawkins, wrote to the Foreign Secretary, George Canning, to ask for the intervention of the British Government to remove his nephew to safety. Trelawny's mother wrote direct to Sir Frederick Adam, the Lord High Commissioner in the Ionian Islands imploring him to 'relieve me from a state of most dreadful anxiety about my son E. J. Trelawny who at one time sailed with your brother'.[4]

But the British Government was unwilling to give assistance to distressed philhellenes – they had forfeited their rights by taking service with a foreign power in breach of the Foreign Enlistment Act. And Sir Frederick Adam saw no reason to intervene on behalf of an unsatisfactory midshipman who had served in H.M.S. *Resistance* under his brother's command – Trelawny was later to describe Captain Charles Adam in his book as a 'red-gilled sycophantic Scotchman' – But even if the authorities had been prepared to stretch a point in Trelawny's favour because of his powerful political connexions, could they do so for a man who boasted of having deserted from the Royal Navy, fought under French colours, killed British soldiers, and sunk British ships? All requests to intervene were firmly refused.

Trelawny's survival was mainly due to the effort of Major d'Arcy Bacon, the imperturbable traveller whose drawers had caused such a sensation at Talanta the previous February. He was at Nauplia when he heard the news of the assassination attempt and, with Captain Hamilton of H.M.S. *Cambrian*, he persuaded Mavrocordato to allow Trelawny a safe passage to leave the cave on condition that he quitted Greece. Bacon himself agreed to go to the cave with twenty five pallikars supplied by Ghouras, and Hamilton sent a corvette H.M.S. *Sparrowhawk* to the gulf of Corinth to pick up the wounded man.

As he wrote to his admiral in justification of his action in helping someone who had outlawed himself:

> It was difficult to determine how far you might approve of my interfering for a person in the situation of Trelawney, against whom there were so many reports and serious accusations; but on the other hand, some of these reports were known to be false, others to be exaggerated, and it was painful for me to think the life of an Individual depended on my determination, and I decided on demanding permission for his embarcation as a British subject, stating at the same time that I did not consider Mr Trelawney entitled to the full protection that that character would have given him under other circumstances, but that I wished it to be extended to him from motives of humanity.[5]

By the time the admiral's report had been sent to the Foreign Office, it was, of course, too late for Hamilton to be overruled.

Bacon found Trelawny lying on a mat in a corner of the cave, pale and emaciated. His right arm was completely paralysed, he had lost three upper teeth, and could only open his mouth with difficulty. Three days later he descended the ladder for the last time, and as he was helped to mount the mule to begin the long journey to the sea, Cameron fired the guns in a last salute to the wounded commander.

The *Sparrowhawk* was waiting at Dystomo and conveyed Trelawny, Tersitsa whose pregnancy was now apparent, Tersitsa's brother, and Major Bacon to Athens where they transferred to the *Cambrian*. Everyone wanted to see the man about whom so many stories had been told and he was happy always to supply more. The chaplain of the *Cambrian* found some too gross for repetition, but he did record his general impression:

> This affair [the release of Whitcombe] so far as it is related to us, tells favourably on the part of Trelawny; and in truth that person requires some palliating circumstance to lighten the huge mass of obloquy which attaches itself to his public and private character. If one half of what is circulated respecting him be true (of which I pretend not to judge) his conscience must be callous indeed, if it remain at rest beneath it: his heart must be as black as it is bold, and unfeeling as it is adventurous! *His wife* is a little girl certainly of not more than *thirteen or fourteen years of age*; of pretty features, but impressed with a deep shade of melancholy. What companionship can such a one have with a man of at least five and thirty.[6]

As soon as he reached the Ionian Islands, Trelawny wrote to all his friends in almost identical terms to tell them of his survival, scratching the words on to the paper with great difficulty with his left hand:

My shattered hulk no longer seaworthy was towed into this port by the Cambrian, Captain Hamilton. I have been near going down – two shots between wind and water – all my timbers carried away – standing and running rigging cut up – two balls entered my back, broke my jaw, breast bone, cut all the nerves of my right arm, and in short, all but did my business. After a two months struggle between my constitution and these severe wounds, by which I suffered daily death, the former triumphed.[7]

The news was published in the English newspapers and Trelawny was delighted to discover how well-known his exploits in Greece had made him, although no brave gestures could conceal that the one great enterprise of his life had been misconceived and disastrous in its results.

The Navy offered a passage to Malta, but Trelawny declined. The heir of Odysseus had hopes of returning to the cave and claiming his inheritance. While they were waiting in the quarantine at Cephalonia, Trelawny showed Major Bacon a few silver drinking bowls – the same that they had used the night the major was captured at Talanta – which Trelawny had somehow managed to bring with him from the cave. They were all that he had of the treasure. Already the tide of history had swept away the last traces of Odysseus's rebellion. Cameron held out in the cave for a few months after Trelawny's departure but then he was killed and Odysseus's family finally agreed to surrender. The Government took possession of the guns and the stores and removed the fortifications, although to their intense disappointment they could not find the treasure.

That treasure now belonged to Trelawny and he alone knew (roughly) where it had been hidden. He never went back to collect it and it was to lie heavy on his mind for the rest of his life. When Sir Sidney Colvin went to see the old romancer, then in his late eighties, in 1881 shortly before he died, he was still talking fondly about the cavern fortress of Mount Parnassus and the buried gold of Odysseus Androutsos.[8]

18

Drifting

> He is a strange yet wonderful being – endued with genius –
> great force of character and power of feeling – but destroyed by
> *being nothing* – destroyed by envy and internal dissatisfaction.
> *Mary Shelley's Journal, 1832.*[1]

It was many months before Trelawny recovered from his wounds. Only a man of immensely strong constitution could have survived. For the rest of his life he moved with a slight hunch, but to everyone's astonishment but his own, he regained fully the use of his arm, and his other faculties were unimpaired. He still carried on his face and body the scars of earlier wounds received in Java in 1811 and liked to show admirers a hard lump on his leg, the size of a walnut, caused by a bullet which had never been extracted. His jaw healed but his lips had a slight twist which resembled a permanent benevolent snarl.

The news of his survival brought two unexpected visitors to see him. Two elder brothers of the young Whitcombe who had fired the near-fatal shot arrived in Cephalonia to discover the facts of their brother's case, and if necessary to 'demand satisfaction' from Trelawny. The authorities took steps to prevent a duel but the brothers seem, reasonably enough, to have been persuaded that Trelawny had not only been fair but generous, and there was no need for the authorities to intervene. One of the Whitcombes decided to join the Greek cause and was severely wounded in the fighting near Athens in 1827. The other went home. The disgraced youngest brother, after spending some time at Hydra where he seems to have suffered a nervous breakdown, returned to England, where Trelawny met him again, and published a strange anonymous book as part of an attempt to come to terms with himself. He shortly afterwards atoned for his crime more directly by accepting a commission in the West India Regiment, a fate reserved for the blackest of black sheep, and – as was expected of officers and gentlemen in these circumstances – died of some tropical disease within a few years.[2]

Trelawny meanwhile remained in the Ionian Islands. At first he seems to have had hopes that he might soon be able to return to Greece, but with the surrender of the cave and the extinction of Odysseus's party, he had no friends there. He waited hoping to attach himself to the expedition which was being sent out from England under the command of Lord Cochrane, but as a result of repeated delays, the expedition did not arrive in Greek waters until the spring of 1827 and Trelawny was unable to join it. Then in October the fleets of the allied powers, Britain, France and Russia suddenly destroyed the Ottoman fleet at Navarino and the outcome of the Greek War was decided. Trelawny paid a short visit to Missolonghi in 1827 but there was clearly no longer any role for him in Greece.

At-Cephalonia he was soon involved in a long-drawn-out divorce suit, the second in his life. A teenage mountain bride might be a useful piece of psychological furniture in a cave in Parnassus, but what position was she to occupy in the mannered drawingrooms of British colonial and military society? Tersitsa bore Trelawny the daughter who had been conceived in the cave (she was called Zella), but not long afterwards the marriage began to break up. The crisis is said to have occurred when Tersitsa – who was forbidden by Trelawny to wear European clothes instead of the Greek dress – took advantage of his temporary absence to wear a Paris dress at a party. Trelawny arrived unexpectedly and in front of the assembled company cut off her hair with his dagger as a punishment. When Tersitsa was pregnant with a second child, she went to live in a convent, and as soon as the baby – a girl – was born, she sent her to Trelawny to be looked after, refusing to have anything to do with her herself. Trelawny made arrangements for the baby to be put out to nurse, but within a short time she died.

Then followed another of those incidents where Trelawny saw himself as invincibly defending a principle but which convinced many of his contemporaries that he was a monster. He sent the body of the dead child back to his wife in a box along with her other things and a letter, and it lay in the convent until it became putrid. Infanticide was suspected and Trelawny was taken to court but he was cleared apart from being fined for illegally removing a dead body.[3] In the divorce proceedings Tersitsa claimed in her petition that 'He failed to treat me with that consideration and nobility of character which distinguish the men of his nation', and he was in no position to deny it. Tersitsa was still only seventeen when she was finally released from the strange man to whom she had been married for four years.

These immediate personal problems absorbed Trelawny's energies for nearly two years after his rescue from the cave in the autumn of 1825. He was in any case in no hurry to move from the Ionian Islands since he needed time for his finances to recover as well as his body. The expedition to Greece, he reckoned, had cost him £1,200, which was obviously far more than he could afford on his income of £300 a year. By 1828, however, when at last he was fully fit again and freed from legal entanglements, the question could no longer be avoided. What was he to make of his life? In particular, a decision had to be taken about his past. He was now a minor celebrity. His exploits in Greece had been widely reported, and whenever his name was mentioned there would be strange stories about India and Arabia trailing behind. Perhaps, having experienced such an extravagance of real romance, Trelawny might have been happy to drop the pretence, but it was already too late. The progressive coalescing of his actual personality with his desired personality was now far advanced. The young man who had been jokingly compared with an illustration to Byron's poetry now looked the part to perfection. No-one thought the resemblance comic, it was too convincing for that. Although still in his thirties, Trelawny looked ageless and indestructible with every wrinkle on that leathern face bearing witness to a life of toil and danger and innumerable troubles bravely undertaken. He no longer needed costume or make-up. He could afford to cut off his long corsair tresses and klephtic moustaches and still convince his audience.

Even if some escape-route had been open to him which would have permitted a retreat from his past without embarrassment, was he any longer capable of taking it? To abandon it would have been like losing a limb or worse for he had come to rely on it. It had sustained him now for six years of his adult life, fulfilling differing psychological needs at each stage with remarkable adaptability. He no longer needed his fantasy as a defence to work off feelings of revenge or frustration against the world, or as a protective costume to wear in a society where otherwise he felt uncomfortable. It was no longer an aid for the weak but a weapon for the strong.

Besides he enjoyed it. Romanticism suited him, he thrived on it, and he wanted more. Like an alcoholic who spends a while in hospital, he found, with returning health, a renewal of the old craving. But where was it to be found? The liberal revolution in Spain had long since collapsed, put down with the help of French bayonets. South America was now independent. The world seemed to be short of suitable trouble spots where a taste for exoticism and violence could be indulged in the name of liberty. He considered going back to India, but though that would no doubt be exciting and colourful, India was hardly the place for a determined anti-imperialist. Mary Shelley may have suggested his name to Frances Wright as a suitable candidate for Nashoba, the settlement carved out of the forests in Tennessee where a new community was being established, peopled by former slaves freed from the conventions of marriage and religion.[4] But if Trelawny seriously considered joining the colony he was fortunate to reject the idea for Nashoba was already on the point of collapse. Trelawny himself thought of Persia. 'If the Russians continue their war against the Turks', he wrote, 'the Persian Circassians and Georgians will, it is believed, renew their hostilities against Russia and make common cause with the Port. If such is the case I have an offer under very favourable circumstances to serve under Abbas Merza, the heir presumptive of the Persian Throne.'[5] Sadly the Turks and the Russians made peace and Trelawny never saw those Circassians.

His restlessness showed itself by a change of name. Edward John Trelawny decided in 1828 to become John Edward Trelawny. There are letters signed by him at different times of his life covering the whole spectrum of variations, E., J., Ed., Ewd., Edward, John, E. J., Edward John, John Edward, Edward J., J. Edward, E. John, John E., E. J.T., T., Tre, and plain Trelawny – to say nothing of Jhon – and I doubt if much psychological significance is to be extracted beyond further evidence of his dislike of too much stability. But the change in 1828, like the change in 1817, was part of a sustained attempt to change his personality and he was to call himself John Edward consistently until 1831, when he reverted back just as abruptly.

He decided to go to England, his first visit to his native land since 1820 when he had spent a few weeks there at the time of his father's death. He arrived in the summer and spent much of his time travelling and visiting relations. He went back to Cornwall and called on his ageing uncle Sir Christopher Hawkins at Trewithen. No longer was he the cringing disobedient boy who brought disgrace on his family by his ungrateful wilfulness but a confident man of the world who could address his rich uncle on equal terms with even a hint of superiority. He was already well-known as the last companion and friend of Lord Byron, and West's portrait which shows him at his most Byronic was exhibited at the Royal Academy in 1829. But he had few friends in England and he found his relations a strain.

His mother still apparently thought that the Government could find a career for her strange son, and hoped that Sir Christopher Hawkins would be able to use his influence as he had done, so unsuccessfully, years before when his nephew was a boy in the navy and again when he was trapped in the cave: 'You have been very kind in your attentions to my Son, and I have no doubt that his Society created some interest, he has acquired much knowledge and having a large share of sense makes him universally liked. Few individuals have made themselves more known in the world. I some time since mentioned to you that he would be a useful person to our government if appointed to some foreign court & I am sure would have done you credit.'[6] It is hard to think of a man less suited to be a diplomat than John Edward Trelawny.

Mary Shelley he regarded as virtually his only friend and in November 1828, shortly before his return to the Continent, he went to see her at Hastings. She was living in virtual isolation there, disfigured by smallpox, and put off seeing him until the last possible moment. It would appear that he wanted to renew the intimate friendship which they had experienced in 1822 and 1823 before he set off for Greece. 'I love you sincerely', he wrote to her before they met, 'no-one better. Time has not quenched the fire of my nature; my feelings and passions burn fierce as ever, and will till they have consumed me. I wear the burnished livery of the sun.'[7] But if he had thoughts of love or marriage – which he started to hint at not long afterwards – Mary's answer was a decisive no. At last she had begun to find the beginnings of a new life in England and to emerge from the long period of depressions and financial worries that had come with Shelley's death. All she wanted was to live quietly with her son Percy Florence and continue her writing.

In one of Trelawny's notebooks there is a passage, written out in his own handwriting, and incorporating his own errors, which appears to be from a letter giving Mary's answer to his proposals at this time:

My whole being was an aching void which refused to give forth any fruits, the fulness of sorrow is great, but how much greater its emptiness, yet sometimes I return to conscientiousness, and lifting my head above this sea of misery, behold the fragments of my shipwrecked life floating around. It is in a pause of this kind that I now write. The huricane of dispair will soon return and I shall be swallowed up again in one abyss of misery after another. Then dear friend when will the swell and storm die away and the dead calm of this great ocean come? When shall I be given up by its depths and be borne unresistingly, upon its bosom, like a weed of the sea to the distant still shores of Eternity.

I live in total retirement, buried, where my mind is sufficiently at ease in my books? The world is now nothing more to me, I am so far from it – at least in emagination, that not even a sound of its distant turmoil and turbulence reaches my ear. I do not like professions. How many covenants equally solemn have I not seen you break – sealed with equal protestations – How strangely unwise in you to talk of me of 'sacred' ties, when I hear that word I know that every outrage of neglect, contempt and selfishness is to follow.[8]

He also turned to Claire Clairmont, the other woman to whom he had offered his love in Italy in 1822, and at a brief meeting in Italy in 1828, he apparently renewed his suggestions that she should live with him. One of her letters giving her answer, so different from Mary's in its outlook on life, and yet so similar in its sense of dawning appreciation of Trelawny's real character, was also entrusted to the notebook:

Is it that you find me so very uncommunicative, in conversation, that you wish to see if my heart will open itself more freely upon paper. You have guessed very rightly. I might have been centuries before I should have [been] able to express by word what I shall now tell you by paper. I have many times endeavoured to discover the reason why my heart shuts up – at every bodys approach, and the only answer I find, is that in its former days when full to overflowing with kindness to all, it was so misunderstood suspected and slandered, that it has taken a refuge in a proud solitude of silence, and their it [wears] away, in such a deep gloom that its very being becomes doubted.

Do not think the melancholy you see sometimes from me is the sign of hopeless wretchedness, I am happy – it is only the shadow of former days, which throws its deep gloom over my mind, which is not yet passed away. How should I not be happy when I possess so many good friends, and see you – restored as by a miracle from out the thousand perils – with which fate had encompassed you. Of all the band which accompanied you in your wild crusade – you return – and return alone. I find you improved, your character has lost much of its original fierceness and wildness – you are softened into something like thoughtfulness – And your passions have died away, and your strong intellect, uncluded by them, lives in wisdom. I wish very much Dear friend to see you married – and I am sure if you were to a beutiful and young woman you would be happy and make her so.

You are fond of beuty – therefore she must be beutiful and as civilization is so much advanced, to these she may early add great instruction and much natural talent, this in the circle you frequent is not difficult to find, Only you must give yourself the trouble to look for it, and that you do not do. I wish you to be settled – and happy. The strongest mind cannot keep out despondancy – which constant inconstancy will let in. Judging of you by myself and abhorring anything that is new, I wish you to marry that you may rest at anchor in a safe harbour.

The two women whom Trelawny had most impressed when he was a bogus corsair, and to whom he had written streams of passionate letters from Greece, were beginning to tire of the extravagance of his emotions. They began to treat him like a favourite but wayward brother with plentiful advice about his health and not getting his feet wet. Perhaps they suspected that he was interested in them not entirely for themselves but because they were the women most closely associated with his beloved Shelley? Or perhaps they realised that although they themselves had become maturer and wiser since the glorious confident days at Pisa, (now, it seemed, an age away), Trelawny would never change. The two letters – the only two which Trelawny ever transcribed – stand side by side in his notebook, twin memorials of disappointed love.

And so he found himself in the situation he had been in so often in the past, that of a corsair without a role. What was he to make of his life? He had no wish to remain in England and at the end of 1828 he left England and returned to Italy. He established himself in a house in Florence, which had once belonged to Petrarch, with Charles Armitage Brown, Keats's friend. Walter Savage Landor and Joseph Severn lived nearby. He had already decided what he wanted to do.

19

The New Corsair

The Corsair and the Giaour, these two giants of modern poetry are none other than Trelawny himself, the hero and the author of these memoirs. He was born to mount a throne or perish on a scaffold.

From the introduction to the French edition of the Adventures, 1833.[1]

He would write a book. It would be the story of his life in the navy and his adventures with de Ruyter, and would lead on to his time with Shelley and Byron. It would be the first major memoir of Shelley to be written. As soon as he reached Italy he set out his plan in a letter to Mary Shelley.

My principle object in writing to you now – is to tell you that I am actually writing my own life – Brown and Landor are spuring me on & are to review it sheet by sheet as it is written; moreover I am commencing it as a tribute of my great Love for the memory of Shelley – his life and moral character – Landor and Brown are in this – to have a hand – therefore I am collecting every information regarding him – I always wished you to do this Mary; if you will not – as of the living I love him & you best – incompetant as I am – & must do my best to show him to the world – as I found him – Do you approve of this? – will you aid in it – without which it can not be done – will you give documents? – will you write anecdotes? – or – be explicit on this, dear – give me your opinion – if you in the least dislike it say so and their is an end of it – if on the contrary – set about doing it – without loss of time – Both this & my life will be sent to you to peruse & approve or alter before publication & I need not say – that you will have free scope to expunge all you disapprove of.[2]

It was a brilliant idea. It promised to satisfy a whole range of Trelawny's needs and wishes. For one thing, it would complete the fusion of his imaginary adventures with the real adventures. Volume 1 could be about the privateering in India, Volume 2 about his experiences with Shelley and Byron in Italy and Greece. Secondly, it would mark Trelawny's debut as a writer – he would at last join the ranks of Byron and Shelley and Leigh Hunt and Mary Shelley and Walter Savage Landor and Charles Armitage Brown. As he told Mary, he intended to come fairly forward in a new character, and lay down the sword for the pen.

His visit to England had also been a reconnaisance. It was all very well to be a corsair among the British colony at Pisa and with a handful of foreigners in Greece. But in England? Would his story hold? Was there anyone who would connect the gawky midshipman put ashore at Woolwich in 1812 with the celebrated friend of Lord Byron of eighteen or nineteen years later? There were his mother and sisters to be considered – they would presumably be surprised, but would they do anything? Sir Christopher Hawkins, his uncle and trustee was old and ill and died almost at the time when Trelawny was forming his plans. But what about his other uncle, John Hawkins? Could his family be persuaded that in the long periods he had been away from England during his naval career, he had in fact been privateering with de Ruyter or fighting Wahabees in the deserts of Arabia? It was, obviously, a daring and dangerous trick to attempt. The risks of exposure and humiliation must sometimes have looked horribly high even for the days of slow communication and imperfect information. But Trelawny reckoned that the risks were worth facing. After all he had carried off the imposture with success for years now with hardly a hint of challenge and very few of his friends knew anything of his life before 1820. Why should his luck not hold?

As far as writing about Shelley was concerned, however, Mary said no, politely but firmly. She would not help Trelawny. She wanted as little publicity as possible, terrified that Sir Timothy Shelley would cut off her income if she again brought the memory of his disgraceful son to the attention of the public. All Trelawny's pleas were refused, and Trelawny's proposed book on Shelley got no further than an advertisement in the *New Monthly Magazine* for November 1830: 'A Memoir of the Life of the Poet Shelley during his residence in Italy will shortly appear from the pen of his friend, Captain Trelawny.'

But if (for the time being) he could not write about his life with Shelley, nobody could stop him writing the first part of his proposed work, the story of his own early life. In fact he felt he had to, for his money problems suddenly became acute. The family responsibilities which he had treated so lightly all his youth now suddenly began to bear down upon him. He had been away from England so long that his two daughters by his first marriage, Maria Julia and Eliza, were virtual strangers to him. Caroline, their mother, had died in 1827 and responsibility for looking after Julia was assumed by Trelawny's mother, Mrs Brereton. Eliza, the younger daughter, had been brought up by the Johnson family and had only recently been told that her strange godfather was in fact her father. Trelawny took his two daughters with him on a visit to France on his way back to Italy at the beginning of 1829 and Mrs Brereton was delighted that at last he seemed to be showing some interest and affection.

Mrs Brereton was now quite old and in uncertain health, although in fact she survived till 1852 when she was 93, but in any case Trelawny did not like the idea of her being responsible for Julia's education. It seemed likely for a time that she would have to come to Italy to live with him at least until he could arrange for her to be adopted. Arrangements had meanwhile been made for Zela, the daughter of his former Greek wife Tersitsa, who was now four, to come to Italy from the Ionian Islands and she arrived in July 1829. All this involved expense which Trelawny was in no position to afford on his fixed income of £300 a year. Then suddenly the Johnson family, who were looking after Eliza, were totally ruined by the failure of a bank in India and they could no longer keep Eliza. Arrangements were made for her to come and live with her father, but before she could come to Italy she unexpectedly died. 'She was the only creature', he told Claire Clairmont, 'the only being, the only tie – from which I expected nothing but sweet remembrances – perfect love – in my love to others, however sincere or ardent, there is and always has been – something or other annexed – which has embittered it ... By her death fortune has expended her utmost malice on me.' With characteristic generosity he gave money to the Johnson family.[3]

He had made it a rule never to refuse money to anyone who needed it no matter how hard his own circumstances might be, and in September 1829 his principle was put to the test. The Swedish baroness whom the much-disliked Medwin had married in 1824 and who was thought to be rich, asked to see Trelawny whom she had only met three times before. When admitted, she declared that she had no money and begged for his help. He gave her the money she asked for, conscious as he did so that his reward from both Mrs Medwin and Medwin himself was likely to be ingratitude and denunciation. It was bad luck to strike

Trelawny at such a time, 'like a stone dropping from the moon upon a man's head', as Claire said in suggesting to Jane Williams that he deserved 'indulgence even petting for his amiable behaviour to Mrs Medwin'.

The energy which he devoted to writing his book, Claire suggested, not altogether playfully, was a preparation for the final catastrophe when he would have given away all his money and would put an end to his own life to escape poverty. The money given to Mrs Medwin would be so much time subtracted from the length of his own life. 'When everything is accomplished he will pile up and set fire to a pyre of wood; into this he will rush headlong and nothing shall be seen of him beyond a wreath of smoke ascending from his burning tomb into the quiet blue sky.'

He might expect £200 a volume for his book, so he was advised by his literary friends at Florence, £600 for the whole book, equivalent to two years' income. And therefore Trelawny began eagerly to write the book which is now called *Adventures of a Younger Son*. He moved out of the lodging in central Florence where he had been staying with Charles Armitage Brown, and established himself in a villa near Galileo's Tower at Arcetti on a steep hill overlooking the city, reflecting no doubt that he too was in the tradition of fighters against church authority. Brown had found Trelawny a difficult lodger – on one occasion when it turned cold he used the furniture as firewood – but their friendship survived and Brown corrected Trelawny's spelling and rough copy into a state fit for a printer.

Trelawny began his book with (reasonably) factual events of his childhood and naval experiences and ended with (reasonably) factual events about his return to England, but for the intervening period he composed a romantic fantasy with imaginary characters and events which projected his own masthead dreams of the young corsair at the side of the legendary Surcouf. It is a good story, wild, violent, and prejudiced, representing in style and arrangement as well as in plot the character which the author had so successfully assumed. Trelawny sent the manuscript to Mary Shelley for her to arrange publication.

There then followed a long correspondence in which Mary pressed him to delete and amend certain offensive passages and Trelawny reluctantly consented. One was a chapter in which the young midshipman is taken on his first run ashore at Portsmouth, another described an unexpected meeting with his commanding officer in a brothel in Bombay. The name *Adventures of a Younger Son* was not chosen by Trelawny himself – he wanted *A Man's Life*. In letter after letter Trelawny insisted that it was the story of his own life – 'the history of my life beginning with my earliest remembrances up the present period – it is to be written to the extent of my ability clearly and fearlessly', 'an honest confession of my life'. But the book, he insisted, must be published anonymously. In one draft the hero was given the old family name of Treloen – hardly the most effective of disguises. Later this was altered to another Trelawny ancestor named Hamelin,* but in the end no name at all was revealed. Trelawny hinted at unspeakable disasters – connected with potential legacies – that would occur if the identity of the author leaked out. His name was not to be told even to the publisher, and everybody else in the know was to be sworn to secrecy. Great care was to be taken about the distribution of copies and Trelawny himself was to be sent one only, to prevent the news of his authorship reaching Italy.

He was already adept at promoting his public image by the well-placed apocryphal story, and he knew that the best way to ensure that his name was generally known would be to tell a few people in strict confidence. Tell the bookseller that the author is a friend of Shelley, he urged Mary. How many privateersmen had Shelley known? The publisher, Henry Colburn, would have been wrily amused at these antics. He had built up his lucrative business mainly through his own skill in puffery, of which he was the greatest master. One of his favourite tricks, which helped sell hundreds of tedious three-decker society novels, was to put it about that the characters were all real people and the authors famous, perhaps even royal, personages whose identity had to be kept secret but might be guessed at by the fashionable.[4]

The process of negotiating Trelawny's book with the publisher and editing and printing was more drawn out than anyone could have wished. Colburn drove a hard bargain, paying only half of what Trelawny had been led to expect and in post-dated bills. Times, as ever, were hard. France lurched into a new phase of her history with the July Revolution of 1830, and for most of 1831 all attention in

---

* Strangely the commander of the French naval squadron in the Indian Ocean during much of Trelawny's service there was called Commodore Hamelin. Did the thought that the enemy commander bore a name so closely connected with Trelawny help to feed his fantasy that his rightful loyalty too was on the French side?

England was concentrated on the great Reform Bill. The country was said to be on the brink of revolution and the minds of the reading public on more important things.

Trelawny waited impatiently in Italy, nervous like any author of a first book but also apprehensive about whether his secret would hold. He had made up his mind to quit Europe for ever, he declared to Mary, making a bolt from embarrassment, one would guess – if his gamble did not come off. He would resume his Arab life, he told her. On another occasion he said he was intending to go to Nineveh where a pillar erected by Sardanapalus still stood. Probably he had been reading Byron's poetical tragedy, *Sardanapalus*.

But worse almost than exposure was the fear of not being taken seriously. Books about Byron and Greece were pouring from the presses and a few contained remarks about Trelawny. For example when the chaplain of the *Cambrian* published his book in 1826 with shocked and shocking stories about Trelawny, he expostulated to Mary Shelley: 'His abuse is of the sacerdotal school, orthodox such as none but these saintly gentry are vulgar or base enough to invent and promulgate – Must these personal slanders be borne? – I suppose so.'[5]

When Count Palma in his book suggested that Trelawny was a paid agent of Lord Byron, Trelawny was as usual ready to fight: 'Call me Turk – savage – pirate – robber, anything but not a hireling – a paid menial of a Lord – thank heaven my right arm is not so wasted of its strength but that it can chastise the liar who asserted it.'[6] Trelawny enjoyed controversies of this kind which drew attention to himself. If he was called Turk he could explain how Odysseus was not a traitor but a betrayed patriot. If called a pirate, he would explain the difference between a pirate and a privateer. As for savage and robber, well no-one could say that corsairs were gentle.

Shortly before Trelawny's own book came out, Dr Julius Millingen, one of the doctors who had helped bleed Byron to death, published his reminiscences of Greece with a sardonic description of Trelawny. It did not call him Turk or pirate but hinted broadly that he was a fraud. Trelawny read a long extract about himself in a review of Millingen's book in the *London Literary Gazette* and was stung to write a violent, personal, prejudiced, and unfair attack on the author which the *Gazette* published.   It did not feel able to publish Trelawny's abusive protest in full, so Millingen remains * * * but the emphasis on his boyish appearance and girlish manners leave little doubt of the nature of the accusation.[7] However, the moment of panic passed. Millingen's lead was not taken up. Trelawny's secret was still safe.

Shortly afterwards, in the autumn of 1831, there appeared the three anonymous volumes of *Adventures of a Younger Son* with its proud quotation from Byron on the title page.

> And I will war, at least in words, (and – should
> My chance so happen – deeds) with all who war
> With thought; – and of thought's foes by far most rude,
> Tyrants and sycophants have been and are.
> I know not who may conquer: if I could
> Have such a prescience, it should be no bar
> To this my plain, sworn, downright detestation
> Of every despotism in every nation.

To a post-Freudian age, the *Adventures of a Younger Son* is more revealing of Trelawny's character than he himself could have realised. Beneath the upper levels of consciousness it is a vivid representation of the romantic dreams which in his actual life were never far submerged. The story of the childhood battle with the raven in his father's orchard with which Trelawny begins is full of mythic associations, forbidden fruit, guardian beast, maiden in distress, and his later story is mainly a series of more violent variations on the same psychological themes – urge towards sexual conquest, self-assertion against established authority, terror of unknown monsters. The world is a rich and fruitful garden where every desire can be fulfilled and every appetite sated. These good things are denied to a younger son by law and custom but are available for the taking to a man with sufficient ruthlessness. The *Adventures* is a celebration of rape and plunder. Anything which stands in the way of self-gratification can be violently smashed aside, and human beings are treated no differently from the exotic beasts and monsters which guard the jungle orchard. In the *Adventures* women do not give birth, they whelp and litter, hands become claws or paws, feet are hooves and flippers and faces are shouts. Trelawny's characters grunt, snarl, purr, and croak, and are compared to over a hundred different kinds of animals including, besides all the more usual species, the sheep tick, the dusky-red scaly cockroach of India, and the draggle-tailed dysenteric cockatoo. At another level the *Adventures* is a lurid advertisement for the riches and excitement of the Eastern lands and a projection of the collective fantasy which in the nineteenth century took European imperialism to every corner of the unknown world. As one modern critic has commented 'The *Adventures* is one of the most impressive nineteenth century examples of the pornography of violence because it is so obsessively imagined'.

The name of the author was known from the start. Almost every review of the book mentioned his name and before long the publisher himself was advertising the book as by 'Captain Trelawny, the intimate friend of Lord Byron'.[8] Almost without qualification the reviews accepted that the book was an autobiography of Trelawny's own life, not an imaginative work. It was violent and shocking, they noted, but praise and admiration poured forth on every side. Walter Savage Landor said there had been nothing like it since the *Iliad*.

Trelawny had done it at last. His fanciful past had been successfully integrated into his real life. His imposture was complete. If anyone knew or suspected that he had made it up, no hint was given. Even Trelawny's mother is said to have been proud of his notoriety rather than shocked at her son's confessions; and when Trelawny returned to England in 1832 he found himself a famous man. He was adopted as one of the literary lions of the day and invited to the dining tables of the great houses. After reading the *Younger Son*, Godwin invited him to supper and he became a weekly visitor, learning direct no doubt from the old philosopher himself the doctrines that had so decisively influenced the lives of Shelley and his admirers. All ears were eager to hear Trelawny's stories of India, of Byron, of the cave.

There seemed to be no limit to his success. Everyone had said from 1817 onwards that he resembled a Byronic hero. Now, with the publication of the *Adventures*, the story was told the other way round; it was not Trelawny who imitated Byron's *Corsair*, so the story ran, but Byron who took Trelawny as his model in composing his romantic poems! It was an extraordinary twist, obviously absurd to anyone who took any trouble to enquire into the dates. *The Giaour* was first published in 1813, *The Corsair* and *Lara* in 1814. Byron did not meet Trelawny until 1822. Yet the story rapidly passed from mouth to mouth and from book to book until it entered the received canon of truth.

It was a good story and why should Trelawny deny it? The circle was now complete. Appearance, character, behaviour, all coincided. In Paris a play ran for a time in 1834 about Lord Byron in Venice.[9] It included one character noted simply as 'Trelawny – Corsaire'. He spends most of the time stamping impatiently about stage wishing he was with his horse in the desert or his pirate ship in India and complaining how stifling civilised society is. To the devil with Europe, he declares; who will give me back the life of Asia, the pleasures of the harem after the joys of combat, love without jealousy, war without treaties? As a representation of the real Trelawny at this time it was not far from the truth.

With the help of Mary Shelley and Charles Armitage Brown he had given every chapter a poetic heading, a quotation from the works of Byron, Shelley, and Keats, the three poets of liberty he called them, the three great romantics who had died young far from England. Effortlessly Trelawny slid into the role of the friend not only of Shelley and Byron but even of Keats whom he had never met but of whom he knew a few stories from Leigh Hunt, Severn, Brown, and others.

The review of the *Adventures* in the *Westminster Review* gave currency to three splendid untruths in one paragraph:

> There seem to have been no pains taken to conceal the fact that the author of these volumes is Mr Trelawny the friend of Lord Byron and the person from whom the poet is said to have taken the idea of the character and exploits of his Conrad . . . Such is the vigour, the freshness and novelty of many parts of the narrative that there can be no doubt that the writer is consulting the deep imprints of experience rather than the brilliant shadows of his imagination. The known European adventures of Mr Trelawny prepared us not to be surprised that marvels should have happened to him in the East, the native land of passion and extravagance . . . It was darkly whispered here and there that there was a mystery about his early life . . . The mottoes of every chapter are without exception from one of three authors Byron, Shelley, or Keats. Trelawny was the friend and favourite of each of these gifted men.[10]

Everything could be turned on its head. How touching of Trelawny to call his Greek daughter Zella after his first (or was it second) wife, people would say, ignorant that the Zela of the *Adventures* was herself a fictitious reconstruction of Tersitsa. No wonder Trelawny knew how to conduct Shelley's cremation in Italy. Did you not read in the *Adventures* how marvellously he had conducted the same ceremony for his Arabian child-bride Zela on the beach at Mauritius?

By the time the stories about Trelawny reached France – where the people were delighted to read the memoirs of a British traitor – they

had become more fantastic than any dream at the masthead. According
to a French journalist who interviewed an English visitor:

> Lara and Manfred really existed. Their living model was a certain
> Trelawny who had been attached to Lord Byron during his time in
> Greece. This Trelawny was a giant, six feet tall with a magnificent head.
> Bold and intelligent, full of controlled passion and bravery, and a body
> of the most perfect proportions it is possible to dream of. He had beauti-
> ful hands with long narrow fingers. He could put a hazel nut between his
> index finger and middle finger, a second between the middle finger and
> the ring finger, and a third between the ring finger and the little finger.
> Then slowly clenching his fist he would crack them open. He could take
> three iron bars each one three or four centimetres in diameter, and twist-
> ing them under his feet, he would transform them without apparent effort
> into a regular plaited three strand rope, as perfect as if it had been made
> by a powerful machine. When his iron rope had attained a certain length
> he would seize it with both hands and twist it to the shape of a corkscrew.
>
> This terrible athlete could speak all the known idioms and dialects
> from the Coast of Coromandel and the point of Ceylon to the Islands of
> Sunda. Bronzed by the Indian sun like the god Siva himself, always
> dressed in silks and cashmeers which draped on him like an ancient
> statue, he was as different as possible from an Englishman. With his tall
> figure and eyes veiled with huge eyelashes, he petrified and thrilled the
> maidens of Abydos, who believed, when they met him, from his beauty
> and poetic physique, that they had found the last of the gods of Olympus
> unexpectedly delayed on the classic earth. Trelawny had however shed
> more blood, ordered more massacres, and stabbed more men then the
> heroes of the Fables he reminded them of. His life as told by Lord Byron
> (whose constant companion he became) was considerably softened and
> sweetened to suit the canvas of the songs of Lara . . . The Conrad of
> Byron is a pale effeminate who would have trembled to meet Trelawny.[11]

William Godwin and Mary Shelley constructed characters based
on the (fictitious) Trelawny for their own novels and stories, and no
doubt he attempted to live up to those parts as well.[12] His life followed
literature, literature followed his life, and his life followed literature
back again. Trelawny stood like a man trying on new clothes in the
tailor's changing booth, surrounded by reflections of himself none of
which fully please him, changing his position, rearranging his cuffs,
adjusting the mirrors, all in a vain attempt to achieve the satisfactory
all round appearance he has seen in the glossy catalogues.

America

I heard steps behind me; – was following me; down, down I sprang, and along the narrow footpath, divided only by a thicket from the tumultuous rapids. I saw through the boughs the white glimmer of that sea of foam. 'Go on, go on; don't stop' shouted–; and in another minute the thicket was passed: I stood upon Table Rock. – seized me by the arm, and without speaking a word, dragged me to the edge of the rapids, to the brink of the abyss. I saw Niagara – Oh, God! who can describe that sight?

From the journal of Fanny Kemble with
Trelawny at Niagara Falls, 17 July 1833.

The success of the *Adventures* meant of course that all possibility of shedding his fictitious past was gone forever. He would have to live with it for the rest of his life. Each succeeding day would be a crisis. Was this to be the day when the truth would come out, the day when his pretensions would be exploded and John Edward Trelawny held up to public ridicule?

If he could not retreat, then he must advance. He would live the part more intensely than before. He would shout down and stamp out without mercy any suspicion from whatever quarter. It should not be too difficult, for although he was acting a part, he was never off stage, he had not had a day off stage for ten years, and it was no longer possible to envisage a real Trelawny different from the role-playing Trelawny. In Greece he had turned fiction into reality. Perhaps it could be done again? Perhaps if he had some real achievement to his credit, the burden of the lie would be more tolerable? He could not get rid of it, but he could perhaps dilute it, smother it, obliterate it with truth? Everyone said he had talents. He was still only forty, apparently at the peak of his powers, and the world lay at his feet. The financial and family problems had eased. Julia came to Italy, to be adopted by Lady Campbell, the wife of a general who was governor of a West Indian Colony, and she was married not long afterwards. Zella too was adopted – by a rich

Italian family – and so Trelawny was fully mobile again. But where was a new field of success to be found?

The *Adventures* had ended with a ringing declaration of political principles. If the noble beings of his younger days had lived, Trelawny declared, meaning de Ruyter, Keats and Shelley, Byron and Odysseus, they would have 'rejoiced at beholding the leagued conspiracy of tyrants broken, their bloodhound priests muzzled, and the confederacy of nobles to domineer over the people paralysed by a blow . . . Yes the sun of freedom is dawning on the pallid slaves of Europe, awakening them from their long and death-like torpor. The spirit of liberty, like an eagle, is hovering over the earth.' The advent of Louis Philippe to the throne of France in the July Revolution of 1830, though doubtless an advance on the previous political situation, would hardly have been recognised by Shelley as the dawn of his millenium. Nor did the final passage of the Reform Bill in 1832 bring about any dramatic redistribution of wealth and power in England or collapse of organised superstition. Yet it was something. There was evidence of political movement. Perhaps Trelawny could play a part in promoting the ideals of his beloved Shelley by joining the great cause of reform? He began to build up contacts among liberal and radical politicians especially those with Cornish connections. Could anyone help to find him a seat in Parliament?

He marked his change of direction, as he had done in 1817 and again in 1828, by a change of name. The short life of John Edward Trelawny came to an end and Edward John Trelawny resumed his career. Again he seemed to think that the success of 1817 could be repeated by performing rites of passage. Then suddenly, on 5 January 1832, without a word to any of his friends, Trelawny left London for Liverpool. He met again his old friend Wright, the builder of the *Don Juan* whose wife Gabrielle had suffered a broken heart over him in 1822, and spent a few days walking round the docks, talking to the captains of the ships, and asking to what part of the world they were bound. He selected the *Tally Ho*, a former privateer, loading with salt and bound for Virginia, and within a few days he was on his way to the New World.

Shortly before the ship sailed, he wrote to Mary Shelley with a partial explanation of his apparent rudeness. The immediate cause of his abrupt departure, he said, concerned some affair of the heart but some later owner of the letter has cut out a few words with scissors – no doubt because of their embarrassing frankness. But the real cause of his departure, Trelawny explained, lay in his own nature:

My inflamable & succeptible nature could never yet – after dreaming – that a woman's sympathy had been awakened – summon resolution, to say, adieu – I am a child of the wandering Jew and doomed to wander – & find no resting place – nor peace nor home – and who can controul his fate! – a ship will decay sooner when laying in harbour, – than at sea – in harbour the silent worm is at work on her hull – eating into her heart of oak – at sea – the foaming billow, and the whistling gale are like dogs who bark oftener than they bite.[1]

Besides, it looked as if civil war might break out in the United States. In 1832 the state of South Carolina, whose interests had been damaged by a Federal tariff, proclaimed the doctrine that the states could, if they chose, nullify any Federal ordinance which they did not wish to apply. The State Government passed a Nullification Ordinance on 24 November 1832 and the Federal Government in Washington, repudiating the doctrine, sent warships to Charleston.

The mere prospect of war would not deter him from going to the United States, Trelawny told Mary, although he wanted to seek peace and quiet there. 'Shelley's maxim is mine, go on till you are stopped and men like us are never stopped.' But who can doubt that when Trelawny decided, among all the ships in Liverpool, to take one to America, it was because he wanted to involve himself in the war? Perhaps in the United States, he imagined, he could have another try at bringing about liberty by direct action?

It is difficult to recall the enthusiasm for all things American which the liberals of Europe felt during the first part of the nineteenth century. Only in the United States, it seemed, and possibly in a few Swiss cantons, was the light of liberty burning. The Americans had no kings or emperors, no lords or titles, they were free and equal before the law, they had freedom of worship and freedom of publication. Their constitution seemed to guarantee their liberties and the people, still largely British in descent and outlook, were happy and prosperous. Reformers throughout Europe held up the United States as their model. The guerillas of Spain and the carbonari of Italy were urged to emulate them, and English Benthamites lectured bewildered Greek klephts on the doctrine of separation of powers. In the chilling repression of Restoration Europe, the United States was a shining symbol of hope to the oppressed of the Old World. Now suddenly in 1832 it seemed that its proud freedom was under attack.

However, it is characteristic of Trelawny and his eagerness to draw his sword for liberty, that nobody appears to have been sure which side he intended to fight on. Mary Shelley apparently was under the impression that he was going to fight for the rights of the South Carolinians to decide their own affairs, including the right to maintain the slavery system. Other evidence suggests that Trelawny had in mind to fight for the Federal Government to maintain the Union. As in Greece he was confused by such matters. Fighting is more straightforward than political analysis.

As events turned out he did not have to kill any Americans at all. The crisis was resolved by a compromise before his ship had docked and there was no war. Having arrived in the United States however, Trelawny decided to stay awhile and look around. It would do him no harm in his political career to have seen for himself what a democracy looked like in practice. Had not Tom Paine, the author of *The Rights of Man*, been to the United States? And Robert Owen and William Cobbett and other heroes of the liberals? Perhaps it would have been preferable if he could have gone there as an exile, driven from his native land for his political opinions – but, failing that, he would go as a tourist.

When he was at Charleston early in 1833 the story went round that he intended to cross to Kentucky and write a book about his observations, but that idea was quickly abandoned.[2] In the early summer of 1833 he was in New York. Like other literary celebrities from England he was invited to the Bread and Cheese Club where he met Fenimore Cooper.[3] He also met the young actress Fanny Kemble,who was playing opposite her famous father in a tour of the principal cities. Trelawny contrived to be a passenger in the same steam boat when the Kemble party set out to visit upper New York State and at Albany he was invited to join their party for the rest of the trip.

The descriptions and anecdotes of him which Fanny wrote in her diary and published shortly afterwards show that he was still the same man who had overwhelmed and charmed the young Mary Shelley on first acquaintance eleven years before:

> Mr – dined with us: what a savage he is in some respects. He's a curious being: a description of him would puzzle anyone who had never seen him. A man with the proportions of a giant for strength and agility: taller, straighter, and broader than most men; yet with the most listless, indolent carelessness of gait; and an uncertain, wandering way of dropping his feet to the ground, as if he didn't know where he was going; and

didn't much wish to go anywhere. His face is as dark as a Moor's with a wild, strange look about the eyes and forehead, and a mark like a scar upon his cheek; his whole appearance giving one an idea of toil, hardship, peril, and wild adventures. The expression of his mouth is remarkably mild and sweet; and his voice is extremely low and gentle. His hands are as brown as a labourer's: he never profanes them with gloves but wears two strange magical-looking rings: one of them which he showed me is made of elephants hair . . . .

The sun set gloriously. Mr – began talking about Greece, and getting a good deal excited presently burst forth into 'The Isles of Greece! The Isles of Greece!' which he recited with amazing vehemence and earnestness. He reminded me of Kean several times: while he was declaiming, he looked like a tiger. 'Tis strange or rather 'tis not strange 'tis but natural how, in spite of the contempt and even hatred which he often expresses for England, and everything connected with it, his thoughts and plans and all the energies of his mind seem for ever bent upon changes to be wrought *in* England – freer government, purer laws, more equal rights.

The main purpose of the voyage up the Hudson – which was already an established tourist route – was to admire the magnificence of nature, especially the Trenton Falls and Niagara, which were reputed to inspire the same feeling as travellers on the older Grand Tour experienced at the Mer de Glace near Chamonix. Everywhere was desolation and wilderness, and the place of man in the scheme of things could be seen in perspective. During a terrifying storm when the Kemble party huddled in their carriage, Trelawny delighted them by writing out on a scrap of paper an Arab description of the attributes of God. 'I do not know whether it was his own or an authentic Mahomedan document,' wrote Fanny, 'it was sublime.'

Near Rochester the carriage was involved in an accident and Fanny was mortified to see Trelawny being carried prostrate and lifeless into a house. Fortunately he was merely stunned and a few minutes later she noticed that – with the same sound dietetic instinct that had saved his life in the cave – he had 'seized on the milk and honey and stuffed away with great zeal'.

They talked eagerly together of life and politics and literature, and to judge from Fanny's diary, her fiancé, Pierce Butler, whom she married very soon afterwards, was consigned to a secondary role. At one town where they stopped Butler ran into a bookseller's shop and bought the *Adventures of a Younger Son* which Fanny had started to read on the voyage over but laid aside. Trelawny immediately snatched the book away saying he was sure Butler would not like it.

The culmination of the trip was of course the visit to Niagara itself. When first invited to join the Kembles Trelawny had characteristically said that he had been there before but he would not mind going again. For some days he and Fanny explored every viewpoint of the great wonder of nature, with Trelawny leading her to ever more dangerous paths, scaring her sublimely, but rather too realistically for her liking.

Trelawny had to impress. He was looking out all the time to see what his audience were thinking, searching for new tricks to raise a gasp of awe or murmur of admiration, and he became more and more derivative. He was the new Shelley. Was that not clear from the way in which he denounced tyrants and priests? He was the new Byron enjoying his hour of literary celebrity. Increasingly he started to look for Byronic things to do, Byronic things to say. But where Byron had been charming and amusing, Trelawny was merely embarrassing. His heavy bams and hurtful practical jokes were a poor substitute for the Byronic humour they were intended to imitate. When he reached a new place that pleased him he would announce his intention of settling there for the rest of his life. Did not Shelley always want to stay in a new place 'for ever'? And was not Byron always overflowing with impressive schemes for new colonies in South America or buying islands in the Aegean? We will start a farm in Canada, he suggested to Fanny Kemble.

Trelawny wanted to talk of politics, but as in Greece, he found that, after an initial politeness, no-one was much interested in his views. The truth was, as it had been in Greece, that he had no understanding of politics and he could not conceal it. He simply mouthed slogans. People were repelled by the hatred with which he scorned anyone who disagreed with him and by his apparent readiness to resort to violence on behalf of virtually any cause, all in the name of liberty. He was more welcome in his old role of storyteller. The young Fanny Kemble and her friends would listen as attentively to his tales as Mary Shelley and Mrs Beauclerc's daughters had done at Pisa, and now he had his Byron stories too which made him a welcome guest anywhere. Gradually however it began to dawn on him, as it had become clear to his friends, that maybe his career was not going to fulfil its promise. He had the appearance, he had the presence, he had the strength, he had the experience – but for what? What was there behind that magnificent exterior? Was there anything of value, or was he all just show?

At Niagara, Trelawny left the Kemble party since he wanted to go to Canada to visit Augusta White – now Mrs Augusta Draper – whom he had not seen since 1819, although it is doubtful whether they actually met on this occasion. On 5 August after the Kembles had moved on, Trelawny was staying alone at the Eagle Hotel and exploring the vicinity. On the spur of the moment the great corsair conceived a typical Trelawnian idea. He would swim Niagara.

There was already a tradition of stunts but it was probably the comparison with Lord Byron that lay behind Trelawny's idea as behind so much of what he did. Had not Byron swum the Bosphorus like Leander of old and written poems about it? Byron had been so proud of that exploit, prouder far than he was of *Childe Harold's Pilgrimage*, and for the rest of his life, he had recalled it with delight:

> As once (a feat on which ourselves we prided)
> Leander, Mr Ekenhead, and I did.

A few miles below the Falls are the Rapids, where no living thing can survive. It was above these Rapids below the Falls that Trelawny plunged in. He swam to the other side and then on the way back, having been swept downstream to a place where the river is full of treacherous hidden currents and rocks, he was almost drowned.

On his return to the hotel he wrote up the episode in his usual grandiloquent style. The would-be great romantic saw himself as the undaunted hero struggling manfully but in vain against an inexorable fate and destined to die young in the attempt:

Why did I attempt to cross a part of the river that none had ever crossed before? There was not even the excitement of a fool on the shore to see or say he had seen me do it. Why had I not spoken to the man at the ferry, he would have followed me in his boat. I remembered too hearing the thing was not practicable; why what a wayward fool I am. These things acted as a spur, these truths crossed my mind rapidly, and I thought of all the scenes of drowning I had seen; of my own repeated perils that way. I heard the voices of the dead calling to me, I actually thought, as my mind grew darker that they were tugging at my feet. Aston's horrid death by drowning nearly paralysed me. Thus I lay suspended between life and death. I was borne fearfully and rapidly along, I had lost all power, I could barely keep my head above the surface, I waxed fainter and fainter, there was no possibility of help. . . . I thought now how much I would have given for a spiked nail so fixed that I could have rested the ball of my toe on it for one instant and have drawn one gulp of air unimpeded, to have swallowed the water that was sticking in the mid channel of my windpipe; nay I would have been glad at any risk to have rested on the point of a lancet . . . My uppermost thought was mortification at this infallible proof of my declining strength, well I knew there was a time in which I could have forced my way through ten times these impediments; the only palliation I could think of was the depth and icy chilliness of the water which came straight from the regions of the frigid zone. This contracted all my muscles and sinews, my head grew dizzy from bending the spine backwards, the blow I had received from the upset I had not recovered; the ball too immediately over my jugular vein retards the circulation; my right arm has never recovered its strength and it was now benumbed. All this and much more I thought of, my body said 'is like a leaky skiff' no longer seaworthy, and 'my soul shall swim out of it' and free myself. I thought the links which held me to life were so worn that the shock which broke them would be slight. It had always been my prayer to die in the pride of my strength – age however it approached, with wealth and power, or on crutches and in rags, was to me equally loathsome – better to perish before he touched me with his withering finger, in this wild place, on a foreign shore. Niagara 'chanting a thunder psalm' as a requiem was a fitting end to my meteor-like life . . .

Gradually, however, as he ceased to struggle so hard, he found he was being carried towards the shore and soon he lay there, panting and unable to stand, but alive. 'I was deeply mortified,' he wrote 'the maxim which has so long borne me towards my desires triumphantly – go on till you are stopped – fails me here. I have been stopped, there is no denying it, death would have pained me less than this conviction. I must change my vaunting crest.[4] But Trelawny's heavy-handed attempts to give symbolic significance to his swim merely emphasised that it was made mainly for appearances, so that it could be talked about later. As with so much of Trelawny's life, it was an act of pure romanticism, but so contrived and artificial as to rob it of the grandeur which he craved.

He wandered sadly back to the East Coast cities, living for a while in New Haven, New York, and Philadelphia, enjoying his growing reputation. From Niagara he went to Saratoga from where news of him reached Anna Quincy, the daughter of the President of Harvard, on 18 August through a Mr Campbell who had just returned:

Gave me a very amusing account of the various lions of the Spring, the greatest of which at this moment is a Mr Trelawney who is said to be the

original of Byron's *Corsair*. It is said that he is the younger son of a
Scottish nobleman, who turned first a privateer, met with a variety of
adventures, *married* a beautiful *Indian* girl, who accompanied him on
various of his honorable expeditions until one day when, as she was
bathing, a *shark* happened unluckily to swallow the unhappy demoiselle.
Upon which Mr Trelawney became so distracted with rage, grief and
Sharkantrophy that he turned Pirate forthwith, and after adventures too
numerous to mention, he returned with a broken heart and a large fortune
to England, became acquainted with Byron, who was so captivated by his
story that he forthwith wrote the Corsair upon it, only giving Medora a
more picturesque fate than befell the hapless Indian beauty. The *marriage*
and the *Shark* are two points in the story that somewhat shake my
credulity. Mr Trelawney has now wandered over to America to seek that
peace which he certainly does not merit, and when Mr Campbell saw him
last week, was endeavouring to forget, for a moment, the Shark and the
Indian beauty in a desperate flirtation with Mary Livingston at Congress
Hall – but doubtless 'The heart, the heart is lonely still'. All the ladies are
quite frantic, of course, about this gallant Rover who, by the by, can be
no chicken if he went thro' all these adventures, Shark and all, before the
Corsair was written.[5]

Anna Quincy was one of the few who ever queried the coherence of
Trelawny's absurd stories. Maybe if she had been exposed to him
direct at the Springs instead of hearing them at second hand, her
critical faculties too might have been put into suspense.

Despite all the attention however, Trelawny was unhappy in the
United States. The social conventions – stricter even than in England –
irked him, and he quickly found that legal freedom of religion did not
imply any approval of atheism. America was not, as he had imagined,
the democratic paradise of the reformers' visions, but still a rather
provincial copy of the England he disliked.

For the winter he moved south to Charleston, South Carolina,
whose climate he preferred to that of Florence, he told Claire, since it
resembled that of China, implying misleadingly that he had been there,
and he seems to have lived in Charleston for some months. Almost
nothing is known of his life there, but it is to be guessed that he
visited cotton plantations and found many enjoyable opportunities to
pass violent comments on the slavery system.

It was during the time that Trelawny was in Charleston that work
began on the great harbour fortress of Fort Sumter where the first
shots of the war between the states were to be fired a generation later.

One of the builders was the brilliant young German-born engineer and industrialist, Christian Edward Detmold, who was to become one of Trelawny's closest friends and one of the men he most admired in all his long life.[6] But no record has been found that they met at this time, and, for the first ten months of 1834, Trelawny disappears entirely – we do not know where he was or what he was doing. Stories that he crossed the continent to California[7] were later inventions intended to impress and cannot be true as they stand.

In a letter to Claire Clairmont written from Charleston on 12 December 1833, shortly before he disappears, we have a hint perhaps of what he had in mind:

> The wealthier classes in America attempt to imitate the English in their social institutions – and that is an absurdity – but they are a small sect – with small means and little influence – Democratic institutions are using up to the stump their goose quills – the Sovereign people are beating down all opposition – they are working out triumphantly their grand experiment – that all men are born free and equal! . . .
>
> Wandering over this country – I see many spots that resemble my rural castles in the air – it is time I should begin to lay the foundation of them – on the earth. – These endless and eternal forests are my delight – so are the rivers.[8]

It had been the dream of philosophers and political reformers since the beginning of the Enlightenment that somewhere in the New World, new settlements could be established in virgin lands where the concepts of political justice and the rights of man could be applied to actual government of real societies. At the time of his crisis in 1817, Trelawny himself had considered going to a new millenarian colony in South America and similar proposals had been revived at various times as each phase of his life came to an end. It was an idea that Shelley would have applauded, and Godwin with whom Trelawny had spent many hours during his last year in England no doubt encouraged him further.

In 1824 the formidable, fearless reformer Frances Wright had invested part of her fortune to buy 2,000 acres of woodland on both sides of Wolf River, thirteen miles above Memphis in Western Tennessee to establish the biggest communistic settlement according to the ideals of Robert Owen that had yet been attempted. She calculated that slaves working on the land saving half their wages, could earn enough to pay for their freedom in about five years after which they could be free colonists. Miss Wright advocated equal rights for women, free unions, as distinct from legally-imposed marriages, contraception, easy divorce and many other liberal, humane, and progressive ideas which made her name anathema throughout Britain and the United States.

When she had been in England in 1828 it had been suggested that Trelawny should go to Nashoba from Greece – and for a time the idea even seems to have been entertained that the main radically-minded survivors of the Pisa circle, Trelawny, Mary Shelley, and Leigh Hunt might all make a new start with Fanny Wright in the new world. As the historian of American socialism commented: 'She invited congenial minds from every quarter of the globe to unite with her in the search for truth and the pursuit of rational happiness.' [9] But by the time Trelawny reached America, Nashoba had been abandoned. Fanny had left for a prolonged visit to Europe, and her followers were devoting themselves increasingly to journalism and politics, demanding free education, organising trade unions, and attacking the influence of religion. It is doubtful if Trelawny ever met her.

But did he, one wonders, during the months in 1834 when his whereabouts are unrecorded, make the long journey up the Mississippi or down the Ohio to Nashoba or to New Harmony or to one of the other settlements? That could be the meaning of a cryptic reference in one of his letters from Charleston to his intention 'to contemplate the White Negur' – i.e. the liberated slaves. And he certainly developed plans – which never carried into action – to visit Haiti where Fanny had sent her liberated slaves in 1830 after the abandonment of Nashoba.[10]

Or did he for a time try to establish in a minor way his own rural castle-in-the-air on the earth – to use his expression to Claire Clairmont? Among the documents found at his death was a Deed of Conveyance dated Charleston 11 January 1834 whereby one Emma Maria transferred to Edward Trelawny for $1,000 a black slave John 'for his use at his new settlement in Virginia or elsewhere'.[11] Did that new settlement, one wonders, ever exist? Or was it another of those passing romantic fancies? In the mountains of Virginia, he told one correspondent half in joke, he had visited a widow with seven daughters, and if one of them were to be given to him, he would never again roam beyond the Blue Ridge.

Whatever it was that Trelawny attempted in 1834, it was a failure.

When he re-emerges in the autumn in Philadelphia, he was racked by indecision about the future and regrets about the past, ill in body and broken in spirit: 'I must now give over this unnecessary kind of life yet I fear me I have gone to far to stop – I should have died ten years ago I should have escaped much suffering – Oh it is a dismal world and after our youth has fled our difficulties deepen – the sunshine which once gladdened my heart no longer warms it – I walk benighted beneath its midday brightness. I long for death and therefore it avoids me.'[12]

Soon however with his usual resilience he recovered his health and emerged from his depression. He met Fanny Kemble again, and the famous actor Charles Mathews who saw him at Philadelphia in December 1834 described him as a sparkling jewel in a huge mine of dullness. But although he considered going on his travels again, his enthusiasm had gone. In the spring he went to New York and left for England. He appears to have taken with him a red Indian girl picked up somewhere on his travels – destined to be discarded as soon as her role of stage-prop was over with as little feeling as he hung up his coon-skin hat. He was forty-three.

21

Politics and Society

> Trelawny is making a name in High Life, from the fresh, frank, savage manner of his remarks. He seems astonished at civilized habits. They tell all sorts of stories. I came home with Mr Cowper and we amused each other in the Cab about him. Mr Cowper said he heard he had murdered two wives, and Mrs Stanhope quizzed him at table by saying he had been making love to some old Dowager with a fortune at Brighton – a 'good thing' said she 'for you know so well how to get *rid* of wives . . .'
>
> *From the diary of Benjamin Robert Haydon, 1835.*

On his return from America, Trelawny threw himself into politics. He became a member of an extreme radical party known as the Philosophic Radicals which included a number of prominent Cornishmen including his cousin Sir William Molesworth. A handful of the group were elected but they had little success. The passage of the Reform Bill had taken much of the momentum out of the parliamentary movement, and the Philosophic Radicals – who were mainly monied men from the landed classes – were soon outflanked by the rise of the Chartists, who not only made them seem irrelevant but gave the upper and middle classes such a scare that they turned increasingly against their political philosophies.

Trelawny made little progress in the party. He was never adopted as a Parliamentary candidate nor did he contribute to the *London Review* which the party ran for a while.[1] He did however take part in the endless discussion groups which the Philosophic Radicals – as is the habit of left-wing intellectuals – were accustomed to hold among themselves, usually over a good dinner at the big house in Putney of John Temple Leader, a rich, radical M.P. In a ringing statement of principle at the end of the *Adventures* Trelawny had declared that he would not be found 'consorting with worldly slaves who crouch round the wealthy and powerful', but on his return from America he had proceeded to do just that. He surrendered himself to the social world and was to be found most evenings at the table of some noble hostess. He wore smart clothes and cut his hair neatly. He frequented Gore House, the home of Lady Blessington, the gorgeous Lady Blessington, who saw herself as a great patroness of literature and herself poured forth a stream of insipid novels about life in high society. It was the era of the silver-fork novel and Bulwer Lytton and Benjamin Disraeli were the rising literary stars.

However, as in Greece, so again in America, few people took Trelawny's views seriously and those few that did were repelled. Beneath the fine clothes of the dandy could still be seen the gunroom bully. How strange Captain Trelawny is, the ladies would whisper as he strove to maintain his adopted character among the chit-chat. The times were changing. Trelawny's political views were like his manners, tolerated by his audience as the necessary but regrettable concomitant of a corsair. As the era of the great romantics passed into history, he saw himself left high and dry by the tide, spluttering helplessly on the beach, a monster out of its element, interesting no doubt but grotesque and possibly dangerous to go too close to. The blues exchanged intimacies about their experiences of the most sought after catch of the season: 'I spent yesterday evening sitting on a sopha with *Trelawney*. There! do you envy me? He amused me extremely. He is not as handsome as he was, because no longer so young but black, sunburnt, bearded and perfectly quiet and gentleman-like in manner. He claimed me at once as an *intimate* acquaintance.' So wrote Anna Jameson, one of the fighters for women's rights, to her friend Ottilie von Goethe. Later she described him in a different mood: 'Trelawny was with me on Sunday and staid from eight till past 12. He did not amuse me (as they say he does others) with a recital of his outrages and murders – perhaps feeling that I am not an admirer of the *Brigand* style. He was very quiet and sensible. I think if he loves any one it is Fanny Kemble who appears to be his *ideal* of womankind.'²

At a party at the Kembles' in May 1837 at which Fanny sang, the wife of the poet Longfellow noted not without a touch of envy that 'in a fauteuil by the fire lolled a beautiful girl, Miss Macdonald, with the Norman blackness of hair picturesquely adjusted, whose dark eyes sought her shoestring 'neath the piercing gaze of the ferocious Corsair Trelawney at her side. He is a ruffian-looking man, with wild mustache, shaggy eyebrows, and orbs beneath them that have the gimlet property beyond any I ever encountered.'³ At the age of forty-five Trelawny the Corsair was still looking for his Medora.

Conrad the Corsair rescues Gulnare from the Turkish palace. An illustration by Edward Corbould to Byron's *Corsair*, also used to illustrate Mary
Shelley's story *Euphrasia* which was based on stories Trelawny told her about
his experiences in Greece

From a sketch by Landseer, *c.* 1835

An engraving by d'Orsay, 1836

From a drawing by E. Duppa, 1837

Trelawny with the Philosophical Radicals.
Temple Leader is in the centre, Trelawny front left,
Molesworth front right

Trelawny returns to nature, 1838

Trelawny the world-weary romantic

Trelawny enjoyed breaking the hearts of the admiring young blue-stockings with whom he loved to be surrounded. 1836 was the year of the great scandal involving Lord Melbourne, the Prime Minister, and the society beauty and lady of letters, the Honourable Mrs Caroline Norton. Week after week the *Satirist* retailed the gossip about the alleged lovers of the 'unblushing one'* who had the misfortune to be married to a boorish husband who created the maximum of misery and scandal before naming Melbourne in a divorce action.

Lord Melbourne's name, William Lamb, provided endless opportunities for jokes at the expense of Mrs Norton – her children, the little *Lambs,* her visits to *Lamb-eth,* and the distraction which was sending her to *Bed-lam.* The Duke of Devonshire and Trelawny could not compete but the scandal-mongers did their best. On 8 May 1836 it was reported: 'The statement that Mrs Norton had gone to *Devonshire* after leaving the house of her husband is untrue – the *Honourable* lady, we are assured, proceeded directly to *Trelawney* in company with her "younger son".'

Before long the jokes were about the new book of poems which Trelawny was said to be writing. He was not doing so of course but the joke required it:

LAST LAYS

"Have you" quoth Seymour "read or seen
TRELAWNEY'S work?" "His *lays*"
Cried Norton "oft the theme hath been
of Mrs NORTON's praise!

A NEW WORK

"What's in the press – what's new begun"
Quoth Tom "what *men*-tal treats?"
"Why" NORTON cried. 'I've only one –
TRELAWNEY's work in *sheets*."[4]

By the spring of 1837 Caroline had decided to have no more to do with Trelawny, as she told Lord Melbourne in a letter which catches unmistakeably Trelawny's style on occasions of high drama and intense emotion:

The least agreeable feature of my life is a threatening letter from Trelawny. I told him in the civilest way possible that he must discontinue his visits

* Mrs Norton wrote a long poem *The Undying One.*

now that I was awkwardly situated and that his name had been used by N[orton] amongst others. I paid him every species of compliment in the course of the few sentences I spoke, tho' I spoke decidedly. He went into the rage of a savage – so much so that he couldn't speak in reply, and *wrote* his answer in the style of the Arabian Nights mixed up with his own novel of "The Younger Son" – mysteriously awful, & vaguely sublime, but very fierce. He did not vouchsafe to say what he would do, but great things are to be done: and I am to be a *skiff*

> Day & night and night & day
> Drifting on its dreary way

without rudder, compass, or pilot "& finally I am to be "a *hulk*", an ungraceful end but it is my doom."5

Like Claire Clairmont and Mary Shelley in earlier years, Caroline Norton found that she could not in the end take seriously Trelawny's mixture of impulsive passion, violence, and theatricality. His particular extreme of romanticism, however agreeable it might be as an occasional change from society manners, was simply unworkable in daily life. It was part of his tragedy that his relationships – especially with women – tended to go in the wrong direction. They did not grow and gain strength from small beginnings, but on the contrary Trelawny after an initial huge impact, was usually fated to go steadily downhill.

During these years of politics and high society his friendship with Mary Shelley came to an end. When he was in America he was still apparently writing her letters proposing marriage to which she – infuriatingly like Claire – now responded by giving him advice about other women who would be suitable. On his return he took to making remarks to her and to her friends which, in earlier years, might have passed as playful banter but which now caused deep hurt. 'Mary I have not seen', he wrote to Claire in November 1835, 'her disease grows upon her with years – I mean her pining after distinction and the distinguished of fortune.' In 1836 when old Godwin at last died Trelawny was amazed and uncomprehending when she decided against catching the market (and promoting the cause) with a biography of her famous father. By August 1838 Trelawny was telling Claire – with a stab at her reliance on Jefferson Hogg for advice and help on matters on which she used to turn to Trelawny – 'Mary is the blab of blabs, she lives on hogs wash – what utter failures most people are'.

At the end of 1837 the Philosophic Radicals introduced the *Custody of Infants Bill* which was designed to establish a right of access for mothers to see their children, irrespective of the married status or past behaviour of the mother. The proposed measure was a direct result of the Caroline Norton affair, for her husband – with the full backing of the law as it stood – had successfully prevented her from seeing her children on the grounds that she lost that right when she left him. The bill was debated in Parliament and in the reviews through much of 1838 with much polemic and counter-polemic on the rights of husbands and the wrongs of women.

Mary, it would appear, declined to lend her name to the campaign. She was a friend of Caroline's but the subject touched her personally in other ways. She recalled no doubt the disbarring of Shelley by the courts from access to his own children and the intense misery which Claire Clairmont had suffered for years in helpless attempts to reclaim her daughter Allegra from her hated former lover Lord Byron. Mary *ought* to have been sympathetic to the cause but she resented the presumption that she must necessarily share the views of the radicals in full. The daughter of William Godwin, the daughter of Mary Wollstonecraft, the widow of Percy Bysshe Shelley had opinions of her own which differed from those of her famous parents, whose names had hung so heavily round her personality from the moment of her birth. It was mainly Trelawny whom she had in mind in this passage when she wrote in her journal – conscious probably that it would one day be read – her self-justification of her refusal to join the cause: 'I have no wish to ally myself to the Radicals – they are full of repulsion to me. Violent without any sense of justice – selfish in the extreme – talking without knowledge – rude, envious and insolent – I wish to have nothing to do with them. It has been the fashion with these same friends to accuse me of worldliness.' Mary felt betrayed by Trelawny and he by her. Their paths diverged and, although they occasionally saw one another, their friendship was – as events turned out – never to be restored. That accusation of worldliness coming from Lady Blessington's prize literary lion must have struck her as particularly cruel and unfair.[6]

The famous friend of Lord Byron was dining out every night on his stories, and when Lady Blessington produced her book of Byron conversations at this time, she put into Byron's mouth a handsome eulogy on Trelawny's sterling qualities. As Claire Clairmont said years later. 'Trelawny made himself quite ridiculous when I lived in London I remember. He absolutely lived, or in any case dined out, on the strength of his acquaintance with Byron. It was always "Byron said this" "Byron did that".[7]

He seemed set to rival his former friend Tom Medwin who in 1824 had published his *Conversations with Lord Byron noted during a residence with his Lordship at Pisa in the Years 1821 and 1822*, one of the most successful and disliked examples of the *I-was-the-Great-Man's-Friend* genre, and Thackeray invented a Byron bore in *Pendennis* who is an amalgam of the two:

> Captain Sumph, an ex-beau still about town and related in some indistinct manner to Literature and the Peerage. He was said to have written a book once, to have been a friend of Lord Byron, to be related to Lord Sumphington; in fact anecdotes of Byron formed his staple and he seldom spoke but with the name of that poet or some of his contemporaries in his mouth, as thus 'I remember poor Shelley at school being sent up for good for a copy of verses, every line of which I wrote, by Jove,' or 'I recollect when I was at Missolonghi with Byron, offering to bet Gamba,' and so forth . . .
>
> 'I remember poor Byron, Hobhouse, Trelawney and myself, dining with Cardinal Mezzocaldo at Rome' Captain Sumph began 'and we had some Orvieto wine for dinner which Byron liked very much. And I remember how the Cardinal regretted that he was a single man.
>
> We went to Civita Vecchia two days afterwards where Byron's yacht was – and by Jove, the Cardinal died within three weeks; and Byron was very sorry for he rather liked him'.
>
> 'A devilish interesting story, Sumph indeed' Wagg said.
>
> 'You should publish some of those stories, Captain Sumph, you really should . . .'[8]

The author of the *Younger Son*, people thought, was perhaps Byron's natural successor. Everyone wanted to hear too the stories of the privateering days, and evening after evening he would tell again of his voyages with de Ruyter in the Eastern seas, his treks across the deserts of Arabia, his reminiscences of the Wahabee Wars.

Nobody apparently was shocked by his confessions of having deserted from the Royal Navy, fought for the French, sunk British ships, and murdered sundry unfortunates of many nationalities. The great war with Napoleon had now been over for twenty years, the treaties had long since been signed, the churches filled up with the appropriate marble monuments, and the admirals and generals had written their memoirs. People were no longer much interested in the issues, and many of Trelawny's audience had been children when the war ended.

But there were still people around who could expose him if they had the mind to, and many others who knew enough to cast the seeds of scepticism. Henry Crabb Robinson, for example, who met Trelawny at Lady Blessington's, tackled Walter Savage Landor:

'You know Trelawny?' 'Oh yes he is my friend.' 'I've heard he was either pirate or smuggler I forget which.' 'For the matter of that I dare say both' said Landor. But Robinson noticed that as Landor answered, he laughed, hinting that his answer was not to be taken seriously.[9]

Medwin was also a potential threat and a potential rival. 'A mesure-less and unprincipled liar.'[10] Trelawny had called him, and indeed in his book on Lord Byron, Medwin had contrived (drawing on Trelawny's manuscript account, errors and all) to give the impression that he had been present at the burning of Shelley's body although he had not in fact arrived until late that night after all was over.

In 1834, when Trelawny was in America, Medwin threw his dart of scepticism at Trelawny in his next book, *The Angler in Wales*:

> I was not at that time a great adept at the pistol [Medwin puts into the mouth of his character R–, who is intended to represent Daniel Roberts,] though I have since practised under Byron, and a more famous shot even than he, an extraordinary, perhaps one of the most extraordinary char-acters of the age, who accompanied him to Greece, whose life has been a tissue of adventures so rare and strange that compared with them reality becomes fiction, and the pictures drawn by the greatest novelists of our times, or of any times, seem pale, lifeless and inanimate copies.[11]

But Trelawny himself was immune to irony and his pretensions were not to be imperilled by such half-hearted assaults. He regarded Medwin with the contempt which the big-time swindler feels for the petty thief.

The ladies of Gore House did not read *The Angler in Wales*, nor would they have taken the point if they had. Like their predecessors, the blues of Pisa, they liked what they heard, they had no wish to disbelieve it, and they wanted more. Oh Captain Trelawny *do* write down some of those marvellous stories, they would insist. We *did* so enjoy the *Adventures of a Younger Son*.

In 1839 he obliged. He contributed a short story, *Sahib Tulwar, Master of the Sword*, to one of the annuals edited by Lady Blessington.

Trelawny and de Ruyter go on an expedition through the jungles of India high into the Himalayas, to meet the famous Indian swordsman Sahib Tulwar. The piece was signed 'By the author of the Younger Son', and a footnote on the first page about Sahib Tulwar insisted that 'Everything herein narrated with regard to this natural-born soldier is true'. It is perhaps a rejected chapter of the *Adventures of a Younger Son*. In the modern fashion Trelawny turned some of the left-overs from his book into an article:

> 'What are they' I said, taking hold of the end of a cord festooned to the tent lines on which some score of shrivelled, dark, odd-shaped things were strung, 'What the devil are they?'.
>
> 'They are the ears of those he has slain,' said De Ruyter, 'they are hanging out to dry. He has some infantine fancies: you observe he wears a massy pair of gold rings in his ears; he says he does so because the soldier brave enough to take his head shall be paid for his trouble.' We now entered the tent; we found the Sahib Tulwar attentively examining the various water-marks on a bundle of damask mettled folardee swords.
>
> 'I am picking out a weapon for that hawk-eyed boy!' said the Sahib Tulwar to De Ruyter; 'I am glad he is here,' gripping me cordially by the hand; 'I will give him a sword and show him how to crop heads as if they were corn cobs.'[12]

Sahib Tulwar is not an Indian but an American from beyond the Allegheny Mountains who joins the Company's service in India. He raises a mutiny and for many years hires himself to a succession of local rajahs, plundering, slaughtering, and burning in a ceaseless war against the British. Through mere restlessness he then takes advantage of an amnesty and joins the British service again, turning his ferocity again on his old comrades. Finally, he decides to go back to the United States. A party is arranged, there is heavy drinking, and Sahib Tulwar is persuaded to give a last display of his amazing horsemanship. He performs one wild trick after another urging his horse on to ever more dangerous feats until 'the maddened horse, overwrought, sprung into the air, and falling heavily (for his heart had burst) killed his bold rider with him'.

Like so many of Trelawny's stories, it is probably an imaginative extravaganza based on something more humdrum, in this case a quotation from a newspaper which had caught his attention and which he had copied into his notebook: 'The late Shakoor Tulwar Singh was shot with his two eldest sons some two months ago in an affair with

our troops – he was considered the ablest man in this part of India –
he was a restless and daring and untameable enemy of British power –
he fortified himself in his house, on his treason being discovered, and
fired on four company of sepoys – then tried to cut his way through
them – all there fell.'[13]

De Ruyter and Trelawny's last expedition together took place
within the blue and gilt silk covers of *Heath's Book of Beauty*, one of the
expensive annuals which, for a few years, it was customary for English
ladies to present to each other at Christmas. It was set among the
engraved portraits of the society beauties of the year, the Viscountess
Powerscourt, The Lady Wilhelmina Stanhope, The Lady Fanny
Cowper, and Miss Cockayne. On one side of the great hero stand
verses *On Seeing a Woodbine growing round a Tree Struck by Lightning in
Shere Wood* by Mrs Torre Holme. Not far away are the lines *On Presenting
a Young Invalid with a Bunch of Early Violets* by Miss Theodosia Garrow.
The corsair who had bammed and shocked the blues was now their
prisoner. He had become a blue himself, a blue who wore trousers and
had a hairy face.

Suddenly in 1839, as in 1832, he disappeared without warning from
London. His smart friends asked one another, what has happened to
Captain Trelawny? He had vanished. Soon the hostesses had found
new celebrities and Trelawny was forgotten. Another phase of his long
life was over.

22

A Long Retirement

> Breakfast bread cheese and apples watercresses and cold water –
> diner at one meat and pudding and water – supper at 7 cheese and
> coffee – to bed at 11 – smoke four pipes a day bathe every morn-
> ing – ride walk and work read in the intervals seldom see any one
> except family – they to are always well and live much in the same
> way . . . and such is the autumn or winter I suppose one may call
> it of life.
>
> *From a letter to Seymour Kirkup,*
> *24 March 1854 from Usk.*[1]

It appeared to be just another of those sudden upsets in his life which
were characteristic of the man. He had been a dandy, a playboy, a lion
of the salons. Well, of course, everyone who knew him thought he must
obviously now want to be the opposite. He moved out of his lodgings
in Duke Street, St James's and installed himself in a large villa on
Putney Hill belonging to John Temple Leader, one of his radical
political friends, who was immensely rich and had two large houses on
Putney Hill besides one in Eaton Square in Westminster. Since Leader
was away a great deal Trelawny had the use of the Upper House in
Putney, with its complement of servants and gardeners, virtually to
himself.

Lady Blessington wrote to tell Walter Savage Landor of the sudden
change in his way of life: 'I had a letter from Mr Trelawny who has
taken to lead the life of a recluse in a villa in Putney never going to see
a single acquaintance or friend and scarcely ever visiting London.'[2]
Landor confirmed in his reply that Trelawny had decided to withdraw
from society: 'I am not surprised at hearing that Trelawny has retired
from society. He possesses a strong and philosophical mind and we
have only the choice of living quite alone or with scoundrels. He might
perhaps have taken the alternative if there had been any genius or even
any pleasantry. I could well be content in solitude as deep in his. . . .'[3]

Occasional reports, reaching London from Putney stressed that he
was tousled and dirty. He had been seen digging or cutting down

trees. He had, it was said, gone back to nature, to the simple life. He ate only vegetables (had not Shelley been a vegetarian?) and proclaimed that hot food was unhealthy. He decided never again to wear stockings or underwear. Whatever the weather he never wore an overcoat, and on his occasional visits to London – he always walked – he could be found standing steaming in front of the fire at the Athenaeum or the Reform Club.

The young blade who could drink everyone under the table now became a strict and ostentatious teetotaller. The great hunter who had gleefully slaughtered the tigers of India and the orang-outangs of Borneo now refused to allow the birds in the garden to be harmed, an astonishing concept to Victorians. Characteristically, when men with guns asked permission to shoot the birds, he told them to go away and shoot one another. The intrepid swimmer who had braved the surf at Madras and the whirlpools of Niagara now took a daily splash in Leader's garden pond.

The real reason why he had moved to Putney, which was known to very few people, was to be with Augusta Goring. They had eloped together. Trelawny might be living with Temple Leader in the big house on Putney Hill and have his mail sent there, but he went every day to see Augusta.

Trelawny's involvement with Augusta Goring was probably the most satisfying relationship of his long life. She was a friend of Mary Shelley and was already separated from her husband, the heir to a baronetcy, when she met Trelawny in 1838, and she caused some scandal by visiting him at his chambers in Duke Street. In August 1838, in order to be with him, she moved to a cottage on Barnes Common, and then, in the spring of 1839, to Farm Cottage on the Upper Richmond Road near Putney. The cottage belonged to Temple Leader and was separated from the house where Trelawny lived by a field which was also owned by Temple Leader. Every day Trelawny would come and spend the day with her and sometimes, when Temple Leader was away, she would stay with him at Upper House.

Their life together in Putney was a strange mixture of open de-fiance of society on the one hand and shame-faced furtiveness on the other. Augusta pretended that her name was Mrs Granby but the servants noticed that she signed her cheques Augusta Goring. They also noticed the name Goring on the name-tabs on her clothes although she later cut them off. When she gave birth to a son on 5 August 1839 she falsely registered him as John Granby, giving her name as Ann Granby and the father's name as John Granby, merchant, her husband.

The sixteen-year-old servant girl Emily Mackenzie, who was employed to help Augusta with the baby, later described how the baby's father behaved on his daily visits:

> I always had a great dislike of going into the room when Mr Trelawny was there – and I used to avoid doing so as long as I could in the hope that he would leave before it was absolutely necessary that the baby should go to Mrs Granby, and at those times I used to wait and watch Mr Trelawny going away before I went in for Mrs Granby. . . . The blinds of the room were almost always down whilst Mr Trelawny was there and I have seen him myself pull them down. He used almost always to do so as soon as he came – to shut out the sun, as he said. He used to say it drew the paper.

They could not go on like that for long. In 1840 Harry Goring, Augusta's estranged husband, sent agents to Putney and collected a mass of evidence from servants and others about every intimate detail of their life together. A petition for divorce was presented, and, for the third time in his life, Trelawny's name was dragged through the matrimonial courts. But if he and Augusta had tried to compromise with society's conventions beforehand, the divorce – which was granted to Harry Goring in 1841 – acted as a release. They decided to marry.

By the terms of his inheritance Trelawny was permitted, with the consent of his trustees, to convert part of the capital which he was not allowed to touch from government bonds to land, and he decided to take advantage of this and settle down to the life of a farmer and country gentleman. The place he chose was Usk, a small country town in Monmouthshire, selected for no other apparent reason than that he had liked it when he had once passed through on a visit.

Yet Usk, he intended from the first, was not to be just another phase of a restless life, but a permanent home. With his family he moved into a house in the town – where a daughter Laetitia was born – but soon afterwards he bought a spectacular site on a cliff outside the town, on which a Roman fort had once stood, and built his own house. The Cot or The Prospect, as he called it, is solidly Victorian and comfortable, with wide windows – like widow's walks – and interesting views in several directions. At the foot of the cliff stands a small church, and Trelawny planted the area with trees, including a fine row of cedars in the churchyard grown from cones brought from the Protestant Cemetery at Rome.[4]

After a time the Cot became too small for his growing family and he took over the house and estate of Cefn Ila which lies on high ground a mile or two from Usk. The farm consisted of 440 acres, and the house was large without being grand. Among other delights it contained Trelawny's library of over a thousand books.

Augusta and he had three children, Edgar, who had been born at Putney as 'John Granby', Laetitia, and Frank. They grew up happily at Usk and the family's occasional eccentricities – such as nude bathing – were considered harmless enough by the villagers. Sometimes his daughter Zella, now Mrs Olguin, would pay a visit from Italy, and the locals would point out this romantic lady, who had been conceived in a cavern on Mount Parnassus, flouncing her way unconcernedly along the river bank, fishing rod in hand, her lace and silk petticoats tearing in the brambles.

Trelawny was a favourite among the children of the village although the younger ones were said to have been frightened by his loud voice and overpowering presence. One of Laetitia's friends was given a pistol when she came to visit, and was told to fire if off on her way home as a signal that she had reached the other side of the wood in safety. When another girl, the daughter of a local solicitor, complained that her long curls were getting in the way, Trelawny simply cut them off and sent her back to her mother without a word of explanation or apology. Liberty, Trelawny believed, should be available to children and when parents became angry with him, he only laughed.

On Sunday mornings the villagers on their way to church would usually see him ostentatiously at work; but in the afternoons the old atheist, the scourge of the existing order, the despiser of established authority, would take tea in large handleless bowls – perhaps the very ones brought from the cave – with his three best friends at Usk, the local doctor, the local lawyer and the local parson. He was always ready with his stories of seafaring days and his stories of Lord Byron, always ready to give his audience what they wanted. 'I often met him whilst in search of botanical specimens on his grounds [wrote J. H. Clark, the historian of Monmouthshire] and he frequently asked me to the house to have a chat and smoke a pipe with him . . . Mr Trelawny gave me a nice assortment of shrubs to plant alongside the conifer path which Mr Dunn and I were at that moment farming on the untidy piece of waste ground adjoining the garden of the Beaufort Arms Inn which formed the approach to the brick wall used for Five Courts in times past . . . He also gave me Lord Byron's ruler and a book "The Tale of a Tub" which had been presented to the poet by Hobhouse, as memorials.'

He was fifty when he married Augusta and went to live at Usk, and he stayed there for a dozen years, the longest period he ever remained settled in one place except when in extreme old age. He dug in his garden, he built walls and outhouses, he cut down trees, he planted trees. He had been lonely and although his secret appeared to be safe, yet the burden of being a sham had weighed heavily on him. Was he really believed, he must sometimes have wondered, or were people quietly making a fool of him? Was the bammer himself being bammed? Did that occasional smile or wink imply scepticism? What were his friends saying about him behind his back? Would his mother let him down by letting slip some chance remark which would be reported back? Now with Augusta he could relax and, if the phrase has any meaning when applied to Trelawny, be himself. In middle age he seemed to have achieved the peace of mind that had eluded him all his life. Ambition had gone, the fear of exposure was remote. It was not an exciting life, but it was a satisfying one.

And so life went on, summer and winter, seed-time and harvest. He and Augusta worked hard at farming, made it pay, and apparently enjoyed themselves, and Trelawny earned a reputation as a good employer. Once a year he went to London by the new railway for a month but for the most part he was content to stay at home.

In 1848 Mary Shelley was visiting the region and apparently it came as a surprise to her to learn that the Trelawnys lived nearby – so complete had been the break ten years before. Later she paid them a visit at Usk and corresponded again with Augusta until a few months before her death in 1851, but the friendship with Trelawny was never restored. In 1857 news arrived that an even older friend, Augusta White, with whom he had shared his crisis of 1817 was coming to England from her home in Canada for a visit. The railway from Milford Haven where she would arrive from Ireland passed within eleven miles of Trelawny's house, and he wrote eagerly to invite her: 'As to our short meeting on this small isle – how could you dream of such a thing, you my earliest oldest and most attached friend – from the first we understood each other, and in age memory is constantly reverting to the past, our sympathy is now stronger than ever – our friendship passed through severe trials and grew stronger, don't let it fly now – your principal duty is to see me, I shall not rest until we meet.'[5] They apparently spent some time together, but by the end of the summer she had returned to Canada.

After so many years at Usk, Trelawny seemed set to live out his days there, content with the life and reputation of an eccentric country gentleman. Yet, despite appearances, the essential man was unchanged. For all Augusta's patient handling, he remained wild and unpredictable. Sometime about 1857, when he was sixty-five, the final crisis occurred. He was engaged in writing a second book, his reminiscences of Shelley and Byron, which he had decided to publish at his own expense, and maybe the remembrance of these days long past set his imagination racing again. Or maybe the experience of meeting Augusta White again recalled the days of his youth when the blaze of literature had dazzled him like an Indian sunrise. A couple of his letters of 1857 are signed J. E. Trelawny instead of E. J. – perhaps the unconscious flicker of his old restlessness which had so often in the past marked a change of life with a change of name.[6]

Suddenly he brought a young woman to the house at Usk and installed her as his mistress. Little is known about Miss B, even her name cannot now be discovered, but the stories of Trelawny carrying her in his arms up the rocks of Usk like Samson with Delilah, suggest that she was the latest of a long line of teenage girls who each for a time irresistibly personified the Byronic heroine of his dreams. Forty years after he had first intoxicated himself on *The Corsair*, he had succumbed again to his old addiction.

For Augusta, patient and tolerant though she must have been, it was too much. She refused to have Miss B in the house. Trelawny insisted. The marriage broke up, Augusta went to live in Italy, and the house, the farm, the furniture and the thousand books were sold.[7] In 1858 Trelawny quitted Wales to return to London with Miss B as his common law wife. It was just at the time when his own book was published and for the second time in his long life he found himself famous.

23

The Friend of Shelley

When he speaks of the poet there is something like tenderness in his accents, something verging on reverence in his looks. The customary formulas of social intercourse are an abomination in his sight. Woe for you if, on first seeing him, you should unfortunately say 'How do you do, Mr Trelawny?'. He will if not rebuke merely grunt out a reply and look as if he thought you a fool. He gives no small change of conversation; every word he utters is stamped with his personality – a personality so powerful that it overtops everything he can say or do . . . He will begin speaking quite abruptly as if only continuing aloud some previous train of thought. 'What' he growled 'is all that rubbish that Symonds writes about Shelley being too beautiful to paint?'

Mathilde Blind who interviewed Trelawny
for the Whitehall Review.[1]

Trelawny's *Recollections of the Last Days of Shelley and Byron* will be read as long as the world is interested in Shelley and Byron, and that promises to be a long time. It is written in the grand manner and all the characters and events have a larger-than-life quality about them. Much of the book is a relating of conversations in which Trelawny had taken part with Shelley and Byron, not real conversations but scraps of anecdote, real memory, and invention worked into a carefully rounded dramatic narrative. Trelawny had the gift of being able to make his subjects appear alive and convincing although many of the details may be inaccurate.

The book begins in Switzerland where Trelawny first hears the name of Shelley and meets Williams and Medwin. It plunges straight in and within a few pages we are at Pisa on that memorable day 14 January 1822 when he is introduced to Shelley, and then the next day to Byron. We have the story of the Pisa circle, the drowning and cremation of Shelley and Williams, the expedition of Byron and Trelawny to Greece, the death of Byron, and the cave. The book ends with the assassination attempt and Trelawny's removal to the Ionian

Islands in 1825. No doubt it is, in essentials, the book about Shelley which Trelawny wanted to write in 1829 when he was prevented by Mary.

But the poet's reputation had suffered more than one sea-change since his death thirty-six years before. In 1822 when the news first reached England, the *Courier* had reported 'Shelley the writer of some infidel poetry has been drowned; *now* he knows whether there is a God or no'.[2] The general judgement of his contemporaries at that time had been that Shelley was a violent revolutionary, a man of loose sexual morals, a destroyer of family life, an attacker of the rights of property, a blasphemer against God, an ungrateful son, and traitor to his class. For twenty years after the poet's death, his father, Sir Timothy Shelley, had done his best to suppress the memory of the unfortunate son who had brought disgrace on the family name.

Although Sir Timothy had agreed to pay Mary a small allowance after her return to England in 1823, one of his main motives was to use the threat of withdrawal as a means of preventing Mary from publishing anything biographical about his son. Each year hopes rose that the snows of winter would carry him off, but the old man who was forty when Shelley was born and nearly seventy when he died, did not finally quit the scene until 1844 at the age of ninety. Despite his efforts, however, interest continued to grow. Shelley's poetry was increasingly admired, and in 1839 Mary – with the consent of the family – published a collection which she herself edited.

When Trelawny received his copy of the book he sent it back to Edward Moxon, the publisher, in a rage. He had become increasingly irritated with Mary and they had quarrelled the previous year over her failure to help the Radicals. It still rankled that she had refused to help him to write about Shelley in 1829 out of fear of the Shelley family, although she had opened herself liberally to the fashionable Thomas Moore for his biography of Byron – and Moore was not even sympathetic to Shelley. But Mary's edition of Shelley's *Collected Works* in 1839 shocked him more than anything she had ever said or done, for Mary, it seemed, had deliberately left out some of the notes to *Queen Mab*, notably those which attacked the evils of organised religion, as well as the dedication to Shelley's first wife Harriet.

The assemblies who had demanded reform and social justice in the great protests of the 1820's had carried quotations from *Queen Mab* on their banners. It was Shelley's most influential work, circulating widely in cheap pirated editions among the disenfranchised. Shelley was a political poet. He wanted to change the world. It had been *Queen Mab* that first aroused Trelawny's interest in Shelley and articulated his own views. It was *Queen Mab* more than any other work which caused Shelley to be held in such detestation in his lifetime. It had been composed in verse in an attempt to escape prosecution for sedition and blasphemy. The notes were of the essence – they provided the justification for the political theory and the poem was a hook on which to hang the notes. Now Mary, it seemed, was censoring her husband's works. It was bad enough that she should accept money from Shelley's family, but to presume to meddle with the dead Shelley's works, that was the final betrayal.

In fact, Mary was misjudged – at least as far as the notes to *Queen Mab* are concerned, if not about the dedication. Shelley himself had regretted some of his comments and Mary's edition was perhaps more in line with his mature thinking than the original text. Besides, *Queen Mab*, even without the full notes, was still technically liable to prosecution, as was to be shown by an action against its publisher Moxon in 1841 for 'seditious and blasphemous libel'. Henry Hetherington, who had been hounded by the authorities using the libel laws to suppress his pamphlets, argued that if he were prosecuted for publishing cheap blasphemy, Moxon should be prosecuted for publishing expensive blasphemy – but the case was never called.

But although Trelawny was unfair to Mary over this matter – he broke with her and their friendship was never to be restored – he was right in a more general sense. Mary had gone over to the enemy. She contrived to get the best of both worlds. She enjoyed and exploited her role as the widow of an increasingly famous poet, and at the same time she was a conformist to the very values that Shelley detested. As Trelawny remarked when he publicly insulted her memory in 1878, she went to church even on weekdays. And she devoted her life to bringing up Shelley's son Percy Florence to be like his grandfather rather than his father.

By her efforts the detestable atheist was to be turned into the divine poet and the sting taken out of his message as a result, and the process was well under way at the time of her death in 1851. After her death, Lady Shelley, the wife of the poet's son, Sir Percy, and a passionate admirer of Mary, took charge of the arrangements and carried them through with thoroughness and efficiency and a fine perception of the psychology of religious forms. A shrine was created at Boscombe Manor, the family home. The domed ceiling was turquoise set with gold stars. Silk curtains hung over the entrance and a red lamp was kept burning inside. Visitors, even ladies, were expected to take off their hats as they entered, and children of the family were expected to cry. A great marble statue group was commissioned as the centre-piece. It represented Mary Shelley supporting the (nearly) naked corpse of the drowned Shelley. It is a Pietà with Shelley as Jesus and Mary as the Virgin. Within the shrine relics were displayed: Shelley's rattle, manuscripts of his poems and letters, locks of his hair set in ornate reliquaries, and most important of all, his heart, the heart which Trelawny had snatched from the fire and which Mary had kept for many years, like a crumbling lavender bag, wrapped with a copy of *Adonais* in a silk-lined box. There were also relics of the disciples, including a portrait and some hair of Edward John Trelawny.

Devotees were discouraged from reading such regrettable stuff as the poet's major works: much better if they concentrate on *To a Skylark* and read suitably edited selections produced, like prayer-books, in elegant gift-market-orientated editions with limp leather or vellum covers. The time was soon to come when a clergyman of the Church of England would read a paper to the Shelley Society proving that Shelley was a Christian. Forged letters appeared in the market and the number of pieces of true bone snatched from the fire continued to rise so that sometimes one wonders if any of poor Shelley's body was cremated on that famous day in Viareggio. The only known portrait was reproduced in innumerable representations throughout the century, becoming more etherial and more epicene at each transformation, but there was a ceaseless quest to find other likenesses until one editor in despair used Leonardo da Vinci's head of Christ as a portrait of Shelley, and it was published as such by Oxford University Press.

The lack of any biography of Shelley was a constant difficulty. It had been Mary Shelley's hope that Leigh Hunt would write it, but his first outline, published in 1828 in his sneering *Lord Byron and some of His Contemporaries* was thin and unsatisfactory. As long as there was no authoritative life, embarrassing stories about Shelley kept being repeated which it was difficult to counter. In 1847 Medwin, who had written his best-seller about Byron in 1824 and a series of articles about Shelley in 1832, appeared again on the scene with a proposed life. He had been digging around in the public records and discovered some of the facts surrounding Shelley's first marriage with Harriet. When pressure to withdraw was applied by the family, he wrote to Mary demanding £250 in compensation for suppressing his work, and although he was not paid and his book did not in the end contain much that was damaging, it was a near-run thing. If there was an aspect of Shelley on which the new orthodox feared heresy more than his atheism, it was his attitude to love.

In 1856 – when Mary had been dead for five years – Lady Shelley decided that the time had come for the long-delayed biography to be written. The circle of people who had known Shelley was growing smaller all the time, those who were left were now old, and some of them were failing. If she did not act soon, many details of the poet's life would be lost for ever. Apart from Claire Clairmont, far away in Italy, and Medwin and Leigh Hunt, who were out of favour, there were only Jefferson Hogg, Thomas Love Peacock, and Trelawny. Lady Shelley, like a professor organising a seminar, invited the three survivors to Boscombe to exchange their reminiscences and Sir Percy Florence Shelley, the poet's son, her husband, made the journey to Usk to talk to Trelawny. But Trelawny was immune to her blandishments. His answer, dated February 1857, was polite but decisive:

> To assemble together under your roof three of the Poets old friends to tell their storeys is a pleasant dream. It is something similar to the plot of Bocacio's Decameron, but the Italian takes care to have youth and summer w[eathe]r.
>
> I told Percy when he was here that I was too old and selfish to leave my den. In my youth I railed at age as hard and crabbed and so I find it.
>
> I dont believe that either of the men you have mentioned will do what you wish. Indolence and excessive sensitiveness to public opinion will prevent it – as it has already done.[3]

But although Trelawny would not co-operate with Lady Shelley, his interest was reawakened. He wrote to Claire Clairmont and Daniel Roberts in Italy to ask them for their reminiscences of Shelley, he looked out his notes, and started to write his own book.

Lady Shelley pinned her hopes on Thomas Jefferson Hogg who had known Shelley since his Oxford days and been indisputably his best friend during the early part of his life. As an added advantage, he had been living with Jane Williams for many years. Hogg was given access to the papers in the possession of the Shelley family and began work on what was to be a four-volume standard biography. But when the first two volumes appeared in print in 1858, Lady Shelley was shocked and horrified, legal action was threatened against Hogg and all further access to the papers was immediately stopped. The Shelley whom Hogg had produced was not the Divine Poet of his dedication, but the rumbustious and comic friend of his Oxford days. The manuscript of the suppressed third volume – which probably contained revelations about Hogg's own love affair with Mary – has never been found.

Hogg, it also turned out, had taken liberties with the documents – 'editing' them unscrupulously to alter the sense, but that aspect of his methods would not have unduly worried Lady Shelley. She used fire and scissors to remove uncomfortable facts from the record and retained Richard Garnett of the British Museum – later Keeper of Printed Books – to give her professional advice on which documents should be mutilated and which destroyed.[4]

To fill the gap left by Hogg's apostasy, Garnett was hired to put together a book which appeared in 1859 under Lady Shelley's name as *Shelley Memorials*. Peacock too was at last persuaded to write down a few respectful reminiscences, and another author, Charles Middleton, who had never known the poet but who had been working away at the sources for five years, also published his biography. But when the *Recollections of the Last Days of Shelley and Byron* was published it was at once recognised as the best. Trelawny stood out as the only true and honest friend of Shelley among the turncoats, the time-servers, and the idolators. Overnight he became the chief expert on Shelley and remained so for the rest of his life. An enterprising publisher brought out a new edition of the *Adventures of a Younger Son*,[5] and Captain Trelawny the literary lion of 1832, was again the centre of attention. He bought a beautiful house at Brompton and decided to enjoy his fame.

He was approaching seventy but still as alert and vigorous as ever, and as one by one the last of Shelley's friends died off, Leigh Hunt in 1859, Hogg in 1862, Peacock in 1866, Medwin in 1869, Trelawny was left in magnificent isolation, a proud survivor from the age of giants.

The London of the 1860s and 1870s to which he now returned was very different from the London of the 1830s. Trafalgar and Waterloo were remote memories. If anyone talked of the war, it was of the Crimea. The age of High Victorianism, earnest Christianity, and Imperial Duty, was far removed from the coarse but fun-loving Regency of Trelawny's youth. The flashy young novelist with the Jewish name, who had been making a reputation for himself when

Trelawny was last in society had climbed the greasy pole to be Prime Minister of England.

When the *Adventures of a Younger Son* came out in 1831 nobody had been much concerned at Trelawny's confessions of murder, piracy, plunder, theft, desertion, treason, mutiny and all the other crimes he persuaded the world that he committed. When he returned to fame, public attitudes had altered. Victorians could hardly be expected to take the same attitude to these matters as their fathers and grandfathers. But in fact no protests were ever made, and Trelawny was even accorded the honour, although of course he did not regard it as such, of being introduced again to Mr Disraeli. The English had already adopted the lazy habit of according respect to the ancient no matter how horrible their crimes in the past.

The Victorians were much more shocked by a very different confession which Trelawny made in the *Recollections* which caused a roar of indignation that was to reverberate to the end of Trelawny's life and follow him for at least two generations afterwards. Like the outrages he committed with de Ruyter, it may not even be true. It is said to have happened at Missolonghi where Trelawny arrived three days after Byron's death in April 1824. When Fletcher, Byron's valet, showed him into the room where the shrouded body of the poet lay, Trelawny sent him out of the room to fetch a glass of water and then lifted the shroud to look at Byron's feet. Which foot, he had wondered, was the withered one that had so affected the course of Byron's life and character? The left or the right? On inspection Trelawny found that *both* feet were malformed! When his *Recollections* appeared with this story in 1858 the world was scandalised at Trelawny's lack of respect towards the body of his friend and even his warmest friends declined to defend him. It is an incident to give pause to anyone who thinks he understands Victorian morals and Victorian public attitudes. A murderer they could accept, but not a cad.

The ladies at Lady Blessington's in the 1830s had been simultaneously shocked and thrilled at his rough manners and unconventional ways. Now it was their children who were the hostesses but their reaction was the same. And of course the more they accorded admiration to his eccentricities, the more he cultivated them. One of his favourite habits, noted by almost everyone who met him over half a century, was to interrupt the small talk of polite conversation with a cry of 'Lies'. This trick usually succeeded in putting a tactful enquirer off his stride. It also, apparently, was of great help in building up Trelawny's reputation for sincerity.

On one occasion when he was staying at a friend's country house, he failed to appear at dinner. A servant was sent to look for him in his room but he could not be found anywhere. At last the butler reported that he had seen Trelawny take his suitcase and leave for the railway station without saying a word. The butler also noted that 'he was sitting in the afternoon in the lake up to his neck in water reading a book, and he remained there until dusk'.[6]

The new generation of poets and writers were delighted at his displays of character. They were passionately interested in Shelley and eager to learn any new detail about him:

> Ah did you once see Shelley plain,
> And did he stop and speak to you.

So wrote Robert Browning. When Trelawny started telling his stories it was like a voice from another age. Browning had made a point of going to see Trelawny when they were both in Italy in 1844 to ask him about Shelley. It so happened that Trelawny was at last having the Java bullet removed from his knee and Browning watched Trelawny ignoring the excruciating pain of the surgeon's probes as unconcernedly as if he were having his hair cut.[7]

His stories of Shelley and Byron were well worth hearing. Trelawny had a tolerable memory for this period of his life. He had notes, he had documents, he had other accounts on which to draw. It is worth emphasising, however, how remote and limited his direct experience was. His acquaintanceship with Shelley and Byron was roughly six months and eighteen months respectively, a tiny part of his long life and a tiny part of their short lives. But of course his audience was not content to hear the same stories of the *Recollections* reported again and again. They wanted more. He was alive therefore he was the expert, overriding all other evidence. Trelawny had been *there* therefore he must know; he must carry the answers to all the unsolved questions about his great friends. Many an old man with a greater natural commitment to the objective truth than Trelawny has wavered in those circumstances. An opportunity to rewrite history is a bribe that few can refuse.

Trelawny pushed his own judgement unscrupulously. Lord Byron, he now knew, had laughed at him behind his back. Now he had his revenge. He would tell how the poet with his hundreds of thousands was so mean with his money that he could not spare the travel fare to Mary Shelley in her distress. He could recount Byron's shilly-shallying in the Ionian Islands and in Greece, his lack of judgement, his jealousy, his pride of rank. Byron could not box well; he was not even a very good swimmer. It was easy to contrast him with Shelley whom everybody liked; with Shelley, the spirit – everyone called Shelley a spirit.

For over twenty years after he had published his *Recollections* Trelawny told his stories. With each passing year his opinions became more set, his stories more elaborate. At each telling Edward John Trelawny took a step nearer the centre of the stage, and he was ready with a forthright opinion on any aspect. 'Did Shelley ever shut himself up to write?' a polite journalist asked. 'Shut himself up!' Trelawny shouted indignantly 'Never! He wrote his poems in the open air; on the sea shore; the pine woods; and like a shepherd, he could tell the time of day exactly by the light. He never had a watch. And I think Byron never had; but if he had one, he never wore it.'[8]

Trelawny knew all about the relationship between Shelley and his first wife Harriet, despite the fact that she had died years before Trelawny met Shelley, and he set himself up as a champion of her reputation against the insinuations of Lady Shelley. He had vital documents, he would say, which could not be published until after his death which would make the whole matter clear. Trelawny knew, too, all about the reasons for Byron's separation from Lady Byron and the paternity of Medora Leigh. Here too he insisted that he was not at liberty to speak but he did in fact say, for what it is worth, that Byron was not the father of Medora but that Lady Byron believed he was.

He much preferred talking about Shelley, shocking his Victorian visitors with his disparaging remarks about contemporary favourites like Tennyson and Browning. 'You are interested in Shelley' he said as soon as one visitor entered the room. 'He was our greatest poet since Shakespeare. And he would not have been the poet he was if he had not been an Atheist'. The visitor noted the evident relish with which he pronounced the word 'Atheist'.[9]

Theodore Watts–Dunton who had rescued Algernon Charles Swinburne from the delights of drunkenness and flagellation at Maida Vale took his protégé to meet the man who had snatched Shelley's heart from the flames. As Watts-Dunton's son reported, his father was not impressed:

> He once summed up Trelawny's personality in two words 'an opinion-ated, vain man, who lived on his reputation as the finder of Shelley's body on the shore in the Bay of Spezia. And then he would relate, as an illustration of the 'Corsair's' marvellous vitality, how, when Swinburne and he one day called upon him in his eightieth year, Trelawny was so violent, not to say obstreperous, that he got into a heated discussion upon some subject connected with Shelley, and thumped the table with such energy that Watts-Dunton began to fear the consequences not only to the furniture and himself, but to his housemate as well.[10]

But Swinburne himself enjoyed every practised Trelawny gesture and was still telling his friends about him months later:

> Always energetic, whenever he speaks of Shelley the especial energy of his affection is really beautiful and admirable to see. There is some fresh air in England yet while such an Englishman is alive. . . .
>
> The present piratical old hero calls me the last of the poets who he thought all died with Byron. To hear him speak of Shelley is most beautiful and touching; at that name his voice (usually that of an old sea-king as he is) *always* changes and softens unconsciously. 'There' he said to me 'was the very Best of men and he was treated as the very Worst.' He professes fierce general misanthropy but is as ardent a republican (*and* atheist) as Shelley was at twenty; a magnificent old Viking to look at.[11]

In 1878, with the help of William Michael Rossetti, Trelawny corresponded with the French painter Gérôme who was engaged on a picture of the cremation of Shelley. Apparently he could remember every detail with absolute precision:

> The iron stand on which the furnace rested was two feet high, the furnace was two feet, making four feet above the ground; and the logs of wood were round. The furnace was five feet long and two feet broad . . .
>
> In the noonday heat in southern climes, all living things but the human seek the shade; in August when Shelley was burnt, the only exception to this was a solitary sea gull attracted by the burning flesh, he hovered a long time above the fire to scare us and satisfy his appetite . . .
>
> I was in my shirt sleeves with nothing on besides white trousers and a cap – Byron in white trousers, a black coat, and a dark blue velvet cap with a gold band round it . . .[12]

But the French had their own ideas about how the cremation of Shelley ought to have looked. The picture, as finished by Gérôme's pupil Fournier, transferred the scene to the symbolically more satisfactory season of winter. Leigh Hunt was brought out of his carriage – to his everlasting embarrassment he had not bothered to witness the actual cremation. Mary Shelley – who was not present – kneels reverentially in a corner and the poet himself has not suffered much in appearance from ten days in the sea followed by twenty-nine days burial in quick lime.

It was William Michael Rossetti who, in 1878 when Trelawny was eighty-six, persuaded him to reissue his book including stories that had not been in the *Recollections*. The result was *Records of Shelley, Byron, and the Author*, a harsher and less balanced book than its predecessor, full of spite and malice and unfair judgements, some of which may have been inserted by Rossetti in the editing since they are not in Trelawny's manuscript notes. He took every opportunity to run down Byron at the expense of Shelley and he was bitterly untruthful and unfair to Mary.

The change of title is significant. It was no longer a book about Shelley and Byron but about Shelley and Byron and Trelawny. By sheer longevity, he had pulled himself up into the ranks of the great romantics. He had patronised the dead for fifty years and this was his reward. Even the detested and pathetic Medwin recognized it, sycophantic to the last. When he died in 1869 his memorial at Horsham recorded as his greatest achievement:

HE WAS A FRIEND AND COMPANION OF
BYRON, SHELLEY, AND TRELAWNY.

Trelawny and Medwin competed for the title of the biggest Byron and Shelley bore in the London of the 1830s. They had each written Byron and Shelley books which exaggerate their own roles while avoiding all but the most indispensable reference to the existence of the other. But Medwin, who once thought his poems were as good as those of his cousin Bysshe, did not have the stamina of Trelawny, and in the end he capitulated. Nobody ever thought of putting HE WAS A FRIEND OF MEDWIN on a tombstone.

When Lady Shelley read the *Records* with its unkind remarks about Mary Shelley she delivered an ultimatum, threatening to excommunicate Trelawny by removing his relics from the Shelley shrine at Boscombe:

The memorial to Shelley
erected at Boscombe by
Lady Shelley

The only known portrait of Shelley, by Amelia Curran and a Victorian engraving of it

This same room is never entered but by kindred feet, or by those in whose hearts Shelley lives – amongst other things in it, there is a glass case containing locks of hair – They belong to those he and Mary valued as friends and with whom they had been most closely associated; Leigh Hunt – Byron – Edward Williams and one marked 'Trelawny 1822', it is black as jet and was given no doubt at the time when Mary possessed in the giver a true and generous friend. But the Trelawny of those days, where is he? Alas! that the snows of age should not only have fallen on his head but should have frozen the heart that beat so warmly in 1822 – There was a picture too – the only one allowed to hang in the same room with those sacred to us – again 'Edward Trelawny'. Hitherto these objects have been cherished under the roof of Shelley and Mary's son, but the time has come when we must ask you whether they have any right to retain their place.[13]

Lady Shelley removed the relics, destroyed some of Trelawny's letters, and clipped off pieces from others with her censorial scissors. But the arch-mythologiser had met her match. Trelawny's place in literary history as the friend of Shelley had long since become unassailable.

24

The Storyteller Part 2

It is a matter beyond dispute that Trelawny was one whose con-
stitutional fearlessness and unimpeachable honour, in every cir-
cumstance of a stirring life, raised him on a pinnacle beyond the
reach of detraction. His masterful bearing and unflinching
honesty compelled respect wherever he went.

Richard Edgcumbe, who knew
Trelawny in old age.

During his earlier years Trelawny knew he was being untruthful and
he lived in fear of being found out, but for his later years it is harder to
be sure. Even when he talked about his Arab bride Zela and his adventures with de Ruyter, it is doubtful whether he was still conscious
that the events he described with such gusto had occurred only in his
imagination. Over the decades his romanticism had eaten away at his
discriminatory faculties like some slow-working disease until he could
no longer distinguish genuine memory from fantasy. He achieved the
ultimate triumph of the impostor – he successfully deceived himself.

Yet surely even in his seventies and eighties there were many
occasions when Trelawny was repeating his old trick of telling deliberate conscious lies out of a straightforward wish to impress, or bam,
or to upstage the rest of the company. The process of self-deception is
not instantaneous even in so practised a performer as the old Trelawny,
and some of his stories were so tall that it would have taken another
lifetime to make them true.

*   *   *   *   *

When one of his admirers, Richard Edgcumbe, remarked that he
was surprised that Trelawny's remarkable career had not been written
down, Trelawny's eyes flashed and he turned on him. 'It *has* been written.
Have you not read the *Younger Son*?" The visitor nodded. 'Well what
more do you want?' On other occasions, Edgcumbe records, Trelawny
loved to expatiate on the many instances of de Ruyter's heroism and
fidelity. 'There never was another like him and never will be', he said
one day, and Edgcumbe noted 'I knew that he meant it'.

William Michael Rossetti was not as uncritical as Edgcumbe, and Trelawny confided to him that, although the famous privateer really had existed, de Ruyter was not his real name. On another occasion, however, Rossetti noted in his diary, someone asked Trelawny's permission to bring out a new edition of the *Younger Son* and 'Trelawny in the course of the evening spoke of his work as not only generally but in detail true'.

At a dinner party he surprised the company by declaring that he had once eaten human flesh (young woman) and had crossed the desert dressed as an Arab Sheik, and he told Joaquin Miller, an admiring visitor from America, that he had circumnavigated the globe and visited California before he was born. He spoke knowingly to him of Captain Morgan and the other pirates of the Spanish Main and, taking Miller aside, 'with increased mystery whispered that he knew to a dot the very spot where a shipload of gold was buried near the harbour of San Diego'.

*   *   *   *   *

Immediately after Shelley's death in July 1822 stories began to circulate that the *Don Juan* had sunk as a result of being rammed – run down, it was said, by one of the large local fishing vessels with sharp prows known as feluccas. Some people thought that there had simply been an accidental collision and the felucca concerned had perhaps not gone to the rescue through fear of the strict quarantine laws. Other people thought that maybe the ramming had been deliberate, since one of the Leghorn feluccas had been seen to follow the *Don Juan* out of harbour on the 8th July 1822 but later unexpectedly came back.

By the time the *Don Juan* was salvaged in September 1822, the theory that she had been rammed was already widespread.[1] Mary Shelley believed it, and it was said to be the opinion of Trelawny, of Roberts who personally superintended the salvage, and of every sailor.[2] In retrospect it is easy to see how, for the people concerned, this interpretation of events, unlikely though it was, provided a psychologically more satisfactory explanation than the obvious one, and, consciously or unconsciously, they were disposed to favour it. For Trelawny and Roberts, who had played such an important part in the design and construction of the vessel, the simple supposition that the *Don Juan* sank because she was unseaworthy carried disturbing implications about their own possible share in responsibility for the disaster.

As for Mary and the others, the ramming theory appeared more worthy of Shelley's tragedy than any explanation based on his ignorance of the sea, his impetuosity, or his lack of elementary care.[3]

Trelawny was a vigorous advocate of the ramming theory from an early date and we may be sure that the hundreds of people who heard him tell his Byron and Shelley stories were left in no doubt that this is what had happened. However when he came to write his *Recollections of the Last Days of Shelley and Byron* in 1858, he found that none of the contemporary documents in his possession gave support to the theory. In fact they tended rather in the opposite direction. There were two letters from Daniel Roberts, one addressed to himself, the other to Mary Shelley which he had evidently been lent at the time to read and not returned.[4]

The letter to Mary came first in time. It was written before Roberts had actually seen the *Don Juan* at close quarters and it is mainly a report of the official inventory which the Italian authorities made at the time. The subsequent letter, addressed to Trelawny himself, contained useful further information about the vessel obtained after she had been brought ashore. But it also contained an implication that Trelawny had been less than scrupulous with regard to some of the stores of the *Bolivar*, a warning about Trelawny's behaviour with Gabrielle Wright, and much about the state of health of Trelawny's horses.

Although Trelawny was naturally disposed to use the Roberts letters, since they showed him at the centre of events, they clearly would not do as they stood. Omission of embarrassing passages without acknowledgement was well within the conventions of the day, and it was also acceptable to tidy up grammar, spelling, and style. But in the *Recollections* Trelawny solved the problem by publishing two 'letters' whose creative editing would have surprised even such practised distorters of documents as Lady Shelley and Thomas Jefferson Hogg. He cut out all the embarrassing material. He pretended that both letters had been addressed to him – although the fact that he was intended to share the one to Mary Shelley is extenuation. He summarised large parts of the second letter. He cut out a few pieces of evidence that did not support his view of the ramming theory – such as that the gunwhale was stove in 'in many places'. And he added a new postscript to reinforce the point about the ramming which is his own invention – though it did represent Roberts's later view – and has no authority in either letter:

P.S. – On a close examination of Shelley's boat, we find many of the timbers on the starboard quarter broken, which makes me think for certain, that she must have been run down by some of the feluccas in the squall.

Here the matter rested for nearly twenty years with successive biographers of Shelley quoting the 'letters' in good faith. In 1875, however another twist was given to the story. Trelawny's daughter Laetitia, on a visit to Italy, heard a rumour that a few years earlier an old sailor on his death bed had confessed that he was one of the crew of the felucca which did the ramming. They were under the impression, he is reported to have confessed, that Lord Byron was on board with money, but when they struck the little boat, it sank immediately and they lost their booty.

Trelawny was now a very old man but his admirers rallied round to give publicity – proof at last that their hero had been right from the beginning. Rossetti arranged for Laetitia's letter to be published in *The Times* and Edgcumbe, after talking to Trelawny, contributed another decisive detail that had not been mentioned on any of the intervening fifty-three years.[5] Trelawny, it was now revealed, had seen oars and spars from the *Don Juan* on board the returning felucca. Trelawny himself contributed to the controversy quoting his own 'edited' version of the Roberts letters in support, and when his book was re-issued in 1878 as the *Records* he introduced further changes to the 'letters'.

The river of historical truth was now as clear as the Arno at Pisa on a winter's day. As with all good myths there were now many versions, and the Italian traditions were independent of the English. When Sir Percy Florence Shelley visited Lerici with Lady Shelley, an old sailor fell and kissed his feet. He showed them Shelley's 'sacred tree' and told how the poet had visited the sick and all those in trouble. The sailor said he prayed night and morning in front of a picture of Mary – Mary Shelley – and recalled that 'he was fair, he was beautiful, he was like Jesus Christ. I carried him in my arms through the water'. Lady Shelley tried hard to achieve a visionary experience of the poet whom she had never known by sleeping in his room in the Casa Magni, but she had no success. Nor did a later owner who built a cenotaph in the garden in hopes of obtaining the sacred ashes from Rome.

In 1890 the commander of the port of Viareggio rounded up all the inhabitants who claimed to be able to remember the great events of 1822 and took written statements. A woman of ninety-three said she was an eye-witness and confirmed the exact spot of the cremation as near the *Due Fosse* (Two Ditches). Some men claimed to have been on board the fishing vessels which salvaged the *Don Juan*. Another old man – who was not alive in 1822 – remembered that as a child the fishermen used to tell him that if he went into the sea, 'he would be burned like the Englishmen at the Due Fosse'. And at least two said that the English had taken the ashes of Shelley and Williams to England so that they could be brought back to life there.[6]

*   *   *   *   *

Trelawny loved to tell of his adventures in Greece and especially of the mountain fortress of Parnassus where, in 1824 and 1825, he had, for the one and only time in his life lived like a Byronic hero. But as the years went by a strange transformation occurred. Odysseus's cave is the Mavre Troupa, on the north side of Parnassus, but there is a much larger and more famous cave on the south side near Delphi called the Corycian Cave which Trelawny never visited but which he had heard of and read about in guidebooks. In an interview to a newspaper reporter in 1860, Trelawny gave a description of Odysseus's cave which shows that he had assimilated the two caves in his mind, into one imaginary cave with all the features of both. He genuinely believed that he himself had lived in the Corycian Cave.[7]

The Corycian Cave is divided into many different grottoes, the length of the first one is two hundred feet and its height forty.

Trelawny's memory is here subdued by guidebook descriptions of the Corycian Cave. 'A chamber 300 feet long, by nearly 200 wide, and about 40 high in the middle.' *Murray's Handbook for Travellers in Greece*, 1854. The Mavre Troupa is far smaller.

The outside light falling on the entrance allowed you to see fully the majestic porch of nature which I often compared with the diverse and decorated architecture of the Gothic cathedrals of Western Europe.

A true memory returns here.

The first things to strike your eyes were irregular stalactites from an irregular roof of sharp stones, with an undulating floor on which babbled a crystal clear spring.

Here we had enough store rooms and chambers for arms, fodder, and living quarters.

At the back of this cave was a large chasm which constitutes the entrance to the second cave of about one hundred feet in length, much darker and making a right angle with the first. This cave is dark and can be walked through with torches, and the more you advance the cooler, the darker and more magnificent it becomes.

You believe truly that you are walking towards the Kingdom of Pluto towards the hall of the infernal gods.

In the light of the torches, the roof and walls give off opalescent crystals and diffuse colours. Curtains of pillars in careless folds, sculptures, projections, borders, the forms of human heads, created by the tears of the earth and covered with evergreen moss in their folds – the transparent and brilliant furniture amidst which Phoebus once played with the Muses, and Pan danced with the Parnassian Nymphs.

Corycian Cave again. There are no stalactites in the Mavre Troupa.

True memory of the Mavre Troupa again creeping in.

Mavre Troupa again.

There is a small inner cave at the Mavre Troupe but Trelawny has transformed it in his imaginative memory into the large inner cave of the Corycian Cave which he has read about. 'The second chamber is 100 feet long'. *Murray's Handbook.*

There are no fantastic stalactites or stalagmites in the Mavre Troupa, only one smallish natural arch. All this section is again a transformation of Trelawny's memory of some description of the Corycian Cave that he had read: e.g. 'The stalactites from the top hang in the most graceful forms the whole length of the roof and fall like drapery down the sides.

'The depth of the folds is so vast and the masses thus suspended in the air are so great that the relief and fulness of these natural hangings are as complete as fancy could have wished. They are not like concretions or incrustations mere coverings of the rock, they are the gradual growth of ages, disposed in the most

simple and majestic form, and so rich
and large as to accord with the size
and loftiness of the cave. The stalagmites below and on the sides of the
chamber are still more fantastic in
their forms than the pendant above,
and strike the eye with a fancied
resemblance to vast human figures.'
Murray's Handbook

*   *   *   *   *

As the century progressed it was clear that, like Shelley, John
Keats was to enjoy the poetic reputation posthumously which had
escaped him during his lifetime. Trelawny had never met him, although
he played a part in preparing the monument over his grave. At the
time of the publication of the *Adventures* in 1831, however, the story
began to take root that Trelawny had known Keats as well as Byron
and Shelley, and he was content to let it grow. His name it was even
suggested, had been considered as a possible biographer.

The painter Holman Hunt reported in his diary a conversation
which took place at Burton Park, Penshurst, in 1863:

When I was painting one morning in the park, I saw him approaching.
When he was nigh I called out "How do you do Mr Trelawny?" He
walked on without answering and coming close threw himself down on
the grass behind me. I repeated my salutation. His reply was "I think
that is about the most foolish thing one man can say to another.". . .

"Besides Byron and Shelley, you knew Keats, tell me what height
Keats was, for the idea prevails that he was extremely short and that does
not correspond with the character of his head as seen in the cast. From
what Keats idly says himself it is inferred he was only five feet."

"No, he was of reasonable height, about your own" said Trelawny.

"Tell me how the character of his face inspired you" I continued:
"He couldn't be called good-looking" he replied "because he was under-
hung [that is had a projecting lower jaw.]

"You use the word in an opposite sense to that in which it is sometimes applied to Charles the Fifth and Philip the Second of Spain, or to a
bulldog?" I said

"Of course Keats was the very reverse" he grunted "and the defect
gave a fragile aspect to him as a man'[8].

*   *   *   *   *

Trelawny had innumerable relics with which he liked to impress
visitors. He had original poems, letters, and other manuscripts of

Shelley and Byron which he had collected since the great days of 1822–1824 without too close a regard for the proprieties. Jane Williams protested in vain for the return of Williams's Indian journal which Trelawny had been permitted to borrow before his death, and Medwin never got back a number of letters addressed by Shelley to himself which he had imprudently lent to Trelawny for his projected biography in 1829. Some of the manuscripts, though not the 'edited' ones, were later presented by Trelawny's daughter Laetitia with nice symmetry to Eton and Oxford, Harrow and Cambridge, the chief places of education associated with the two poets.

On Trelawny's wall hung portraits of two of the women who had meant most to him, Claire Clairmont and Mary Shelley, by the same artist, Amelia Curran, who had painted the girls and Shelley himself in 1820. Trelawny had been asked by Mary long years before to obtain these pictures for her from Italy – she had no portrait of herself at the age when she was with Shelley – and although he had taken possession of them, he never handed them over. One of Mary's last recorded actions in 1850, shortly before she died, was to write in vain to Trelawny begging him to return her picture.

On the other hand, to people he liked, Trelawny showed his life-long characteristic generosity. William Michael Rossetti was showered with gifts, books, manuscripts, pictures, and a huge bed fetched specially from Italy in which Shelley was thought to have passed his last night. Rossetti, the Inland Revenue official, discovered to his pleasure and surprise that the corsair regarded him as one of his best friends.

One evening when Rossetti and his brother Dante Gabriel were showing Trelawny their beloved Japanese prints he remarked disingenuously that he had been to Japan in his youth. As a mark of appreciation they decided to make him a present of two fine Japanese swords, but to their horror, he told them a few days later that he had given them away. They were not genuine, Trelawny said, and invited them to admire instead another sword which he said he had personally looted from a Chinese junk. Then there was the sword he liked to show which Byron had given him at Cephalonia with the words 'Here take this, Tre, and use it either like Childe Harold or Don Juan'. And the dagger which a blind beggar had thoughtfully pressed into his hand at the crisis of the Masi incident at Pisa, in 1822. He was also said to have had 'various dried heads of pirates, and others among his treasures' although nobody has recorded actually seeing them, and he apparently had unlimited pieces of charred bone for distribution to favoured admirers of Shelley.

Trelawny's relics like his stories spanned the spectrum from the absolutely genuine to the absolutely bogus with interesting mixtures in the middle.

25

Last Years

I thank you for your prompt answer to my letter, and commission you to put my tomb in thorough repair; and when I know the cost I will remit you the payment. As my body will undergo Cremation, my ashes will be enclosed in a box about the same size as my friend the Poet's. I have completed my 88th year. I shall commission some friend to bring my ashes to Rome and to see you. There was a rumour that the Poet Shelley's ashes had been removed; but I did not believe you would have permitted such a sacrilege. The Poet Shelley wrote many verses in admiration of your Cemetery. Thanking you again for the honourable way in which you have fulfilled the duties of your office.

A letter to the Custodian of the Protestant Cemetery at Rome, 1880.[1]

Sometime about 1870 Trelawny bought a house at Sompting, a mile or so from Worthing on the south coast of England. Although it was called a cottage, it is in fact quite a large house with garden front and back, and was at that time set in the midst of extensive fig orchards. Trelawny painted it red on the outside, and in the main room he painted the ceiling bright blue – it was as like his beloved Italy as he could make it. A high hedge was planted round the garden to give privacy, it was said, for naked sunbathing, and in the middle of the front garden he planted a cypress tree, as he had done at Usk, from a cone from one of the cypress trees he had himself planted over Shelley's grave in Rome.

By his own count he had been married four times – to Zela his Arab girl, to Caroline, to Tersitsa, and to Augusta, and for a while in London Miss B. had passed as Mrs Trelawny without benefit of ceremony. During the last years however she too had to give way to a younger woman, Emma Taylor, the last of the Byronic heroines who had filled Trelawny's life, who lived with him at Sompting and at London, according to the coy convention of the day, as his 'niece'.

Of his seven known children two had died in childhood.[2] Julia, his elder daughter by his first wife, seems after her marriage to have drifted away from her father whom, after all, she had only seen for a few weeks at most during the whole of her life. Zella, the daughter who had been conceived in the cave at Parnassus, was brought up in Italy by an English lady, Jane Boccella, who was married to an Italian marquis, but she came to England sometime in the 1830s to be looked after by Trelawny and by his mother, Mrs Brereton. It was apparently while she was on a prolonged continental tour to remove her from the scene during Trelawny's involvement with Augusta Goring, of whom she initially disapproved, that she met a Mr Olguin, a South American doctor whom she married. In the early 1850s she and her husband fell into debt – Trelawny refused to help – and they emigrated for a while to the Argentine, but in 1870 she and her family were back in London. On one occasion soon afterwards when Trelawny was visiting her house and he made some unkind remark, she rang the bell for the servant and said with great firmness 'Show Mr Trelawny out'. That, it seems, was the end of their relationship.[3]

Only with his last legitimate wife Augusta did Trelawny enjoy anything approaching a regular family life and he was in his sixties when his children were growing up. There were three, Edgar, Frank, and Laetitia, and Trelawny took a close interest in his sons' education. They must learn foreign languages, he decided, recalling his own unhappy experience, and be trained in a practical profession such as engineering. Both boys were sent to military academies in Germany.[4]

It was a strange choice for the lifelong anti-authoritarian, but we may guess that what lay behind it was Trelawny's admiration for his old friend Christian Edward Detmold whom he had probably first met in Charleston, South Carolina, in 1833, and who during Trelawny's later years seems to have become his current hero.[5] Detmold, who was born in Germany, and educated there at a military academy, emigrated early in life to the United States and became one of the greatest engineers of the American industrial revolution, being responsible not only for laying many of the new railways but for building new steel mills and designing the New York crystal palace which was built there to rival the London original in 1856. Detmold was interested in art and music, he had a fine collection of paintings, and he published a translation of Dante. Detmold was the best human being he had ever met, Trelawny would tell his friends in later life, as well as being his oldest friend, – a better man even than Shelley.

But if he thought that by giving his sons a repeat of Detmold's education he could turn them into men like Detmold, Trelawny suffered a bitter disappointment. The younger boy, Frank, whom Trelawny seems to have loved dearly, acquired a taste for the military life at his school in Germany and to his father's despair decided to become a professional soldier in the Prussian Army. Then when he was still a young man he died of consumption.

The other son, Edgar, was destined to cause his father intense pain all his life. He never got over his resentment that when he was born to Trelawny and Augusta at Putney in 1839 before they were married they had given him a false name. In revenge, when he was grown up, he told people that he was not the son of Edward John Trelawny, but of Sir John Trelawny the current baronet, a deception which Edward John, the despiser of hereditary wealth and power, must particularly have abhorred. He also became an ostentatious convert to Roman Catholicism. After Germany Trelawny sent Edgar to America, where Detmold himself was asked to help him, and Augusta Draper, too, tried to take an interest in the son of her old friend. But Trelawny's annoyance gave way to anger and then to despair. As reports came back of his behaviour he refused to write to him, then he disowned him and declared he would never see him again. In his attitude to his own son Trelawny showed the same wild hatred for which he had so despised his own father. As he wrote to Augusta Draper:

I know Edgar he is a cunning fellow a great actor – he saw thro' Detmold at a glance and has to my disgust made a dupe of him – he has once before play'd the same game – I told Detmold to send him on to you under the conviction that you with your strong good sense would judge for yourself and see thro' Edgar's acting and artifice – he is acting a part his fits are assumed theire is nothing the matter with him phisically but he disliked his birth and used the means he has to gule those about him – if you will see him yourself I shall be most thankfull – return *here he shall not* with my consent & if he comes to England I will *not* see him. If you do see him read him this my opinion of him which his mother joins.[6]

But maybe Trelawny's own experience was repeating itself in more ways than he knew. For Edgar, from what little is known of him, evidently shared some at least of the characteristics of the Trelawny who had successfully bammed his way into the society of Byron and Shelley a generation before. At the end of 1858, Trelawny, unconscious of the irony, was writing of him to Augusta Draper in terms which

Brereton could have used at one time of Edward John: 'I told Det. that Edgar was a *rogue* & *vagabond* ... I moreover warned him as to Edgar's duplicity – art & cunning & that from his childhood he had never been known to speak a word of truth – you have been behind the scenes and saw the force – Edgar saw what flats he had to deal with & by playing one of his old doges hoaxxed you all – persuaded you that I was a rascal & that he was a clever amiable sensitive noble-minded & ill-used young man.'[7]

Edgar went his own way. In 1872 he married the rich widow of a baronet but within a few months he was taken to law and his wife left him. He died suddenly soon afterwards without apparent cause – 'A monster' according to his father's summing up, writing about him without a tinge of regret within a few months of his death.

And so as the aged Trelawny prepared to settle down for his last years at Sompting there were few to give him comfort. He had seen four children die and quarrelled with two of the survivors. Of all his multifarious relations only his youngest daughter Laetitia was still in touch with him and in 1878 it was her turn to bring the tempestuous name of Trelawny before the gaze of the bewildered British public for the last time in his long life.

In 1875 when she was living with her father at Sompting, word arrived of the death of her mother Augusta who had gone to Italy in 1858 following the break-up of her marriage to Trelawny. It happened that Augusta's son by her previous marriage, Sir Charles Goring, lived not far away and Laetitia made contact with him – they were not previously acquainted – to tell him the news. The result was that Sir Charles fell suddenly and deeply in love with Laetitia, and his passionate appeals to his half-sister featured high in the well-publicised divorce case of 1878 when Sir Charles's wife produced a long list of scandalous charges against him most of which, including all accusations against Laetitia, were later withdrawn.[8]

Trelawny's own reaction to these events is not known. Maybe he would have enjoyed the Byronic flavour or maybe he would have wanted to call out young Sir Charles to fight a duel. He himself did not change. Every day, summer or winter, he walked to the sea to swim and he still refused to wear the socks that Claire and Mary had fussed about on his return from Greece in 1828, half a century before. He was a teetotaller and a vegetarian. Every morning he would rise early to chop the wood, but he would not allow the fire to be lit before noon.

Instead of cushions in his home he used old newspapers. The villagers were overawed by the strange figure striding about the Downs or feeding the ducks in the village pond. 'The Greek', they called him and perhaps, when he heard it, Trelawny remembered his nickname of sixty years before, 'The Turk'.

Even at Sompting the old man found ways of keeping his public image well polished. One day when he was out for a walk wearing a new overcoat he met a tramp and, more generous than St Martin, he took it off and gave it to him. On another occasion when frost lay on the ground he did the same with a pair of new boots and came home barefoot through the streets.

Occasionally he would go to London, but more often visitors came to see him, to hear him talk of the great days of the past. He had an opinion on every subject, and a forthright one. The old atheist could be relied on at any time to denounce the Pope. The old republican and anti-imperialist could be relied on to support every revolutionary movement in Europe and beyond. As ever, killing the tyrants – especially the Emperor of Russia, nicely misspelled the Scar – was his main remedy for all political problems.

In 1874, at the age of eighty-two, he sat as a model for the old man in the famous picture by Millais, *The North West Passage,* which was one of the sensations of the year and was soon to be seen in innumerable reproductions all round the world. The moral of the picture is given in the caption, 'It can be done and England should do it' which is obviously meant to represent the sentiments of the old man. As a likeness of Trelawny, all accounts agree that it is a good picture, and he was flattered to be commemorated by one of the leading artists of his day. But, as so often in the past, Trelawny missed the point. He went thundering round to Millais as soon as he saw the picture to try to challenge the artist to a duel for painting a glass of grog at the old teetotaller's elbow, but the lifelong revolutionary was apparently unaware that he had lent himself to an exercise in propaganda for British imperialism.

He was an original, so people thought, in the tradition of the English worthies, and so, obviously, in a sense he was. But his character in old age was also an accumulation of the various Edward John and John Edward Trelawnys of the past. He was the rebellious son, the insubordinate bullying midshipman, the Byronic hero, the corsair, the successor of Shelley, the imitator of Byron. The ingredients of his character were visible to anyone (but there was none) who knew his story. In the *Recollections* he had recounted a comment of Byron's when first he appeared at Pisa in 1822. Do not go to the Shelley's, Byron said, 'for they will mould you into a Frankenstein monster'. Fifty years later he had become just that, a monster composed of pieces of the dead, crudely botched together.

On 6 November 1876 an unexpected visitor arrived by train to spend the day with him. Augusta Draper, now herself seventy-eight and in poor health, was on a visit to England and came to call on her old friend. For the last time they talked again about the terrible events of 1817 which had shaped Trelawny's character so decisively and cast him on his extraordinary career. Why, she teased him, with his spirit of freedom, had he cut down unsparingly some trees in the garden that surely had a right to grow as they liked. After sixty years, she noted in her diary, they had both changed but not in their perfect understanding of one another.

One of the last visitors who met him shortly before he died was Sidney Colvin who had made the expedition to Sompting in February 1881 to shake the hand that had snatched Shelley's heart from the flames, and he has left a vivid account of Trelawny in his eighty-ninth year:

> The veteran received us in a small, old-fashioned room on the ground floor where he sat in an armchair with a couple of black-and-tan terriers playing at his feet. I had been accustomed to hear much of his extraordinary vigour . . . I was therefore somewhat surprised to perceive in him at first sight all the appearances of decrepitude. He scarcely moved himself in his chair on our entrance, but sat in a shrunken attitude, with his hands on his knees, speaking little, and as if he could only fix his attention by an effort. He wore an embroidered red cap, of the unbecoming shape in use in Byron's day, with a stiff projecting peak. His head thus appeared to no advantage; nevertheless in the ashen colour of the face, the rough grey hair and beard and firmly modelled mouth set slight awry, in the hard, clear, handsome aquiline profile (for the nose, though not long, was of a marked aquiline shape) and in the masterful, scowling grey eye, there were traces of something both more distinguished and more formidable than is seen in Sir John Millais's well-known likeness of him as an old seaman in his picture 'The North-West Passage, – a likeness with which the sitter himself was much dissatisfied . . .
>
> By and by he began to rouse himself, and then his conversation became, at least at intervals, curiously impressive. His moral and social recklessness, his defiance of current opinions, his turbulent energy, his

Passage by J. E.
Millais, 1878.
'It can be done
and England
should do it'

Trelawny in old age, from a photograph taken about 1871

sure eye for character and his no less sure instinct for literature, all made themselves felt along with the extraordinary interest of his experiences. From time to time he would rise, almost bound, up in his chair, with his eyes fastened on yours like a vice, and in tones of incredible power would roar what he had to say to your face. I never heard in human conversation a voice so energetic as that which burst from the old man in these explosions; explosions which subsided quickly, and in the intervals of which his accents were quiet and muffled as before . . . It was the hour when the long negotiations between the British Generals and administrators and the Boer leaders had failed, and the operations of the Transvaal War (of 1881) were in full swing. Trelawny defiantly declared his hope that the English would be beaten. 'If I were a younger man' he shouted in a strong *crescendo* 'I would go and fight for the Boers – fight for the Boers – fight for the Boers.'

Trelawny talked of Shelley and the sinking of the *Don Juan*, of Odysseus and his treasure in Parnassus, and told again stories that he had been repeating for half a century. As the visitors said their good-byes and one of them congratulated Trelawny on looking so well for his age, he was heard to growl 'S'very well, s'very well: that's the kind o'lies I was talking of: lies, lies, lies.'[9]

The end finally came on 13 August 1881, a day he had been more or less genuinely wishing for, like a good romantic, since at least 1822. He had fallen when out on one of his walks, was taken to bed, and died a few weeks later, insisting emphatically on his death-bed that he remained a confirmed atheist. The preparations for his funeral had been scrupulously made in advance with the help of William Michael Rossetti, and everything was ready and waiting for him. The body had to be embalmed and sent to Germany to be cremated. Emma Taylor then took the ashes in a walnut box to Rome where they were buried in the grave he had purchased in 1823.

At this own request, some lines from Shelley were carved on his tombstone:

> These are two friends whose lives were undivided.
> So let their memory be now they have glided
> Under the grave: let not their bones be parted
> For their two hearts in life were single-hearted.[10]

And there he still lies, in more senses than one, destined to be forever described in the reference books as Edward John Trelawny, adventurer, friend of Shelley.

Bibliography
Notes
Index

Bibliography

The sources for Trelawny's life are widely scattered, and it seems best to include a full bibliography although some of the books mentioned contain only a little about him.

MANUSCRIPT SOURCES

The following is a list of the main collections which contain materials relevant to Trelawny. There are of course numerous relevant documents in other libraries and in private hands some of which are referred to individually in the notes.

Papers relating to the Hawkins and Trelawny families. Cornwall Record Office, Truro.

Papers relating to the Hawkins and Trelawny families. East Sussex Record Office, Chichester.

Log books and muster books of ships in which Trelawny served. Public Record Office, London.

Letters and other documents relating to Trelawny. Carl H. Pforzheimer Library, New York.

Letters and other documents relating to Trelawny. Keats-Shelley Memorial Library, Rome.

Letters and other documents relating to Trelawny. Bodleian Library, Oxford.

Lord Abinger's collection of papers relating to Shelley, including numerous letters of Trelawny, and the microfilm of other documents not deposited. Bodleian Library, Oxford.

Letters and other documents relating to Trelawny. British Library.

Copies of official documents of the Tuscan and Lucchese governments relating to the wreck of the *Don Juan*, the cremation of the bodies, and the salvage of the vessel. Municipal Museum, Viareggio.

Journals and letters of George Finlay and Frank Abney Hastings. Library of the British School at Athens.

Copy of a Journal of James Forrester '*Reminiscences of Visits to Various Places in and round the shores of the Mediterranean*'. Columbia University Library, New York.

Journal of Major d'Arcy Bacon, Bodleian Library, Oxford.

Archives of the London Greek Committee including letters by Trelawny. National Library, Athens

Letters and other documents relating to Trelawny. Collection of Mr John Murray, London.

Manuscripts of *Adventures of a Younger Son*, and *Records of Shelley, Byron and the Author*. Houghton Library, Harvard.

Letters and other documents relating to Trelawny. Beinecke Library, Yale.

PRINTED SOURCES

Armstrong, Margaret – *Trelawny, A Man's Life*, 1941

Athoe, G. B. J. – 'Trelawny's Cottage', a letter to the *Times Literary Supplement*, 2 August 1941

Biagi, Guido – *The Last Days of Percy Bysshe Shelley*, 1898

Blind, Mathilde – 'Mr Trelawny on Byron and Shelley', *Whitehall Review*, 10 January 1880

Boase, George Clement – *Collectanea Cornubiensia*, Truro, 1890

Boase, George Clement and Courtney, W. P. – *Bibliotheca Cornubiensis*, 1874–82

Bray, Mrs A. E. – *Trelawny of Trelawne*, 1845

Brown, Charles Armitage – *Letters* ed. Jack Stillinger, Harvard, 1966

Mrs Brookfield and her Circle, 1905

Browne, James Hamilton – 'Narrative of a Visit to the Seat of War in Greece', and 'Voyage from Leghorn to Cephalonia with Lord Byron', *Blackwood's Magazine*, 1834

Buxton, John – *Byron and Shelley*, 1968

Byrde, M. B. – 'Trelawny at Usk', *The Athenaeum*, August 1897

Carpenter, Edward – *My days and dreams*, 1916

Chorley, Henry Fothergill – *Autobiography, Memoir and Letters*, 1873

Clairmont, Claire – *Journals* ed. Marion Kingston Stocking, Harvard, 1968

Clark, J. H. – *Reminiscences of Monmouthshire*, Usk, 1908

Cline, C. L. – *Byron, Shelley and their Pisan Circle*, 1952

Cobbe, Frances Power – 'Letter to the Editor on a Recent Article on E. J. Trelawny', *Temple Bar* 64, p. 317, 1882

Colvin, Sir Sidney – *Memories and Notes of Persons and Places*, 1921

Crosse, Andrew – *Memorials Scientific and Literary*, 1857

Crosse, Mrs Andrew – *Red-letter Days of my Life*, 1892

Dowden, Edward; Garnett, Richard; and Rossetti, Wm. Michael – *Letters about Shelley*, 1917

Down, T. C. – 'Pirate Trelawny', *Nineteenth Century*, May 1907

Edgcumbe, Richard – 'Edward John Trelawny' a letter in *The Athenaeum*, 2, p. 814, 1901

Edgcumbe, Richard – *Edward Trelawny (A Biographical Sketch)*. Plymouth, 1882

Edgcumbe, Richard – 'Letter to the Editor on a recent Article on E. J. Trelawny. *Temple Bar* 66, p. 431, 1882

Edgcumbe, Richard – 'Talks with Trelawny'. *Temple Bar* 89, 1890

Emerson, James; Pecchio, Count; and Humphreys, W. H. – *A Picture of Greece in 1825*, 1826

Gamba, Count Peter – *A Narrative of Lord Byron's Last Journey to Greece*, 1825

Garnett, Edward – Introduction to his edition of *Adventures of a Younger Son*, 1890

Gisborne, Maria, and Williams, Edward E. – *Their Journals and Letters* edited by Frederick L. Jones, Norman, Oklahoma, 1951

Graham, William – *Last Links with Byron, Shelley and Keats*, 1898

Grylls, R. Glynn – *Mary Shelley*, 1938

Grylls, R. Glynn – *Trelawny*, 1950

Hausermann, H. W. – *The Genevese Background*, 1952

Haydon, Benjamin Robert – *Diary* edited by Willard Bissell Pope, IV, Harvard, 1963

Hill, Lady Anne – 'Trelawny's Family Background and Naval Career', *Keats–Shelley Journal*, V, 1956

Hill, Lady Anne – *Trelawny's Strange Relations*, privately printed, 1956

Holmes, Richard – *Shelley, The Pursuit*, 1974

[Humphreys, W. H.] – 'Adventures of an English Officer in Greece', *New Monthly Magazine*, 1826 (See also under Emerson)

Hunt, W. Holman – *Pre-Raphaelitism and the Pre-Raphaelite Brotherhood*, 1905

Jameson, Anna – *Letters to Ottilie von Goethe*, 1939

Jarvis, George – *Journal and Related Documents*, Thessalonika, 1965

Jones, Frederick L. – 'Trelawny and the Sinking of Shelley's Boat', *Keats–Shelley Memorial Bulletin*, 1965

Kemble, Frances Ann – *Record of a Girlhood*, 1879

[Kemble] – *Journal of Frances Anne Butler*, 1835

Kennedy, James – *Conversations on Religion with Lord Byron and Others, held in Cephalonia, a short time previous to his Lordship's death*, 1830

Landor, Walter Savage – *Imaginary Conversations. Fifth Series, Odysseus, Tersitza, Acrive, and Trelawny*

Lappas, Takis – *Odysseas Androutsos*, Athens n.d. [in Greek]

Lewis, Michael – *Social History of the Navy 1793–1815*, 1960

Looker, Samuel J. – *The Worthing Cavalcade, Shelley, Trelawny and Henley, A Study of Three Titans*, 1950

Lovell, Ernest J. – *Captain Medwin*, 1962

Marchand, Leslie A. – *Byron, a Biography*, 1957

Marchand, Leslie A. – 'Trelawny on the Death of Shelley', *Keats – Shelley Memorial Bulletin*, 1952

Massingham, H. J. – *The Friend of Shelley, A Memoir of Edward John Trelawny*, 1930

Miller, Joaquin – *Trelawny with Shelley and Byron*, Pompton Lakes, New Jersey, 1922

Millingen, Julius – *Lord Byron and his Doctors*, London n.d. [1861]

Millingen, Julius – *Memoirs of the Affairs of Greece*, 1831

Moore, Doris Langley – 'Byron, Leigh Hunt, and the Shelleys', *Keats–Shelley Memorial Bulletin*, 1959

Moore, Doris Langley – *The Late Lord Byron*, 1961

Moore, Doris Langley – *Lord Byron, Accounts Rendered*, 1974

Norman, Sylva – *Flight of the Skylark, The Development of Shelley's Reputation*, 1954

Olguin, Francisco J. de – *El Libro de Andres Maurois sobre Lord Byron, Rectificacion a sus conceptos sobre John Edward Trelawny*, Buenos Aires, 1930

Origo, Iris – *The Last Attachment*, 1949

Parkinson, C. Northcote – *War in the Eastern Seas 1793–1815*, 1954

Parry, William – *The Last Days of Lord Byron*, 1825

Robinson, Henry Crabb on Books and Their Writers, ed. Edith J. Morley, 1938

Rolleston, Maud – *Talks with Lady Shelley*, 1925

Rollins, Hyder Edward – *The Keats Circle*, Harvard, 1965

Rossetti, William Michael – *Rossetti Papers 1862–1870*, 1903

Rossetti, William Michael – *Some Reminiscences*, 1906

Rossetti, William Michael – 'Talks with Trelawny', *The Athenaeum*, 1882

St Clair, William – *That Greece Might Still be Free, The Philhellenes in the War of Independence*, 1972

Sanborn, F. B. – 'Odysseus and Trelawny', *Scribners Magazine*, April 1897

Sharp, William – *The Life and Letters of Joseph Severn*, 1892

Shelley and his Circle, 1773–1822. Manuscripts in the Carl H. Pforzheimer Library, Volumes V and VI edited by Donald H. Reiman, Cambridge, Mass, 1973

Shelley and Mary, for private circulation only, 1882

Shelley, Mary – *Journal*, Edited by Frederick L. Jones, Norman, Oklahoma, 1947

Shelley, Mary – *The Letters of Mary W. Shelley*, edited by Frederick L. Jones, Norman, Oklahoma, 1944

Shelley, Percy Bysshe – *The Letters*, edited by Frederick L. Jones, 1964

Shelley, Lady – 'Letter to the Editor on a Recent Article on E. J. Trelawny', *Temple Bar* 64, p. 319, 1882

Sketches of Modern Greece . . . by a Young English Volunteer in the Greek Service, 1828

Stanhope, Colonel Leicester – *Greece in 1823 and 1829*, Second edition, 1825

Surcouf, Robert – *Le Corsaire Malouin, Robert Surcouf*, Paris, 1890

Swan, Rev. Charles – *Journal of a Voyage up the Mediterranean*, 1826

Swinburne, A. C. – *The Swinburne Letters*, edited by Cecil Y. Lang, 1959–62

Temple-Leader, John – *Rough and Rambling Notes Chiefly of My Early Life*, Florence, 1899

[Trelawny, Edward John] – *Adventures of a Younger Son*, 1831

Trelawny, Edward John – *Adventures of a Younger Son*, edited by William St. Clair, Oxford English Novels, 1974

Trelawny, Edward John – *Letters*, edited by H. Buxton Forman, 1910

[Trelawny, Edward John] – A Description of the Cavern Fortress of Mount Parnassus', *Examiner*, 13 November 1825

Trelawny, E. J. – *Recollections of the Last Days of Shelley and Byron*, 1858

Trelawny, Edward John – *Records of Shelley, Byron and the Author*, 1878

Trelawny, Edward John – 'Reply to an article by Richard Garnett in the *Fortnightly*', *The Athenaeum*, 1878

[Trelawny, Edward John] – *Reminiscences of the Greek Revolution*, an interview with Stephanos Xenos in *Bretannikos Aster*, 1860 [In Greek]

[Trelawny, Edward John] – 'Sahib Tulwar (Master of the Sword)', *Heath's Book of Beauty*, 1839

[Trelawny, Edward John] – *The Trial Between Lieutenant Trelawney Plaintiff and Captain Coleman, Defendant for Criminal Conversation with the Plaintiff's Wife*. London n.d. [1817]

Trelawny, J. E. – 'Letter to the editor commenting on a review of Millingen's "Memoirs of the Affairs of Greece" ', *London Literary Gazette*, 12 February 1831

Villemessant, H. de – *Mémoires d'un Journaliste*, Paris, 1872–75

Villeneuve, Eugène de – *Journal fait en Grèce pendant les anneés 1825 et 1826*, Brussels, 1827

H. E. W. – 'Edward John Trelawny', *Temple Bar* 63, 1881

White, Newman Ivey – *Shelley*, 1947

Williams, Edward Ellerker, *See under* Gisborne

Notes

The short italicised titles refer to printed books and manuscript collections described in the Bibliography. Other works are mentioned in full. References to the *Adventures of a Younger Son* are to the 1974 edition.

I. THE YOUNGER SON *pp.* 3–9

1 *Adventures*, p. 1.
2 Trelawny's date of birth is usually given as 13 November 1792 although a sprinkling of other dates are also mentioned, and I have been unable to find official confirmation. In a letter published in *Shelley and His Circle*, v. p. 323, Trelawny says that 13 November is his birthday. In a letter dated 15 November 1821 due to be published in a forthcoming volume, he says the day is the 29th anniversary of his birth. It is not known where his family were staying at the time of his birth and I have been unable to trace the baptismal record. It is sometimes said that he was born at the family house in London, 9 Soho Square, but they did not inherit that until 1798 when Owen Brereton died. His grandfather, General Trelawny, also lived in Soho Square.
3 In the *Adventures*. For Trelawny's family see *Hill: Strange Relations* and *Lovell's Medwin*, pp. 130 and 135f. There are other references which tend to confirm his picture of his parents (e.g. in the *Hawkins Papers*) apart from the evidence of their behaviour.
4 John Hawkins to his wife, 7 March 1808, *Hawkins Papers at Chichester*.
5 *Adventures*, p. 14.
6 John Hawkins to his wife, 7 March 1808, *Hawkins Papers at Chichester*.
7 *Massingham*, p. 4.
8 *Adventures*, p. 1.
9 *Lovell's Medwin*, p. 135.
10 *Adventures*, p. 5. This was one of the stories which he told to Shelley and his friends at Pisa. See *Williams's Journal* for 18 February 1822.
11 *Adventures*, p. 15.
12 The details about Trelawne as it was in Trelawny's day are taken mainly from the description by *Mrs Bray* who visited the house in 1833.
13 *Adventures*, p. 8. It is clear from references in his mother's letters that the choice of school was made after more lengthy consideration than Trelawny implies. Trelawny describes his schooldays in the *Adventures* and there are a few scattered references to him at this time in his mother's letters among the *Hawkins Papers* some of which are quoted in *Hill: Family Background* and *Strange*

Relations. Seyer is in the *Dictionary of National Biography* and there is other useful information in obituary notices. The conditions at the school in Trelawny's day are described by Trelawny's contemporary *Andrew Crosse* and an engraving of the school building is reproduced with the article by P. E. Barnes in the *Bristol Evening News* of 13 December 1935.

14 *Andrew Crosse.*

15 Rev. Samuel Seyer, A. M. *Latium Redivivum, a Treatise on the modern use of the Latin Language and Prevalence of the French,* London, 1808.

16 The story of Trelawny's expulsion from the Seyer School has to be treated with a good deal of caution since it is drawn entirely from the *Adventures.* Yet it is certain that a violent incident involving a rebellion of the boys did occur when Trelawny was there. Robert Southey alludes to it in his *Commonplace Book,* fourth series, 1851, p. 363:

> They were taught that they ought to resist their natural enemies, and by an easy and obvious logic, discovered that their natural enemies were the master and usher whom they accordingly resolved to shoot. Some accident discovered the plan and prevented murder; but it was necessary to call in the military to reduce them. This was hushed up, so many families of consequence here were concerned.

He dates the incident 1797, but more probably it occurred during the later invasion scare of 1801. *Andrew Crosse,* p. 23 has a somewhat different version:

> On one occasion we got up a rebellion; we resolved to stand out for longer holidays. We arranged to barricade the schoolroom; we provided ourselves with muskets . . . However the plot was discovered before it was ripe for execution, the muskets were seized, the ringleaders expelled, others flogged . . . One of these lads was afterwards midshipman in Nelson's squadron and was cut down while bravely boarding an enemy's ship.

Since there were only about thirty or forty boys at the school, it is possible that the midshipman is a mismemory of Trelawny. Although Crosse records the later progress of other contemporaries he was apparently unaware that Trelawny – who was then famous – had been at school with him. Whatever in fact happened, the incident was well covered up – there is no reference to it in Seyer's voluminous surviving papers – nor have I found any mention in the newspapers, although it was said to have been reported in the Irish press as an example of anti-war sedition in England.

2. THE NAVY *pp.* 10–16

The chief sources for Trelawny's naval career are the log books and muster books of the ships in which he served, nearly all of which survive and are preserved in the Public Record Office, London. Lady Anne Hill who was the first to discover the facts of Trelawny's early life and reconstructed his naval career in *Family Background,* kindly made available to me her notes and transcriptions of material which was not included in the article. For the customs and regulations of the Navy in

Trelawny's day, see *Lewis*. For the campaigns in the Indian Ocean in which Trelawny served, see *Parkinson* and William Thorn's *Memoir of the Conquest of Java*, 1815.

1 Quoted in *Massingham* p. 13 from an original document.
2 *Massingham*, p. 21; *Adventures* pp. 19 ff. and 62 ff. These chapters were suppressed from earlier printed versions.
3 *Adventures*, p. 33.
4 James Prior. Quoted in *Parkinson*.
5 Mrs Brereton to John Hawkins, Helston, 16 October 1812, *Hawkins Papers at Chichester*.

3. AT THE MASTHEAD *pp*. 17–23

Trelawny describes his punishments at the masthead and his dreams of escaping from the Navy in the *Adventures*. He mentions too his reading about the mutiny in the *Bounty* and about John Paul Jones. Much of this chapter is however necessarily conjecture.

1 *Adventures*, p. 34.
2 John Hawkins to his wife, undated but before 7 March 1808. *Hawkins Papers at Chichester*.
3 *Newton Forster*, 1897 edition, p. 181. In this book Marryat also describes a fictional encounter with Surcouf.
4 *Adventures*, p. 85.
5 For Surcouf's life see *Surcouf*; Lord Russell of Liverpool, *The French Corsairs* 1970; C. B. Norman, *The Corsairs of France*, 1887. For Surcouf's terrifying reputation see *The Memoirs of William Hickey*, volume iv, 1925, and contemporary news from India such as the *Asiatic Annual Register*. There is enough evidence to make the identification of de Ruyter with Surcouf virtually certain. The conjecture is further confirmed by a remark Trelawny made to W. M. Rossetti in 1872. Talking of the *Adventures* he is reported to have said 'The person there named de Ruyter really existed. He was of Dutch extraction named Senouf (as I understood the name) and had a commission from Napoleon as a privateer'. ('Talks with Trelawny', *Athenaeum*, 29 July 1882). It seems from the parenthesis that Rossetti was uncertain whether he had heard the name right and that Trelawny actually said Surcouf. There is no record of any privateer called Senouf (or de Ruyter or de Witt) in the Mauritius, French, or Dutch archives. For the degree of correspondence between Surcouf and de Ruyter, see my note in the *Adventures*, p. 472.
6 Quoted in *Surcouf*.
7 Quoted in *William Hickey*, op. cit. iv, p. 414.
8 *Asiatic Annual Register*, 1808, p. 34.

4. REJECTED *pp*. 24–30

The main sources for this period of Trelawny's life are his letters of the time to Augusta White most of which have now been published in volumes V and VI of

Shelley and His Circle. The information in these letters can be correlated with the evidence given at his divorce trial (see *The Trial between Lieutenant Trelawney* . . .) and his own account in the *Adventures*. There are also letters among the *Hawkins Papers* by members of his family which refer to him at this time and two important letters by Trelawny himself.

1 *Adventures*, p. 462.
2 E.g. at his divorce trial.
3 Trelawny to his uncle John Hawkins, 6 May 1817. *Hawkins Papers at Chichester*.
4 In one of his letters to his uncle John Hawkins, Trelawny says that his father made the family break completely with him, yet one of his letters to Augusta White is apparently dated from the family house in Soho Square and there are other references to his seeing his family.
5 Mrs Brereton to Sir Christopher Hawkins, 6 August 1818. *Hawkins Papers at Truro*.
6 Trelawny to John Hawkins, 1 May 1817. *Hawkins Papers at Chichester*.
7 Trelawny to John Hawkins, 6 May 1817. *Hawkins Papers at Chichester*.
8 *Shelley and His Circle*, v. 79.
9 *Ibid.*, v, p. 101.

5. BOOKS *pp.* 31–35

1 A story told by George Finlay to Richard Monckton Milnes in 1832. See James Pope-Hennessy: *Monckton Milnes, The Years of Promise*, 1949, p. 60. There are other versions. See note 11 to chapter 9.
2 The examples of misspelled words in this passage are of course all taken from Trelawny's actual letters. Unfortunately some of his writings are now available only in edited versions so that it has not always been possible to give other quotations in his own words.
3 The spelling of the letter in *Letters*, p. 62, has been discorrected. In the original reproduced in the *Keats-Shelley Memorial Bulletin*, i, p. 52, Trelawny – as always – addresses him as 'Dear Robers'. In a letter of 9 September 1867 to Seymour Kirkup in the Pforzheimer, he refers to him as 'Old Robers': it may be a joke.
4 Letter to Jane Williams, 28 January 1823, *Abinger collection*, 'My dear Gane'.
5 Letter to John Murray, 15 January 1833, *Murray Collection*, 'I read the Bironic satire in Frasers Magazine . . .'
6 This astonishing example comes from a letter of Trelawny to the Johnsons in the Pforzheimer Library, due to be published in a forthcoming volume of *Shelley and His Circle*. It is clear from the context of the letter that Trelawny, in this case at least, was not deliberately misspelling his name. To the end of his life he was uncertain about John and Jhon, Johnson and Jhonson. It is tempting to connect Trelawny's spelling difficulties with the effects of heavy-metal poisoning which is being increasingly associated with the problems of dyslexia and with difficult and disturbed behaviour. Lead poisoning occurs in areas where there is no chalk to provide a protective fur inside the lead pipes which

carry the drinking water, notably in areas of acidic peat moors. Is this part of the explanation of the Celtic (and Cornish) temperament with which Trelawny was so liberally endowed?

7 *Lovell's Medwin*, p. 135. I have been unable to confirm the story. Maybe Trelawny's alleged letter in the *Morning Post* may one day be discovered although the newspapers did not often publish letters from members of the public at this time.

8 *Shelley and His Circle*, v, p. 278.

9 *Ibid.*, v, p. 276.

10 In the Pforzheimer account book due to be published in *Shelley and His Circle*. For the travel book on Greece see also Note 7 to Chapter 24.

11 This detail is in Chapter 15 of the *Records*.

12 *Monthly Review*, 73, 1814.

13 He was called 'The Turk' by Mrs Prout and others at Bristol. *The Trial between Lieutenant Trelawney* . . . A letter of 18 November 1817 published in *Shelley and His Circle*, v, p. 232 refers to Trelawny's friends drinking the health of 'The Grand Turk' at his birthday party.

6. SWITZERLAND *pp.* 36–43

Trelawny's life from 1817 to 1822 has to be reconstructed from scattered references. Two important letters in the Pforzheimer Library are due to be published in a forthcoming volume of *Shelley and His Circle* together with an interesting account book. There are a few references in *Williams*, which can be tied in with his own brief account in the *Recollections*. A few more can be found in the unpublished journal of Daniel Roberts for 1820/21 in the Keats Memorial Library, Rome. *Hausermann* quotes a few relevant extracts from official documents.

The evidence for Trelawny's finances is scattered but since a man's income is almost as important a determinant of character as his libido, it may be worth setting it out in some detail. In a letter to John Hawkins in 1817 (quoted at the beginning of the chapter) he says his income is £300 p.a. This is also the figure left him by his father in 1820. In the Crim. Con. trial his allowance at the time of his marriage was said not to exceed £300 p.a. In 1822 a great uncle John Heywood left him £500 which would have yielded about £15 *per annum* if invested. In May 1823, when pressing Claire Clairmont to live with him, he said that his income 'is reduced to about £500 a year' (*Letters*, p. 58) and there are other indications that he may have had an additional income beyond the £300 a year left him by his father.

The Pforzheimer account book shows vividly that he calculated his living expenses down to the last *quattrino*, equivalent to about a tenth of a penny, and kept daily accounts.

From scattered references in letters it appears that in the late 1820s Trelawny had expectations from his aunts, and fear that they would cut him off was high among his worries when he was contemplating publishing the *Adventures*. The book brought him £300 in 1831 or 1832. His mother, by a will dated 1841, left him £3,750 when she died in 1852. There are references to further legacies when he was older.

Brereton's will permitted Trelawny, with the consent of the trustees, to convert some of the capital into land, and this was apparently done when, in middle age, Trelawny went to Usk. He was, understandably, pleased that his farming activities were profitable. His own will is summarised in *Boase*.

By adjusting Trelawny's money income to take account of taxation changes, changes in English prices (as measured, for example, by the Gayer Rostow Schwartz Index), and changes in the comparative purchasing power of the foreign currencies of the countries where Trelawny lived, a curve can be derived of his 'real take-home income'. This helps to confirm other evidence about the extent to which considerations of money played a part in determining some of the important decisions of his life, notably the decision to leave England in 1818 (where his real income was falling); the decision to move to Tuscany (where his real income more than doubled); and his reluctance to leave the Ionian Islands or Italy after his Greek adventure because of the drastic fall in living standards which this involved. In 1836 his real income was no higher than it had been in 1821. Trelawny did not become financially secure until he was nearly 50 after which he enjoyed a comfortable income and correspondingly increased self-confidence.

1 Trelawny to John Hawkins, 6 May 1817. *Hawkins Papers at Chichester*.

2 Exchange rates and relative price levels are taken from the guide books of the time especially Mariana Starke: *Information and Directions for Travellers on the Continent*, sixth edition, 1828.

3 *Life and Letters of Maria Edgeworth*, 1894, i, 283.

4 *Recollections*, pp. 1ff. I have let the story stand although it is unlikely to be quite true, since in this case Trelawny's error is, I think, understandable and venial. In the *Recollections* Trelawny puts the incident in 1819 although he corrected this in the *Records* to 1820 which was in fact the year he went on his tour of the Lake of Geneva with Roberts. It is extremely unlikely that a copy of *Queen Mab* could have been available there at that time since the first published (pirated) edition came out in 1821. However, I do not think Trelawny invented the story – that was not his way. More probably it was *Rosalind and Helen* that he came across as he says and the story is otherwise as he relates. We know from his 1820 book list that he owned a copy of that book before he left for England at the end of his tour of the Lake, and the priest's alleged remarks about *Queen Mab* could apply equally to *Rosalind and Helen*. On his return to England in 1820 – still before he ever met Shelley – Trelawny went to Ollier's to buy all his published works. *Letters*, p. 272.

5 Trelawny calls the house Plangeau which cannot be identified. From a letter of Medwin it appears to have been at Schloss Plongeon.

6 This work, with the date of 1821, is mentioned in *Boase and Courtney*, and (wrongly transcribed) in *Williams's Journal*, p. 112. Despite a wide-ranging search I have been unable to locate any copy.

7 *Recollections*, p. 7.

8 *Shelley: Letters*, ii, 242.

9 Public Record Office, Prob. 11/1635, f. 553.

10 *Letters*, p. 108.

11 Trelawny to Mrs Johnson 15 November 1821, due to be published in a forthcoming volume of *Shelley and His Circle*, where the whole chronology of this
period of Trelawny's life will be discussed.

7. BAMMING THE BLUES *pp.* 44–53

For the life of Shelley the biographies by *White* and *Holmes*, though very different,
are both excellent. Much of the detail of Shelley's life at Pisa is given in full from
primary sources by *Cline*.

1 From the unpublished *Vie de Lord Byron en Italie*, copy kindly provided by Mr
Leslie Marchand. See also note 4 below.
2 It is interesting to compare the financial accounts of Trelawny's life at Pisa in
the Pforzheimer account book with Byron's accounts for the same period
quoted by Doris Langley Moore: *Lord Byron – Accounts Rendered*.
3 *Recollections*, p. 20.
4 *Ibid*., p. 26. The meeting of Trelawny and Byron is described vividly by *Origo*,
p. 298, although her translation of documents is very free. The source, a passage
in the Countess Guiccioli's unpublished *Vie de Lord Byron en Italie*, which is
quoted in translation at the head of this chapter, is suspect as a historically
accurate account since it was written many years afterwards when Trelawny's
reputation had long since been established. It does however tend to confirm
what some authors had believed happened on that occasion even without the
benefit of her evidence.
5 It is possible of course that Trelawny had already begun to assume his imaginary
persona before his arrival at Pisa. However it is unlikely that he had gone far down
this road before 1822, since in Switzerland he was closely associated with
Roberts, with a relative called Molesworth, and with the St Aubyn family all
of whom had known him for many years. Only when he reached Pisa was he
truly freed from connexions with his past. This is not to say that of course he
had not practised shooting the occasional tall story to suitable audiences in the
past.
6 *Lovell's Medwin*, p. 101, is interesting on bamming. See also *Graham*, p. 56. The
word seems to be a slang abbreviation for bamboozle. For a naval example see
Marryat's *Kings Own*, Chapter XLIX.
7 Apparently an unused passage intended for the *Adventures* written by Trelawny
in Williams's notebook 'Sporting Sketches in Hindoostan' in the Bodleian
Library. It may be intended to refer to another occasion, such as his entry into
society after the success of the *Adventures* in 1832.
8 *Mary Shelley's Journal*, p. 165, with a few small additions and corrections restored from the manuscript in the Bodleian.
9 Unluckily the main source, the journals of *Williams* and *Mary Shelley*, although
they are full of references to Trelawny telling his stories, give few indications
of what the stories actually were. The raven story is one of the few that can be
closely documented. Some of the stories embedded in Medwin's *Angler in
Wales*, 1834, seem to derive from Trelawny.

8. TRELAWNY'S STORY *pp.* 54–58

It cannot be demonstrated in detail that the stories which Trelawny told at Pisa were those later collected and written up as the *Adventures of a Younger Son,* but the probability is high. Scattered evidence survives for other stories in the Trelawnian epic cycle which existed only in oral form – Trelawny in the Wahabee Wars, Trelawny's Circumnavigation, Trelawny in the Himalayas, Trelawny's Voyage to Japan – but Trelawny the Privateer was always the favourite. Some of the stories in the *Adventures* appear to owe their origin to events which occurred after Pisa and could not, obviously, have been in his repertory at that time. For example the funeral cremation of Zela owes much to the cremation of Shelley, the story of the sailor who said 'frite' for 'freight' occurs in both the *Adventures,* p. 419, and the *Recollections,* p. 192, and much of Trelawny's writing about Zela is based on his actual experience of Tersitsa.

It has been suggested to me by a prominent Cornishman that Trelawny and his listeners knew that he was indulging in 'fictionalised autobiography' like George Borrow, or telling travellers tales like *The Adventures of Peter Wilkins,* but there is overwhelming evidence that he wanted his stories to be regarded as the literal truth.

1 *Adventures,* p. 60.
2 Here and elsewhere I have called Trelawny's imaginary Arab bride Zela (in accordance with the original spelling in the *Adventures*) to distinguish her from his real daughter Zella. In fact however Trelawny wanted Zela's name to be spelled Zella with the accent on the a.

9. THE PISA CIRCLE *pp.* 59–69

The main events of this period are carefully reconstructed by *Cline.*

1 *Letters,* p. 83.
2 *Williams,* p. 131. An interesting picture of Jane wearing her oriental headdress is to be published in the forthcoming new edition of Mary Shelley's journal.
3 *Mary Shelley: Letters,* i, 155.
4 *Shelley Letters,* ii, 439.
5 *Ibid.,* ii, 436.
6 Mary Shelley to Mrs Gisborne, 10 October 1822. *Shelley and Mary,* p. 872.
7 Usually called *Fragments from an Unfinished Drama* in editions of Shelley.
8 Quoted by *Origo* from *Murray Papers.*
9 *Kennedy,* p. 297.
10 The nature of the relationship between Byron and Trelawny in 1822 is well seen in the series of letters by Trelawny dealing with the boat among the *Murray Papers* – careful, businesslike, orthographic, and respectful.
11 The first recorded version is in *Millingen,* pp. 150ff., published in 1831, where it is noted that Lord Byron 'observed of him he could not even to save his life tell the truth'. Many of Trelawny s acquaintances who later repeated the story must have read it in *Millingen* or heard it from others who did, and clearly it

struck a chord. George Finlay, who knew both Byron and Trelawny in Greece and stayed on in Athens after the Greek Revolution, is said to have passed on a remark by Byron that Trelawny could not spell or tell the truth to Monckton Milnes (noted at the head of Chapter 5). He is also said to be the source of the other version 'if we could only make Trelawny wash his hands and speak the truth we might make a gentleman of him' (*Cobbe* in *Temple Bar* also in *Life of Frances Power Cobbe by Herself*, 1894, i, 236). The other family of Byron quips about Trelawny also probably have a common ancestor, this time in *Kennedy*, p. 314, published in 1831, 'Lord Byron ... used to say T was an excellent fellow till his Lara and Corsair spoiled him by his attempting to imitate them'. This story was often repeated notably by the Countess Guiccioli (see *Moore, Late Lord Byron*, pp, 434ff. for full quotations) and latterly by Claire Clairmont. This story too sounds plausible.

Trelawny had some reputation as a liar early on. See the ponderous joke at the burial of Shelley's ashes in Rome noted in *Sharp's Severn*, p. 122, 'Here lies Edward Trelawny for he is still living', and the mocking remarks of Byron recorded in *Kennedy*, pp. 297f., about Trelawny's exploits being, like Falstaff's, 'by Shrewsbury clock'. The astonishing thing is not that a few sceptical eyebrows were raised but that, by and large, Trelawny carried off his deception with almost total success.

12 *Williams*, p. 160 from the *Recollections*.

13 *Adventures*, p. 139.

14 *Hill: Family Background*, p. 25.

15 *Williams*, p. 128.

16 *Letters*, p. 1, with the spelling discorrected.

17 All these details are taken from *Williams, Mary Shelley's Journal, Trelawny's Recollections*, and contemporary documents. The evidence for associating the design of the *Don Juan* with Trelawny's fantasies is therefore strong. See also Diana Pugh: 'Captain Roberts and the Sinking of the Don Juan', *Keats–Shelley Memorial Association Bulletin*, 1975, although she understandably did not realise that 'letters' quoted by Trelawny could not be treated as reliable transcriptions. See Chapter 24.

The privateers were usually rigged as hermaphrodites – in other words the top sail of the foremast was square-rigged (see illustrations). One would almost guess that Shelley – had he heard the name – would have wanted this for the *Don Juan* too if she had been big enough because of his fascination with real hermaphrodites. The illustration in *Williams* and the plan in *Grylls* are unlikely to represent the *Don Juan* since they show only one mast. The drawing of a full-rigged ship by Williams commonly reproduced as the *Bolivar* cannot represent Byron's schooner.

18 Quoted in *Cline*, p. 74, from an original in the Pforzheimer Library no longer accessible. From a letter of Trelawny to Roberts in the Keats Memorial Library, Rome, postmarked 31 Gen[naio] it would appear that the names *Don Juan* and *Bolivar* were already decided upon in January 1822.

19 *Shelley: Letters*, ii, p. 435.

10. THE STORYTELLER PART I *pp.* 70–76

1 Claire Clairmont to Jane Williams, 13 February 1830, *Abinger Papers*, quoted in *Lovell's Medwin*, p. 236.

2 Log of H.M.S. *Cornelia*, 29 March 1809, Adm. 51/2045.

3 Log of H.M.S. *Akbar*, 5 August 1811, Adm. 51/2080. Quoted in *Hill: Family Background*, p. 29.

4 *Adventures*, pp. 47ff.

5 Mrs Brereton to John Hawkins, 25 March 1807 *Hawkins Papers at Chichester.*

6 Log of H.M.S. *Woolwich*, 3 September 1807, Adm. 51/1736.

7 *Adventures*, p. 286.

8 *Records*, i, p. 72.

9 *Adventures*, p. 43.

10 *Ibid.*, p. 73.

11 *Ibid.*, p. 411.

12 Trelawny to Seymour Kirkup, 4 January 1857. *Pforzheimer*. Aston may be connected with the Allsopp that Trelawny knew in 1817 (*Shelley and His Circle*, v, pp. 324f.) who apparently went to South America. Trelawny also claimed to have recalled the drowning of Aston in his own swim at Niagara. See p. 144.

13 The Williams notebook is now in the Bodleian Library. Trelawny subsequently used the blank pages to keep his own notes. For Jane's request to have it back see her letter to Mary Shelley in *Williams*, p. 164.

14 *Adventures*, pp. 405ff.

15 *Shelley and his Circle*, v, p. 326. This was a traditional Trelawny motto not one of his own invention. Trelawny's tendency towards combativeness might have been helped along by the old Cornwall tag 'A Trelawny never lacked courage, nor a Godolphin wit, nor a Grenville loyalty'.

16 Pforzheimer account book.

17 *Kennedy*, p. 297.

11. THE DEATH OF SHELLEY *pp.* 77–84

It is difficult to establish for certain exactly what happened on and after the fatal day of 8 July 1822 despite the wealth of relevant material. Many of the participants were concerned within a short time of the disaster to vindicate their own conduct, to blame others, or to lay claim to credit, and all but the most contemporaneous documents have to be treated with caution. The *Viareggio official records* of which many are quoted in *Biagi* give a framework of dates and facts which there is no reason to question. The records of Lord Byron's expenses quoted in *Moore: Accounts Rendered* are also presumably reliable although their interpretation is difficult.

Trelawny wrote about a dozen accounts of his role in these events, some of them very nearly contemporaneous, others more than half a century later. See *Marchand*. In many of the accounts there is a good deal of confusion, running together of incidents, exaggeration of his own part, romantic ornament, and plain error. Even in the baldest and earliest accounts, for example, Trelawny painted into the cremation scene the islands of Elba and Capraia which can never be seen from Viareggio, and these errors were plagiarised by Medwin and Leigh Hunt when they drew on Trelawny's accounts for their own books. In one of the earliest versions written in September 1822 (Keats Memorial Library, Rome – quoted by Marchand) Trelawny specifically discounts the ramming theory. For an example of how quickly the story altered in the telling, see the version by John Carne reporting Hobhouse reporting Byron in John Carne, *Letters*, privately printed 1885, p. 151.

See also Chapter 24.

1 *Mary Shelley Letters*, ii, p. 205.
2 Trelawny's 'Bocca Lericcio' which has failed to puzzle many commentators is a mistake for 'Bocca del Serchio' caused by false attraction with 'Lerici'.
3 *Recollections*, pp. 132ff. This is one of the purple passages of romantic literature and deservedly so.
4 From *Brown's Letters*. An edited version is in *Sharp's Severn*.
5 *Letters*, p. 53.

12. MARY AND CLAIRE *pp.* 85–89

1 From a letter to Mary Shelley, 28 March 1830, quoted in *Claire Clairmont's Journal*, p. 285, from the *Abinger papers*.
2 Trelawny's letters to Byron about the *Bolivar* are among the *Murray Papers*. The incident of the 'old clothes' is referred to in several letters of Trelawny, Byron, Roberts, and Mary Shelley. See T. G. Steffan: *Byron and Old Clothes*, *Notes and Queries*, November 1969, p. 416.
3 *Shelley and Mary*, pp. 944, 950, 969.
4 The episode with Gabrielle Wright is referred to in Trelawny's *Letters* and in letters in *Shelley and Mary* although the name is not always given. See also *Williams*, p. 164 and note. Trelawny's attitude can be seen from his letter to Jane Williams of 25 January 1823, *Abinger papers*, from which the quotation is taken.
5 Trelawny's *Letters* contains most of his known love letters to Claire. The editor left out a few passages from the originals which can be read in the British Library. Claire herself was apparently responsible for obliterating other passages and they have not yet been read. Henry James's masterpiece *The Aspern Papers*, the ultimate condemnation of literary biographers, is based on the later struggle between Silsbee and Forman for the papers of the aged Claire. Forman eventually won, but instead of unknown works of Shelley and Byron, he found that he had acquired Trelawny's letters to Claire. In the course of the contest Silsbee apparently offered to marry Trelawny's daughter Laetitia. See *Keats–Shelley Memorial Bulletin*, 1955. *Graham*, p. 42, reports Claire as declaring in her old age that Trelawny was never her friend, but he is unreliable. It is possible however that Claire – in the language of her day – was telling Graham that Trelawny was never her lover.
6 See *Claire Clairmont's Journal*, p. 356.

13. TO GREECE *pp.* 90–95

1 *Letters* p. 61.
2 *Shelley and Mary*, p. 943.
3 *Recollections* pp. 160ff.
4 Mrs Brereton to Sir Christopher Hawkins, 6 August 1823. *Hawkins Papers at Truro*. Obviously Trelawny in his letters to his mother was as usual exaggerating. It would be interesting to know whether he deliberately gave her the wrong name of the ship. 'Hypernea' is probably not Greek but a Trelawnian spelling of 'Hibernia.'
5 *Letters*, pp. 65, 170.
6 *Shelley and Mary*, p. 950.
7 This and other incidents on board ship are recorded in the *Recollections*, and *Records* and by *Hamilton Browne*.
8 See Note 11 to Chapter 9.
9 *Journal of Frank Abney Hastings*, 7 October 1823, British School at Athens.

14. A DREAM COME TRUE *pp.* 96–102

The sources for Trelawny's reconnaissance on behalf of Lord Byron are his *Recollections, Records,* and *Letters; Hamilton Browne;* letters in *Shelley and Mary;* the interview with Xenos; the Hastings Journal in the British School at Athens; and letters from Trelawny and Hamilton Browne among the archives of the London Greek Committee preserved in the National Library in Athens.

1 *Shelley and Mary*, p. 986.
2 The song in *Childe Harold's Pilgrimage,* canto ii.
3 *Letters*, p. 82; *Shelley and Mary*, p. 1003.
4 Hamilton Browne to Byron, 13 September 1823. *Greek Committee Archives.*
5 Trelawny to Byron, 14 September 1823. *Greek Committee Archives.*
6 *Shelley and Mary*, p. 983.
7 *Ibid.*, p. 986.
8 For the stories of Odysseus's early days see George Waddington *A Visit to Greece,* 1825 p. 78, and the note to Landor's *Imaginary Conversations* which Trelawny claimed to have written himself. See note 1 to chapter 17. There is useful material about the removal of the guns in *Stanhope,* and *Parry* and in the *London Greek Committee Archives,* and in Edward Blaquiere's *Narrative of a Second Visit to Greece,* 1825.
9 See, for example, *Shelley and Mary*, p. 1003. Blaquiere to Bowring, 6 May 1824, *London Greek Committee Archives.*
10 *Letters*, p. 89.

15. THE DEATH OF BYRON *pp.* 103–111

1 *Jarvis*, p. 236.
2 Some scholars have doubted whether Trelawny could in fact have looked at

Byron's feet as he claimed, arguing that Byron's coffin was sealed before Trelawny arrived at Missolonghi. The date of the sealing is not certain – the date of 25th April is given in the official document printed in Nicolson's *Byron*, p. 269, but the authenticating signature is dated 20th April so one date of these two cannot be right. It was perhaps a belief that the second date was a mistranscription for 29th April that caused *Gamba* who was there (and who had access to the document later) to date the sealing to the 29th. As for the date of Trelawny's arrival, *Gamba* says '24th or 25th'. *Millingen* has 23rd and says explicitly that Trelawny saw the body. Since both these witnesses were present and both were working from journals written at the time it is hazardous to override their evidence without strong cause. This is not to say of course that Trelawny definitely did look at Byron's feet, only that it has not been proved that he did have the opportunity. See also p. 176.

3 Trelawny to Stanhope, 31st March 1824 (OS), *Greek Committee Archives*.

4 *Kennedy*, p. 312.

5 *Letters*, p. 80.

6 *Ibid.*, p. 73.

7 Trelawny to John Cam Hobhouse, 30th April 1824. *Murray Papers*. Also in *Shelley and Mary*, pp. 1006ff.

8 *Shelley and Mary*, p. 1026.

9 *Millingen*, pp. 150ff.

10 *Forrester*.

11 Trelawny to Stanhope, 2nd May 1824 (OS), *Greek Committee Archives*. Typically Trelawny liked to date his letters in the old style although most documents in Greece at the time had already adopted the new calendar.

12 Quoted verbatim by Blaquiere in a letter to Stanhope, 8th June 1824, *Greek Committee Archives*.

13 Discussed in the same letter.

14 *Sketches of Modern Greece*, i, pp. 108ff. I have no doubt that the author of this strange book is William Guise Whitcombe who, in 1825, fired the shot that nearly killed Trelawny in the cave. The work is fictionalised autobiography based on his own experiences in Greece and on stories heard from people he met there. Most of the characters mentioned under pseudonyms can be identified with real people whom Whitcombe met and there are secure links with a number of good external sources. But the internal evidence is almost strong enough by itself to confirm the identification. The author makes several disguised references to the incident in the cave and there is much about the unspecified sin that brought about his disgrace. However much Whitcombe tried to disguise his experience, numerous authentic autobiographical details unrelated to his fictional story crept into his narrative (e.g. the mention of his arms and ankles being bruised by chains, ii, p. 150). The author calls himself Nastuli, a diminutive of Anastasius, the hero of Thomas Hope's novel that Whitcombe took as his model.

As far as Simpkins as a caricature of Trelawny is concerned, some of the author's hits are very near the mark (compare for example the extract quoted here with the letter quoted at the head of chapter 16) and obviously not much exaggeration is involved. Although Whitcombe makes fun of Simpkins and unhistorically (for Trelawny) has him slinking off from danger, he also stresses that he is a good hearted and likeable fellow for all his absurdities. One of his characters, modelled on the American Jarvis declares at one point (i, p. 179) 'You have probably been acquainted for some length of time with Mr. Simpkins and you have found him no doubt well informed and communicative. The poor fellow to be sure, is sometimes flighty, and inclined to give too great a scope to his faculties of imagination; which however should not detract from his other merits'. It is striking that Trelawny could be represented as claiming to be the original of *Lara* so early. See chapter 19 for the development of this story. The book was published in 1828 well before the appearance of the *Adventures*.

16. THE CAVE *pp.* 112–119

Trelawny's own description of the cave published in the *Examiner* is fairly accurate. It is also described by *Humphreys*, by *Major Bacon*, and by *Landor* who drew on Trelawny for his information. Latterly Trelawny's memory of the cave underwent a sea change – see Chapter 24.

The cave described as Odysseus's cave in some guidebooks and in the article by *Sanborn* is not the Mavre Troupa. For Tithorea and its locality see Leake's *Northern Greece* and Frazer's *Commentary on Pausanias*. There is much of interest in *Lappa* and Trelawny's interview with Xenos from which many of the details are taken.

1 *Letters*, p. 89
2 Xenos interview. See also Chapter 24.

17. THE ASSASSINATION ATTEMPT *pp.* 120–125

1 *Landor*. Trelawny helped Landor in preparing this *Imaginary Conversation* and claimed to have himself composed the historical note. His letter to Sir Christopher Hawkins, 3rd February 1829, *Hawkins Papers at Truro*. 'In the 4 volume of Landor's Imaginary Conversations published by Ebers, Bond Street, there is a conversation between Odesseus, his Sister and Myself – with a brief sketch of the life of Odesseus annexed – written by me.' Although it is mainly a long political tract, it also contains much useful information about the way in which Trelawny wished his stay in the cave to be regarded. The characters of Odysseus and Trelawny are drawn on a heroic scale. Tersitsa is terrified of the tall stranger yet at the same time irresistibly attracted towards him.

2 For example, *The Globe and Traveller* of 16 May 1825, reporting that Odysseus had joined the Pasha of Negropont, commented 'The story that one of our countrymen, Mr. Trelawny, who was some time with Odysseus has accompanied him in his apostasy is utterly incredible.' For a while the newspapers reported that the cave was in the hands of Odysseus's brother-in-law without realising that Trelawny was meant.

3 *Claire Clairmont's Journal*, p. 332, 24 June 1825. 'I read in the newspapers that Odysseus has been defeated four times near Atalandi by Gura, that he has given himself up prisoner and has been conveyed to Napoli. What this means I cannot make out – I cannot believe that the chief Edward has chosen is one capable of betraying his country; but I am naturally extremely low spirited at this news tho' I do my best to believe it is false.'

4 See *Grylls, Trelawny*, pp. 135f., from manuscripts in the British Museum.

5 FO 78/139 Public Record Office.

6 *Swan*, ii, p. 172.

7 *Letters*, p. 91. The original is in the Keats–Shelley Memorial Library at Rome and more accurately published in the *Keats–Shelley Memorial Bulletin*, I p. 57. Trelawny wrote in similar terms to Leigh Hunt and the letter was printed in the *Examiner* for 26 February 1826 and the *Globe* for January 1826.

8 *Colvin*, p. 246.

18. DRIFTING *pp.* 126–132

1 *Mary Shelley's Journal*, p. 202.

2 For the visit of the two Whitcombe brothers to Trelawny at Cephalonia see *Down* who drew on the original documents in the Public Record Office. The journal of the brother who became a Philhellene is in the Gennadios Library, Athens. The young Whitcombe served as a Lieutenant in the 2nd West India Regiment in the West Indies and in Central America. In 1832 he is reported as sick and he died in 1833 at the age of about 27. It is not known when Trelawny met him in England, if indeed this claim is true. For his book, *Sketches of Modern Greece*, see note 14 to chapter 15.

3 For Trelawny's divorce from Tersitsa, see *Down*, who disposes of a misreported story in *Sharp's Severn*.

4 See the convincing conjecture in Perkins, A. J. G. and Wolfsen, Theresa, *Frances Wright*, New York 1939, p. 198, commenting on a letter in *Shelley and Mary*. But this passage may refer to another mutual acquaintance, the philhellene Dutrone.

5 Trelawny to Sir Christopher Hawkins, 3 February 1829. *Hawkins Papers at Truro.*

6 Mrs Brereton to Sir Christopher Hawkins, 21 September 1828. *Hawkins Papers at Truro.*

7 *Letters*, p. 111.

8 This and the following quotation are taken from two longer passages copied in Trelawny's handwriting into Williams's 'Sporting Sketches' which Trelawny had taken possession of and used as a notebook. It seems certain that they are letters, although undated, and there is evidence to suggest that one is by Mary and the other by Claire, besides the fact that they fit the style and character of the two women. For example Mary often used the image of the weed of the sea in talking of herself, and Claire is known to have been advising Trelawny to marry and settle down – but not with her – at this time. See *Claire Clairmont's*

Journal, p. 417. Claire, in many ways the most perceptive of people who knew Trelawny well, teases him in the same letter about his 'Medora' – showing that she at least was aware of the Byronic heroine syndrome in his character.

19. THE NEW CORSAIR *pp.* 133–142

The arrangements for editing and publishing the *Adventures* can be followed in detail in Trelawny's *Letters, Mary Shelley's Letters,* and letters in *Shelley and Mary*. A few other letters of this correspondence remain unpublished. For a summary, see my introduction to the *Adventures*. When he was an old man Trelawny denied publicly that Mary Shelley had helped him in any significant way with the publication of the *Adventures*. There is an interesting critical review of the *Adventures*, as a document of the romantic imagination, by Thomas Philbreck in *Nineteenth Century Fiction*, 1975, on which I have drawn a good deal.

The information about Trelawny's children is taken from scattered references in Trelawny's letters (many unpublished in the Pforzheimer) which can be compared with other references in letters by his mother) *Hawkins Papers at Truro, Mary Shelley's Journal,* and elsewhere. Landor composed some bad verses in commemoration of Trelawny's problems with his children at this time. There is a pathetic letter in the Pforzheimer from Eliza which suggests that he did not pay her much attention. Most of the information about his dealings with Medwin and much else of relevance is from a long letter from Claire to Jane Williams postmarked from Dresden 13th February 1830, among the *Abinger Papers*. His relationship with Godwin can be seen from numerous references in Godwin's Diary, in the Bodleian.

See also *Brown's Letters* for Trelawny in Florence. The manuscript of the *Adventures* (Houghton Library) is in Brown's handwriting. At the time of my edition I had not identified the erased name Hamelin.

1 Translated from *Mémoires d'un Cadet de Famille par Trelawny, Compagnon et Ami de Lord Byron*. There were also German, Swedish and American editions.
2 *Letters*, p. 177, with a few misspellings reinserted from the original in the *Abinger Papers*.
3 See his letter to Mary Shelley, 5th January 1832. *Shelley and Mary*, p. 1154. 'A year back I wanted money to relieve a friend who was suddenly plunged into extreme distress, and I think that was my principle inducement to do so foolish a thing as to hazard the publication in question.'
4 For Colburn see Leslie A. Marchand: *The Athenaeum*, 1947.
5 *Letters*, p. 106.
6 *Letters*, p. 105, Palma's book is *Greece Vindicated*.
7 The full title of Trelawny's article is in the bibliography. It is reprinted in his *Letters*.
8 For example, the *Westminster Review* quoted at the end of this chapter; the *London Literary Gazette* for February 1832, 'We believe the celebrated Trelawny to be the author'; *New Monthly Magazine* April 1832, 'Mr. Trelawny, the reputed author of the present work'; *Quarterly Review*, 48, 1832, 'But the Younger Son

is not a work of fiction. It is we are assured a fragment of the autobiography of a man of remarkable talents who has chosen to live a most extraordinary life . . . With Mr. Trelawny's general strain of opinion and sentiment it is impossible not to be grieved and pained . . .'

9 Ancelot: *Lord Byron à Venise*, Paris, 1834.

10 *Westminster Review*, 1832. For Trelawny's interest in Keats see also H. Buxton Forman's edition of Keats's *Works*, 1883, iv, p. 381. For Trelawny as possible biographer see *Sharp's Severn*, p. 195.

11 *Villemessant*, i, pp. 301ff, translated. Trelawny when he saw the book in old age insisted that the story of breaking the nuts was true.

12 For example Borromeo in Godwin's *Cloudesley* and De Faro in Mary Shelley's *Perkin Warbeck*. Much of *Falkner* is taken from Trelawny. Mary Shelley also incorporated stories about Trelawny into her short stories, notably *Euphrasia* in the *Keepsake* for 1839. In August 1881 when many obituaries of Trelawny were appearing, Robert Louis Stevenson was putting together his ideas for *Treasure Island*. He decided to incorporate 'a fine old Squire Trelawney (the real Tre, purged of literature and sin, to suit the infant mind).'

20. AMERICA *pp.* 143–154

The sources for Trelawny's visit to North America are sparse and his movements have to be reconstructed from sporadic references. There are three important letters addressed to Mrs. Stith (who met Byron in Italy and whom Trelawny may have met there) in the Beinecke Library, a few letters in the Pforzheimer, one in the Folger Library, Washington, and one published in *A Continuation of the Memoirs of Charles Mathews*, 1839 with other references. For 1833 there are numerous references to him in *Kemble's Journal* although he is not referred to by name and in a few places it is not absolutely sure which – is intended to represent Trelawny. In addition there are references in the usual source books.

1 From a letter to Mary Shelley, 9th January 1833, in the Huntington Library. There is a letter to Murray from on board the *Tally Ho*, dated 15th January 1833, among the *Murray Papers*.

2 From a ms letter by Rebecca Rutledge to her husband dated El Dorado 10 April 1833 in the South Caroliniana Library.

3 This detail, by Dr John Francis, is from the *Memorial of James Fenimore Cooper*, New York 1852, p. 95. *Sanborn* says he met Wendel Phillips at Philadelphia without giving a primary source reference.

4 *Letters*, pp. 178ff.

5 Quoted by *Grylls, Trelawny*, p. 181 from *The Articulate Sisters* ed. M.A. de Wolfe Howe, Cambridge, Mass., 1946, pp. 240ff.

6 For Detmold see note 5 to chapter 25.

7 E.g. in *Miller*.

8 *Letters*, p. 187.

9 Noyes, quoted by George B. Lockwood: *The New Harmony Movement*, 1905. For the suggestion that Trelawny should go to Nashoba in 1828 see note 4 to chapter 18. The direct evidence connecting him with Frances Wright's schemes

in 1833–5 is slim although, in my view, the likelihood that he took a close interest is great. Curiously in the letter to Claire quoted he says some minds are as difficult to unroll as a Herculaneum manuscript – this is probably a reference to or a remembrance of the fact that Frances Wright's famous first book on political idealism, *A Few Days at Athens*, was published under the fiction that it came from a Herculaneum ms.

   For the idea that some of the Pisa circle might go to America see Waterman, William: *Frances Wright*, Columbia, 1924, p. 122 who deduced it from primary sources. It is highly doubtful if Mary ever seriously considered going to America although she may have given Robert Dale Owen polite encouragement to think otherwise.

10 Letters to Mrs Stith in the Beinecke. Trelawny was intending to go to Haiti in the winter of 1834/35 but there does not appear to have been time for him to have done this within the fixed points of his reconstructed timetable.

11 Quoted by *Massingham* p. 235 from an original document.

12 To Mrs. Stith, 27 November 1834.

21. POLITICS AND SOCIETY *pp.* 155–163

There are numerous references to Trelawny in the chronicles of the period, notably *Robinson, Haydon, Jameson* and *Chorley*.

 1 A letter of Trelawny's of 2 July 1838, reprinted in *Anna Jameson: Letters and Friendships*, 1915, p. 165, suggests that he had a hand in a work or article to be called *Wrongs of Women* but I have not been able to identify this for certain.

 2 *Jameson*, pp. 36, 45.

 3 *Select Letters and Journals of Fanny Appleton Longfellow*, 1956, p. 41.

 4 *The Satirist* 8 May 1836, 17 July 1836 and elsewhere.

 5 *Letters of Caroline Norton to Lord Melbourne*, Ohio 1972. I have amended 'last' to 'least' without authority since this makes better sense.

 6 The breakdown of Trelawny's relationship with Mary Shelley can be seen in their letters and in Mary's *Journal*, especially the unpublished passages. Yet the immediate cause of the break in 1838 remains to some extent conjectural. Mary's long entry in her journal for October 1838 is a carefully considered apologia for her attitudes to a wide range of political and moral issues on which she felt vulnerable to criticism because of her deviation from Shelley's principles. The break was worsened soon after by Mary's edition of Shelley's poems. See chapter 23.

 7 *Graham*, p. 43.

 8 *Pendennis*, 1850 edition, i, p. 393 and p. 403. Captain Edward Strong, another character in *Pendennis*, also has a whiff of Trelawny about him.

 9 *Robinson* p. 631.

10 Quoted in *Cline* p. 196 and *Lovell* p. 98 from the *Murray Papers*.

11 *Angler in Wales*, 1834, ii, p. 153. There is another reference to Trelawny (unnamed) on p. 214.

12 *Heath's Book of Beauty*, 1839.

13 Copied by Trelawny into the Williams notebook, Bodleian Library.

22. A LONG RETIREMENT *pp.* 164–169

Much of the information about Trelawny and Augusta comes from the divorce trial record of the Court of Arches of 1840 preserved at Lambeth Palace. LR H593/1–13. I am grateful to Mrs Doris Langley Moore for drawing this source to my attention. There are a few letters between Mary Shelley and Augusta among the *Abinger Papers.* For Trelawny at Usk see *Clark* and *Byrde.* There are interesting letters from this period of Trelawny's life in the Pforzheimer.

1 *Pforzheimer.*
2 Quoted from *The Literary Life and Correspondence of the Countess of Blessington,* 1855.
3 *Ibid.*
4 A typed notice in the porch of the church still notes that the trees were the gift of 'a Mr Trelawny'.
5 Trelawny to Augusta Draper, 3 July 1867. *Pforzheimer.*
6 *Pforzheimer.*
7 There are advertisements about the sale of Cefn Ila in the *Usk Observer* for 20 March 1858 and 22 May 1858 which list the farm stock and tools and mention the thousand volumes of books. The house was burned down in 1973.

23. THE FRIEND OF SHELLEY *pp.* 170–181

The best general account of the development of the Shelley legend is in *Norman,* see also *Rolleston.* For Mary Shelley during this period see especially *Grylls, Mary Shelley,* and her *Journal,* of which much of interest is omitted in the currently available printed version.

1 *Blind.* John Addington Symonds's *Shelley,* first published in 1878 enjoyed an enormous readership for many years through being included in the cheap *English Men of Letters* series. The remark about Shelley being too beautiful to paint is in chapter II.
2 Quoted in *White* ii, p. 391.
3 Quoted in *Grylls, Mary Shelley* p. 284.
4 A letter by Garnett to Lady Shelley of 3 August 1898, when he was keeper at the British Museum Library, leaves no room for doubt that he did this. *Abinger Collection. Quis custodiet ipsos custodes?*
5 The Parlour Library edition is undated. Sadlier suggests 1856 but it may be earlier.
6 *Holman Hunt,* ii, p. 242.
7 *Life and Letters of Robert Browning,* 1891, p. 137.
8 *Blind.*
9 *Carpenter,* p. 121.
10 *Life and Letters of Theodore Watts-Dunton,* 1916, ii, 19. Lady Anne Blunt, whose ms journal is in the British Library, also noted on a visit to Trelawny on 20 October 1878 how he would rise from a chair, throw himself back violently, and bang the table with his fist.

11 *Swinburne Letters* ii, 332; iii, 16.

12 *Letters*, pp. 268ff.

13 Quoted in *Grylls, Mary Shelley*, p. 287. The picture of Trelawny was the one by Severn reproduced following p. 60. In the catalogue of Shelley relics prepared by Lady Shelley now in the Bodleian, there is no mention of Trelawny. Some of the Trelawny letters in the Abinger Collection have been physically mutilated to remove passages containing sentiments or facts of which the family disapproved. For the total destruction of others see *White*, ii, p. 625.

24. THE STORYTELLER PART 2 *pp.* 182–190

There are numerous examples of Trelawny's later storytelling and his listeners' comments in the articles and comments by *Edgcumbe* (which are much the same), the various books by *Rossetti*, and *Miller*. See also *Brookfield* and *Carpenter* and a few stories collected from primary sources by *Massingham*.

1 A copy of the inventory is among the *Viareggio official papers*. None of these papers discuss the possible cause of the disaster.

2 *Mary Shelley Letters*, i, p. 197 and i. p, 223.

3 The feeling that great events must somehow have great causes still clings to the Shelley story. I have heard it seriously suggested that Shelley was assassinated by the Austrians and that Lord Byron was implicated.

4 The two originals are in the British Museum Add Mss 52361 having been acquired in 1963. Trelawny's daughter Laetitia made donations from Trelawny's papers to numerous institutions connected with Byron and Shelley and sold some others. She refused absolutely to give access to the papers which she kept. It is difficult to avoid the conclusion that she must have been aware of the damage which the revelation of these two particular letters would cause to her father's reputation and deliberately held them back. Since these letters are so important it is worth quoting them in full.

Pisa Sepr 14th 1822

My dear Mrs Shelley

We have got fast hold of the Don Juan at last and she is safe at anchor at Viareggio. She has been got up entire but much damaged from being so long under water. Everything is complete in her and clearly proves she was not upset but I think must have filled by a heavy sea – Contents found are – The 29 Piggs of Iron Ballast (which is complete) Seven sails – Awning, a Trunk containing two hundred + forty five dollars of Tuscany – shirts pantaloons etc etc – 7 tea spoons – A second trunk or Valice which was yr husband's containing books & cloathes – all the boys things safe in the fore peak etc – I shall see Ld Byron and arrange for paying the expenses of getting her up – I of *all things wish to keep the Boat* for remembrance of my good friends. Ld Byron no doubt will sell her by auction and I hope to be able to outbid any that may feel inclined to put up for her – She is as yet in quarantine. I go to her tomorrow morning as I have obtained the papers at Leghorn to give her pratique – you shall have the particulars when everything is arranged – I wrote to stop your Desk – send to Stow for it – remember me to Mrs Williams – believe me yr affectionat freind.

Daniel Roberts

Dr Trelawny

You must have heard thro' Mrs S. that the Don Juan was found & therefore concluding she would make you acquainted with the contents of that letter of mine, I beg in return you will give her the extracts of this to you. I went to Viareggio after consulting with Ld Byron upon what was most advisable to be done with the fellows who found her – It was agreed to put up everything for sale – the half of the profits for them the other for our friends. On Monday the sale commenced – the only thing knocked down to me was the shell of the boat for 300 livers – The sails where rotten and some of them completely in peices – the rigging all that I saw not worth a Napoleon. The two masts carried away just above board – bowsprit off close to the bows – Two Gaffs good – boomb good, pump good, false stern carried away – the rudder lost, the Gunwhale stove in in many places – the boat half full of a blue mud among which we picked out Cloths of all sorts (mostly rotten) books & spy glass broken/all the bottles of Marsalla Wine (that was bought as a present to the harbour Master at Lerici) were found in the basket – the corks half forced out and the Wine impregnated with Salt Water (perhaps you are acquainted with the wonderful effect that the pressure of Salt Water has upon a full bottle in any depth of water – if so you will not be surprised at the phenomenon). The books I had washed and put into reading order some of them too much rubbed to separate the leaves. In the MSS we found there were two Memorandum books of Shelleys – quite perfect and another not to be separated – the Memo's of Williams quite perfect writen up to the 4th of July, all in Lord B's possession except that of W – I gave that and all the letters a peice of stuff he bought for Jane and all private papers in charge to Hunt as I saw many sworn objurations on Ld B among them – I thought that step most advisable. After paying all expenses and with as damd a set as ever breathed I cleared for our dear friends Widows – 101 Dollars 300 livres of Genoa – 7 Tea spoons & the books.

The boat I have here and am consulting Reid about selling her etc but find that it will cost me much money – At all events I will put the hull in condition – paint her and fit her and if I find I get on tolerable cheap I will then rigg and fit her. The ballast I could not afford to buy – but Ld B has found out that you left behind some of his ballast and told me to sell it for him (what a damd close calculating fellow he is) *You* are so *biggoted* in his favour that I will not say more – only God defend me from ever having anything to do with him again.

Now my dear fellow let me enter upon another subject to a Man of your quick comprehension! I need but say *"report spreads fast"* do not let a few

paltry seconds of *lust* (for it is nothing else) get the better Man of you –
farewell

and believe me
Your obliged and affectionate friend
Daniel Roberts

Shelley's Desk arrived today – I have sent it on to Lord Byron – I hope I
have done right.

18th Sept[r] 1822

The Rockfort is more and enough for Genoa Willm B – is in the tiller – Ld
B told me he should send for the Schooner to Lerici to take him to Genoa
as the roads are bad – I rode yr horse Sarzana to Via reggio – he is in good
condition – poor Alf looks very bad he had kicked his feet all to peices
against the stone stabling – so I ordered them to *shoe* him again with a light
iron. The landlord advised so doing but if you think we have acted wrong
return word and I will order the shoes off again. The hoofs stick horribly
but there is no appearance of grain. When you have time send me a line
DR[4]

The texts Trelawny printed in *Recollections* were:

Pisa Sept. 1822

Dear T.

   We have got fast hold of Shelley's boat, and she is now safe at anchor
off Via Reggio. Every thing is in her, and clearly proves, that she was not
capsized. I think she must have been swamped by a heavy sea; we found in
her two trunks, that of Williams, containing money and clothes, and
Shelley's filled with books and clothes.

Yours, very sincerely
DAN ROBERTS

Sept 18, 1822

Dear T

   I consulted Ld. B., on the subject of paying the crews of the felucca
employed in getting up the boat. He advised me to sell her by auction, and
to give them half the proceeds of the sale. I rode your horse to Via Reggio.
On Monday we had the sale, and only realised a trifle more than two
hundred dollars.

The two masts were carried away just above board, the bowspit broken off
close to the bows, the gunwhale stove in, and the hull half full of blue clay,
out of which we fished clothes books, spyglass, and other raticles. A
hamper of wine that Shelley bought at Leghorn, a present for the harbour-
master of Lerici, was spoilt, the corks forced partly out of the bottles and
the wine mixed with salt-water. You know, this is effected by the pressure
of the cold sea-water.

We found in the boat two memorandum-books of Shelley's quite perfect,
and another damaged, a journal of Williams's quite perfect, written up to

the 4th of July. I washed the printed books, some of them were so glued together by the slimy mud, that the leaves could not be separated, most of these things are now in Ld. B's custody. The letters, private papers, and Williams's journal, I left in charge of Hunt as I saw there were many severe remarks on Ld. B.

Ld. B. has found out that you left at Genoa some of the ballast of the 'Bolivar', and he asked me to sell it for him. What a damned close calculating fellow he is. You are so bigoted in his favour that I will say no more, only God defend me from ever having anything more to do with him.

[The postscript quoted in the text p. 185 follows here]

In the *Records* Trelawny omitted the references to his being bigoted in favour of Lord Byron which were clearly inappropriate in 1878 however true they might have seemed in 1822 or 1823 when he had been called 'Lord Byron's jackal'.

5 The controversy took place in *The Times* and other newspapers in December 1875 and January 1876.

6 *Biagi*. The full results of his investigations in 1890 are among the *official papers* at Viareggio.

7 The Corycian Cave was rediscovered by Edward Daniel Clarke who asked the villagers about it, and he was also aware of the Mavre Troupa on the other side of Parnassus. But he himself never visited either. Raikes the first traveller to go to the Corycian Cave published an account of it which was to remain the source for the guidebooks in the nineteenth century. Strangely, the book in which Raikes published his account, *Walpole's Travels*, was virtually the only travel book which Trelawny possessed in 1820. His interest arose no doubt because his uncle John Hawkins, another noted early traveller in Greece, had contributed to the same volume, and possibly because he was considering going to Greece himself with Medwin, Williams, and Shelley at that time.

Many later accounts of Odysseus and Trelawny have had them living in the Corycian Cave. I am greatly indebted to Mr A. C. Lascarides for translating the *Xenos* interview.

8 *Holman Hunt*.

25. LAST YEARS *pp*. 191–197

Much of the material for Trelawny at Sompting is collected in *Looker*. There are some relevant unpublished notes among the *Murray Papers*.

1 *Letters*, p. 274.

2 I raise a small doubt about the number seven because in a letter of 1831 (*Shelley and Mary*, p. 1152) Trelawny refers to the ease with which he has had his four children adopted. At that time the total only reaches four if one counts (besides Maria Julia, Eliza, and Zella) the second daughter born to Tersitsa who died within days of birth or a child born to the fictitious Arab girl Zela, neither of which explanations is totally convincing. In the letter Trelawny says that only two were surviving at the time, Maria Julia and Zella.

3 The little that is known about the later life of Maria Julia (Mrs Burley) and Zella comes from the unpublished notes made by the late C. M. Trelawny-Irving of conversations with his grandmother Zella. (Private collection). These were also drawn on by *Massingham*.

4 The facts about Frank and Edgar (with some about Zella) are largely deduced from a few contemporary unpublished letters of Trelawny in the Pforzheimer, two of which are quoted below. See also *Sharp's Severn*, p. 264.

5 Detmold is in the *Dictionary of American Biography*. There is no positive evidence that Trelawny met him on his visit to America in 1833–5 but it is difficult to see at what other time the friendship could have been established. In a letter to Millais dated 23 June 1873 (private collection) Trelawny wrote 'My friend Detmold has a well cultivated mind and taste for art so I send you his criticism . . . Have you not a son educating in Hanover – if so you should have told Detmold – he knows everyone in that country worth knowing and is now there – of all the humans he is the best'. William Michael Rossetti noted in his copy of the *Records* (private collection) that the 'enthusiastic simpleton, referred to on p. 152 was meant for himself. Rossetti did not ask Trelawny whether he considered Shelley a *perfect* man but whether he considered him the best man he had even known. 'He replied No he considered Detmold the best.' In writing to a prospective biographer of Trelawny, F. W. Hoyt, on 4 April 1882 (private collection) Rossetti advised that the three people most able to help were Miss Taylor, Laetitia, and Detmold, the engineer who knew Trelawny for 35 or 40 years and was regarded by him as the best man he had ever known. This last point gives weight to the conjecture that Trelawny first met Detmold on his visit to the United States in 1833–5.

6 Trelawny to Augusta Draper, 24 February 1858. Pforzheimer.

7 Trelawny to Augusta Draper, 25 December 1858. Pforzheimer.

8 The Goring divorce case from which the facts were extracted was reported in, for example, *The Times*, 2–7 February 1878.

9 *Colvin*, pp. 240ff.

10 This is a misquotation since Mary misread Shelley's difficult handwriting in publishing the fragment after his death. The last line should read 'For their two breasts . . .'. Trelawny himself felt a touch of residual diffidence at applying these verses to his own case. In a letter of 15 July 1869 to Adelaide Kemble in the Pforzheimer he says that he has selected the epitaph but wants to make an alteration

These are two friends in life devided
Death has united, so let their memory be
Now they have glided under their grave
Let not their bones be parted
For their two hearts in life were single hearted

I doubt if many people would find this an improvement on Shelley's verse even if the sentiment accords better with the facts. After Trelawny's death there was a dispute between Laetitia and Lady Shelley over the ownership of the burial plot. Lady Shelley wanted to erect there the large marble statue of the drowned poet by Onslow Ford but discovered too late that she had no rights. The statue was donated instead to University College, Oxford, who reluctantly accepted it in part expiation for having expelled the most distinguished man ever to attend the college.

Index